# The Wright Stuff

# The WRIGHT STUFF

## Reflections on People and Politics by Former House Speaker Jim Wright

James W. Riddlesperger Jr.,
Anthony Champagne,
Dan Williams,
*editors*

TCU PRESS

*Fort Worth, Texas*

Library of Congress Cataloging-in-Publication Data
Wright, Jim, 1922-
The Wright stuff / [edited by] James W. Riddlesperger Jr., Anthony Champagne, and Dan Williams.
p. cm.
ISBN-13: 978-0-87565-506-2 (cloth : alk. paper)
ISBN-10: 0-87565-506-8 (cloth : alk. paper)
ISBN-13: 978-0-87565-571-0 (paper : alk. paper)
ISBN-10: 0-87565-571-8 (paper : alk. paper)
1. United States--Politics and government--1945-1989. 2. United States--Politics and government--1989- 3. United States--Foreign relations--1945-1989. 4. Wright, Jim, 1922- 5. Statesmen--United States. 6. Legislators--United States. I. Riddlesperger, James W., Jr., 1953- II. Champagne, Anthony. III. Williams, Daniel E. IV. Title.
E839.5.W76 2012
973.92--dc23
2012038199

TCU Press
P.O. Box 298300
Fort Worth, Texas 76129
817.257.7822
www.prs.tcu.edu

To order books: 1.800.826.8911

*Designed by Barbara Mathews Whitehead*

# CONTENTS

## II. DOMESTIC POLICY



## III. POLITICS: RAW, MEDIUM RARE, AND WELL DONE



## IV. DEFENSE AND FOREIGN POLICY

# ACKNOWLEDGMENTS

NO BOOK IS EVER singly authored, even a book that contains the writings of one author. This book, which collects various published and unpublished pieces by Jim Wright, former Speaker of the House, is the result of a strong thread of collaborations and contributions, and there are many people to thank. Three years ago Dr. Dan Williams, director of TCU Press, approached Jim Wright about the possibility of collecting some of his speeches, articles, and newspaper columns. With Jim's approval and gracious help, he then approached Drs. Jim Riddlesperger and Anthony Champagne to help select from the massive amount of materials available from the Jim Wright Collection housed in the TCU Mary Couts Burnett Library, which includes books, speeches, columns, editorials, and unpublished writings. When further winnowing was needed, Klay Kubiak, TCU English department graduate student, offered invaluable help in taking on the task of organizing and helping to edit the materials. Lisa Pena of the library's Special Collections department lent her expertise and willingly spent hours researching photographs and locating additional materials for this volume. Norma Ritchson, Mr. Wright's longtime assistant, and Mary Swain, also with the Mary Couts Burnett Library, both contributed their valuable time and talent. Kathy Walton, the TCU Press editor, worked with Jim Wright on the final shape of the book, and Melinda Esco, the TCU Press production manager, worked her magic with last-minute changes and reorganizations. Rileigh Sanders, assistant editor, and Becca Allen, marketing coordinator, equally contributed their time and expertise.

# FOREWORD

For most of the past forty years, Jim Wright and I have worked together either for the betterment of our city, for our nation, or for the university that we've both come to love.

Jim is one person who has risen to the very heights in our nation's legislative branch without forgetting for a moment where he came from or the folks at home who sent him there.

As mayor of Fort Worth for ten years of that time, I never failed to find in Congressman Wright a willing listener with an open and creative desire to find solutions, whether the problem involved a critical need for flood control, restitution of an economically blighted area, broader educational opportunities, or a need for improved highway, rail, or airline service for our people.

Jim Wright served thirty-four and a half years in the US Congress, ten as House majority leader and the last two and a half as Speaker before his retirement in 1989. For nineteen years he has taught a three-hour course in "Congress and the Presidents," highly popular with students at Texas Christian University. He also wrote weekly editorial columns for the *Fort Worth Star-Telegram* which also appeared in a number of other newspapers, including the *Miami Herald*, the *Kansas City Star*, and the *Los Angeles Times*, among others.

One great reason for this book is to share with a wider audience what we who know him have seen as Jim's great gift in the use of words, sometimes to express an entirely new concept that can turn into a workable idea.

One outstanding example in this volume is a somewhat whimsical idea Jim expressed in a newsletter to his constituents in 1958. It was Christmastime, and Jim was just finishing his second term in Congress. The biggest, starkest reality of the era was the Cold War, which had divided the whole world into two hostile camps. In this angry and restrictive atmosphere, Jim did a wholly unexpected thing. He wrote a letter to a mythical "Ivan," meant to represent some average citizen in Russia, our relentless Cold War enemy.

In the letter, he showed why both sides, without even trying to understand one another, were squandering billions on nuclear weapons (in a doctrine called Mutual Assured Destruction, aka MAD)—while leaving necessary work at home undone. The letter attracted some attention and was applauded by then Senate majority leader Lyndon Johnson, but was gradually forgotten.

Almost twenty-nine years later, in the spring of 1987, the new leader of the Soviet Union, Mikhail Gorbachev, read a copy of Jim's almost three-decades-old "Letter to Ivan," and was so impressed that he asked Wright, then Speaker of the US House, if he'd like to speak directly to the whole Russian people via the nation's national broadcasting chain.

Never before had the Russian government allowed, let alone invited, a US Congressman to speak freely to their public. The US State Department was thrilled at the prospect of the USSR's new, tentative interest in exploring peaceful relations with the United States.

Encouraged by our secretary of state, Jim delivered a renewed appeal, a speech of his own creating, and invited his Russian listeners to write their own thoughts to him. The result was an avalanche of letters from ordinary Russian citizens, the overwhelming majority of them friendly.

The event encouraged both sides to continue the peace talks that, some months later, resulted in the end of the Cold War.

The author of these works, a Democrat, served with eight American presidents, five of them Republicans. His essays not only reflect history in the making, but offer an acute commentary on today's political landscape. Whether writing about Goldwater or

Nixon, Kennedy or Carter, Wright's clear-eyed view isn't shuttered by rigid ideologies (see "Legislation and the Will of God"). He understands the vicissitudes of politics and doesn't shy away from revealing its dark—and occasionally comical—episodes, but he respects and celebrates honest practitioners from both sides of the aisle. His is a hopeful vision of a government where conciliation and compromise are integral to the art and science of governing, and recognized as the very fabric of what may be the greatest conciliatory instrument of all time: the Constitution of the United States.

Read and enjoy.

Bob Bolen
Mayor of Fort Worth, Texas, 1982-1991
President, National League of Cities, 1989-1990
Senior Adviser to the Chancellor,
Texas Christian University, 1991-2013

Young Jim Wright at his childhood home.
SPEAKER JIM WRIGHT COLLECTION, SPECIAL COLLECTIONS, MARY COUTS BURNETT LIBRARY, TCU.

# INTRODUCTION

Words are the weapons of peace, the instruments by which we convey thought, the very stuff of which civil discourse is made. Actions speak louder than words, we are told. Yet very often the most dramatically heralded deeds have been either inspired or provoked by words. Since time began, words have started and ended wars.

It is to me, therefore, both gratifying and deeply humbling that educational colleagues at TCU Press should consider some few of my own written words and the thoughts they convey worthy of republishing selectively in this beautiful volume.

Throughout my life, perhaps in unconscious mimicry of my mother and father, I've striven for words adequate to my most cherished thoughts and ambitions. To whatever extent I may've occasionally succeeded, I owe thanks to the tireless examples of those two wonderful people.

My mother, before her marriage, taught English literature and poetry. Through much of her life, she was popularly sought out to give periodic public book reviews.

My dad, while largely self-educated, was a voracious reader, skilled wordsmith, gifted sloganeer, effective salesman, sales manager, and leadership exemplar. In his midforties he founded, and for a quarter century directed, a nationwide sales-promotion company with paying clients in more than a thousand cities and towns across the United States.

Mother and Dad were both bibliophiles, and our family library was a frequent amazement to my childhood contemporaries.

From preschool years, books were among my cherished presents. At age seven, I received from Dad my first real "man's book." It was

*Jack Dempsey, the Idol of Fistiana* by Nat Fleischer, then editor of *The Ring* magazine. Written for adults, it contained photos and tales of Dempsey's personal and professional history as well as blow-by-blow accounts of the famed boxing champion's major bouts. When I'd devoured the book and even memorized several of its most thrilling sequences, Dad favored me, one at a time, with a series of Edgar Rice Burroughs's Tarzan books, beginning with *Tarzan of the Apes.* Heady stuff at ages seven and eight!

Mother admired an expressive vocabulary and insisted within the family on proper grammatical usage. "You may meet and talk with someone for no more than five minutes," she'd say, "and that person may have no idea how learned you are in math or geography, but your new friend will know right away whether or not you speak proper English!" First impressions are important, she'd remind us.

Both parents encouraged meaningful intrafamily conversation at the dinner table. Some of the subjects, far from boring us, aimed at stretching our imaginations. We children were never scolded or made to feel stupid for an expressed opinion. My two younger sisters (Mary Nelle and Betty Lee) and I were encouraged to share at the evening meal some new story, joke, or—even better—a poem we'd memorized. Each offering was to be greeted by an appreciative audience. I was never allowed to make a disparaging reference to any serious comment of a younger sibling. And none of us were permitted to leave the table until all had finished.

## The 1930s and The Great Depression

THE TWO BROAD external events that made the deepest impression in the formation of my lifetime goals were the Great Depression and World War II. Trying to cope with the needs of our growing family in America's ravaged economy in the 1930s forced several potentially disruptive family moves. We went, of necessity, to wherever Dad could make the best living. During the formative public school years, I attended nine different schools in seven different

At around age six, with his younger sister Mary Nelle.
SPEAKER JIM WRIGHT COLLECTION, SPECIAL COLLECTIONS, MARY COUTS BURNETT LIBRARY, TCU.

cities–Houston, Fort Worth, Dallas, Weatherford, Duncan, Seminole, and Oklahoma City. When finally allowed to study for the last three years continuously in one place, Dallas's W. H. Adamson High School, I felt almost as though I'd been embraced by a heavenly familiarity.

The year of 1931, when my father made his first attempt to found a national company, would be remembered later in wry family jest as "the year we ate the piano." As it turned out, we "ate" the family car, too. We wouldn't own another auto for the next six years. We got a second-hand one in 1937.

Something else, even more traumatic, happened in 1931. It was in that early Depression year that my maternal grandfather, who'd successfully represented a nationwide lumbering-supply company for twenty-two years, was arbitrarily terminated—as were all of that

Wright at age seven or eight.
SPEAKER JIM WRIGHT COLLECTION, SPECIAL COLLECTIONS, MARY COUTS BURNETT LIBRARY, TCU.

organization's other employees who'd earned at least twenty years of seniority. This mass dismissal was performed in a transparent effort to avoid making good on a company pledge to provide retirement incomes for employees upon individual completion of twenty-five consecutive years of employment with the company.

Watching my grandfather's earnest but dismayingly unfruitful daily attempts at age sixty-three and older to find other employment made an indelible impression upon me at ages nine, ten, and eleven. He was a proud man. I could read the hurt in his face.

These grandparents weren't wealthy. But my granddad had always enjoyed steady employment, and they'd never faced the kind of crisis that loomed upon them so suddenly and unexpectedly now in their sixties. My mother was their only child. To prevent imminent foreclosure upon their home in Fort Worth, my mother and father moved our immediate five-member family from Weatherford to Fort Worth, where we took residence in a portion of the house and paid rent to the elder couple, providing them with the necessary cash for mortgage payments and saving the grandparents' dwelling from foreclosure.

It was, under the circumstances, the only available way to assist in their economic salvation. There was then no such thing as Social Security, no unemployment compensation, no WPA projects. Certainly no food stamps! These and other benignly beneficial programs came late—too late to have saved my grandparents' home. But I thanked God in later years for the privilege of helping to strengthen such programs—and for the strong sense of family unity that permitted my parents to help the elder generation through those terribly tragic times.

As for us, my sisters and I were never permitted to think of ourselves as "poor." We were reinforced, rather, with constant reminders of how "fortunate" we were to have enough to eat and wear, a comfortable dwelling in which to live, good work for our hands and minds, and enough at times to help others.

Aside from the inconvenience, not owning a car actually had

some compensations. Walking almost everywhere was an unrealized physical boon. Family journeys afoot were longer and, for me at least, more enjoyable.

My parents were religious, though not sanctimonious. In Duncan, when I was eleven, we'd walk every Sunday morning to the Presbyterian Church for Sunday school and worship services and return via downtown, often for a "store-bought" Sunday lunch. On Sunday evenings, Dad and I often would walk together to one or another of Duncan's other churches to "sermon sample" and observe their order of worship. My folks were fairly ecumenical by nature. Enroute homeward afoot, my father and I would discuss the pastor's sermon along with other weighty matters. "Man talk"! I reveled in it and felt mighty mature.

## World War II Abrewing

AS FOR WORLD WAR II, the second stimulus to my life's ambitions, it began to affect my life and planning in the four or five years leading up to Pearl Harbor. In an unusual way I, though only fourteen at the time, became acutely conscious in 1937 of that war's menacing encroachment upon us.

Like a lot of boys my age, I aspired at ages fourteen and fifteen to athletic achievement. My career goal: to be a football coach. That was the guy my crowd admired the most! Having transferred from school to school, I'd skipped a couple of grades. As a consequence I was at least a year younger than my class contemporaries and defensively self-conscious lest they discover that fact. The dismal trouble, so far as it concerned my football prowess, was that I wasn't big enough not to be faster than I was, nor fast enough not to be bigger than I was. I weighed about 137 while several teammates were between 160 and 170. I tried to compensate by running harder and driving harder! In an early season game that year, I suffered a right knee injury. A chipped cartilage and "water on the knee." I was required to wear a

Wright and girlfriend Geraldine Brazeale, 1935.
SPEAKER JIM WRIGHT COLLECTION, SPECIAL COLLECTIONS, MARY COUTS BURNETT LIBRARY, TCU.

knee cast for the next six weeks.

Coach Robert B. Harris, my hero, said: "You're unfortunately benched for the rest of this season, Jim. But what our school needs, even more than a great halfback, is somebody to represent us in debate competition with other schools. And I think you're the best prospect we've got!"

Harris was the world history professor. In the process of trying to impress him with my prowess, I became incurably hooked on history. When our studies came to World War I—in which my father had served as a captain and infantry commander in France, and during which he had greatly admired President Woodrow Wilson—I became profoundly convinced that the US Senate had made a dreadful and costly mistake in rejecting the League of Nations covenant and retreating into isolationism.

The fruits of that monumental error were becoming unmistakably apparent by the late 1930s. Japan, after invading Manchuria in September of 1931, was now beginning to run rampant in the far East over a succession of weaker peoples. Italy's dictator, Benito Mussolini, had invaded and overthrown militarily pitiful Ethiopia, scoffing at the League of Nations as a "crumbling artifice." Adolf Hitler, having invaded the demilitarized Rhineland, had thrust his forces into the Sudetenland, Czechoslovakia, and Austria. Clearly, Wilson's 1920 prophecy was coming true: another, more devastating world conflict in twenty years.

It came to me that year in world history class. Better even than being a great football coach would be to go to our US Congress someday as an elected member and make major contributions to world peace! As that conviction crystallized into a near obsession, I devoured several political biographies and a book of Woodrow Wilson speeches. I developed a fascination with President Franklin Roosevelt and his battles to lift our lagging national economy, and gained increasing satisfaction from participation in interscholastic debates.

In the spring of the following year, my debate colleague and I represented Adamson High in a daylong, statewide elimination tournament sponsored by North Texas State Teachers' College in Denton. We made it to the semifinal arguing the question of fair taxation. It was a chest-swelling experience!

Along with a pal named Joe Irwin, I organized a new campus club called The Progressives. We promoted extracurricular discussions on how to achieve our three announced alliterated objectives: *Peace, Progress, and Prosperity.* To top it off, my senior year, classmates chose me as president of the graduating class. By now, my career ambition was set. It never wavered.

The ensuing six years—at Weatherford College, the University of Texas, and flying with the US Army Air Corps in World War II—built upon my increasing desire to strike blows in Congress for world peace, and for more widely shared domestic prosperity.

As I hungrily viewed my future, words would be my tools in the pursuit of public policy, and I greedily gobbled each opportunity to try them.

At Weatherford College, I was editor of the school's weekly newspaper and tried with abundant ambition but limited success to expand its readership to the wider community. Weekends I earned pocket money by covering sports for the *Fort Worth Star-Telegram.*

At the University of Texas, while majoring in government and economics, I represented my alma mater in intercollegiate debate competitions, and pocketed thirty dollars a month working for Texas Attorney General Gerald C. Mann in fashioning a card file system for referencing Texas court cases and attorney general opinions. Words, ideas, and public policy: my meat and potatoes.

## The War

THEN CAME PEARL HARBOR. My world, like everyone's, was suddenly transformed. Words were not enough. More was expected of guys like me. Let Roosevelt and Churchill speak the magic words —I was their willing disciple.

On December 31—less than three weeks after Pearl Harbor and nine days following my nineteenth birthday—I volunteered and was sworn into the US Army Air Corps, where I spent a goodly part of 1943 and '44 flying combat missions against Japanese forces and fortifications in the Southwest Pacific. Words would wait. Action alone counted! Oh, well, I did manage between missions to wiggle in time to write a few carefully censored and unpaid dispatches to hometown newspapers. But that's beside the point.

After the war, I had the good fortune to join my father in the family business, earn a highly satisfactory living, build a home and start a loving family of my own, and make time also to serve for two terms as mayor of our hometown, Weatherford. It was these life experiences that provided the background for my thinking when I was elected to Congress and served thirty-five years in the US House of Representatives. I never forgot those experiences and, although there were hitches and glitches along the way—lots of them—I remain grateful for this career path. Through the better part of thirty-five years in Congress, I wasn't always on the winning side. But my life was filled with opportunities to broaden the gates of economic opportunity, promote upward mobility for the humblest of Americans, and occasionally to make some specific contributions, however small or incomplete, to world peace.

## Public Office and Its Opportunities

IN SO MANY WAYS HAVE I BEEN BLESSED. Really, a very lucky guy. To realize at least a few of my youthful and admittedly grandiose ambitions—while enjoying two happy marriages and helping to rear a family of wonderfully loving children, grandchildren, and great-grandchildren—what supreme good fortune!

If any of the written words or spoken thoughts preserved in this volume have any capacity to enlighten or inspire, or if they contribute even slightly to my cherished lifetime goals of a vibrant American economy, a healthy living environment, respect for human rights, or the even broader goal of peace on earth, I shall consider my imperfect labors to have been richly rewarded.

Jim Wright
March 15, 2012

# I

# Presidents and Personalities

With former Speaker of the House Sam Rayburn.
SPEAKER JIM WRIGHT COLLECTION, SPECIAL COLLECTIONS, MARY COUTS BURNETT LIBRARY, TCU.

## In Memoriam: Sam Rayburn

*Below is the eulogy Wright spoke on the House floor after Mr. Rayburn's death.*

MR. SPEAKER, eulogies have been spoken from the well of this House in memory of Sam Rayburn. Books will be written in tribute to his life and career. None can fully do him justice.

By any standard of measurement, Sam Rayburn ranks as the greatest lawmaker in the history of this nation. More truly significant legislation bears the stamp of his authorship than that of any other man. He served longer in the Congress than any other man in history, and presided over this body twice as long as any other Speaker in the history of the US House of Representatives.

Because of legislation sponsored by him, the average people of America live more comfortably and work more productively. Because of his concern, the blessings of our national prosperity are shared by the humblest family on the most unpretentious farm in America.

It was his lone vote that extended the draft in 1941 and saved us from being caught wholly unprepared by the sneak attack of the Japanese which catapulted us into World War II. It was his singular influence which prevailed upon the Congress to finance the development of the atomic bomb without divulging its secret, and thus hastened the end of that conflict with the attendant saving of untold thousands of American lives.

With the death of Sam Rayburn, who filled the Speakership longer than most of us have served in the Congress, an era has come to an end. Nothing will be quite the same. The stern visage, the courtly manner, the firm hand, and the painstaking fairness which were the Rayburn hallmarks had seemed inseparable parts of the House Chamber—as much so as the mace, the microphones, the galleries, and the cloakrooms.

No man or group of men can take his place or fill the void his passing leaves. For Sam Rayburn was more than a personality, and the leadership he exercised was more than inhered in the office he occupied. Mr. Rayburn was an institution, unique in the history of American government.

I remember a lazy Sunday in late summer, just before he left Washington for the last time. Eight or ten of us had gone out to Jefferson Island near the mouth of the Potomac for an abbreviated weekend away from the telephones, a weekend of fishing and visiting with the Speaker.

He sat there on the screened-in sun porch of the lodge dressed in his Sunday's best—dark blue suit and vest. The others of us just sat around and listened while Sam Rayburn talked. Occasionally someone would interject a question, but essentially it was a monologue, little vignettes and episodes called up out of the rich store of his memory.

Mr. Rayburn did not preach, but it was one of the finest sermons I have ever heard. It was almost a reverie, and throughout his reminiscences of the great and the near-great there ran the threads of his own great kindliness, his great faith in America, and his great hope for the future. I think the rest of us knew, although we did not want to admit it, that this was probably the last such opportunity we might have. Maybe he knew it, too.

Two years ago, on his birthday, he spoke to a small group of the things he held nearest his heart. Mainly, he spoke of Bonham and of Windom and of Flag Springs. He burned through to the very seat of man's folly as he related how, when he was a boy, the people of Windom thought those of Flag Springs to be fundamentally different from themselves in nature because Flag Springs was eight miles away. With his sweeping view of history, he applied this to man's view of the world in 1959.

He spoke of Bonham, and it was easy to tell that this was where his heart truly lay. Sam Rayburn said he loved Bonham because it was a place where people know it when you are sick and where they care when you die.

To what may we attribute the unprecedented success as a lawmaker experienced by this plainspoken and unpretentious man from Bonham? There might be as many answers as there are people who knew him. For my own part, I have tried to analyze the secret of the immense Rayburn influence. Essentially, I think it boiled down to three or four things.

The first was an almost uncanny judgment of people. The Speaker could pretty well size up a person and the person's intentions. Maybe this came from experience and a great deal of it. But it was a tremendously important asset in the job he held. He was seldom deceived by glib talk, false exteriors, or specious reasoning.

Secondly, he had a marvelous facility for burning through the outer dross to the heart of a matter. Often have I heard Speaker Rayburn utter a few sentences which summed up the matter at hand after others had spent many precious hours beating around the perimeter of the issue. He almost never wasted words, and so succinctly could he state the single overriding consideration involved in a question under discussion, that the rest of us often found ourselves nodding in agreement and thinking, "That's just what I was trying to say."

But principally I believe the secret of Sam Rayburn's greatness lay in his reputation for dealing in complete honesty and fairness, and his devotion, amounting almost to consecration, to the United States. These were the qualities which so endeared him to his colleagues that, in a body of 435 self-styled leaders and not a few prima donnas, Sam Rayburn was chosen unanimously time after time to be the spokesman and leader for his fellow members.

You never had to guess where Mr. Rayburn stood. His word, once given, was as good as gold. You could count on it and never look back. Members knew this, and it meant more than almost anything else. He never forgot the people, the plain average people who put their trust in him. Nor did he ever once lose faith in America and its future. Patriots have died for their country, and such devotion awes us. Sam Rayburn did a less dramatic but perhaps even more difficult thing. For the better part of a century, he lived for his country.

## Honor Washington, Lincoln, and Thirty-Eight More

PRESIDENTS' DAY primarily commemorates our former presidents with February birthdays. In the broader sense, it's a time to think of that whole variegated assortment of forty-four American males from George Washington to George H. W. Bush who've served us with dedication and varying degrees of grace in the highest office of our land.

American presidents have come in odd shapes and sizes. There is no physical stereotype. They've been tall and short, fat and lean, relatively young or old, charismatic and occasionally dull.

Most, if not all, have had a sense of humor. They've needed it.

They have had one thing in common: all of them without exception have wanted earnestly to do the right thing for this country. I do not believe there was an essentially bad man among them.

Wrongheaded, perhaps. Or stubborn. Ill-informed. Heedless. Inadequate to the task. But not evil.

Lyndon Johnson said the presidency has made "every man who occupied it, no matter how small, bigger than he was; and no matter how big, not big enough for its demands."

To be president is to occupy the most honored and most criticized office on earth.

Thomas Jefferson called it "a splendid misery." To Theodore Roosevelt it was "a bully pulpit." Harry Truman said, "The buck stops here."

George Washington in retirement wrote that he'd rather be "dead and in my grave" than to suffer again the indignities heaped upon that office by the press.

But John F. Kennedy quipped that "the pay is good and I can walk to work." Being president, said Lyndon Johnson on another occasion, is like being "a jackass in a hail storm. There's nothing to do but stand there and take it."

All of us have our favorites. My boyhood pantheon of heroes included Lincoln, Jackson, and Franklin Roosevelt. As far as I was concerned, FDR could have been president forever. With maturity, I developed increasing appreciation for Jefferson, Wilson, and Harry Truman.

During thirty-four years in Congress, I got to know and observe eight presidents at close range. I admired each of them. I watched six of them age visibly. Each year in the presidency, I am convinced, exacts at least a three-year toll upon the nervous system and bodily reserves. It is the man-killingest job on earth.

Only one in my observation, Ronald Reagan, seemed physically impervious to its demands. I think he refused to worry.

Reagan charmed official Washington with his personality, his sense of humor and of the dramatic. However one might quarrel with the accuracy of his "facts," his timing was flawless. He was to television what Franklin Roosevelt was to radio—the consummate performer.

Dwight D. Eisenhower, the same age as my father, was president when I went to Congress. He was the most universally respected of the lot. He also may have been the least partisan.

Kennedy was to me the most inspiring. He made my generation ask what we could do for our country and believe we could make a difference. His last speech, on the morning of his assassination, was to an audience I'd helped assemble for him in my hometown.

I'll be forever scarred by the trauma of that day. One of the New Frontiersmen said, "We'll never laugh again." Larry O'Brien replied, "We'll laugh again, but we'll never be young again."

The way some in the media treated a succession of four presidents—Johnson, Nixon, Gerald Ford, and Jimmy Carter—reminded me of Pacific Islanders who tried to appease the pagan gods by periodically selecting their choicest maiden and hurling her into a live volcano.

Once I was in Mexico with President Carter. He addressed a joint session of the national Congress for thirty minutes in Spanish. No American president ever had so honored an official foreign audience by addressing it entirely in its native tongue.

When Kennedy in Berlin spoke four words in German, he became the toast of the Free World. But Carter? His remarkable feat wasn't even reported to most of the American people. The media were too busy gloating over an unfortunate turn of phrase in a toast at an earlier luncheon.

And Carter never got the full credit he deserved for the dynamic personal diplomacy that produced the Camp David Accord, the peace settlement that still endures between Egypt and Israel.

Richard Nixon, whatever the faults of the Watergate affair, deserves to be remembered as the president who opened the diplomatic door to China and started the long, tortuous process of winding down the Cold War. It began with him.

Students sometimes ask who was the "best" president with whom I served. That's a hard evaluation to make.

Lyndon Johnson was the busiest, the most effective with Congress. Surely he was the most complex. I believe he was the smartest, not in the graceful patina of academia but in sheer native intelligence. He was superbly persuasive in a small group.

He had an uncanny ability to read what other people were thinking. And there was another side to him, a side that biographer Robert Caro never saw. Johnson believed in government as an instrument of beneficial change and wanted desperately to make life better for plain people, people without any political influence and without the independent means to help themselves.

That more than anything else is what drove him. And that, in my reckoning, is what makes a president great.

*Fort Worth Star-Telegram,* February 16, 1992

## The Words "Best" and "Carter" Often Said in Tandem

"JIMMY CARTER is the best former president we've ever had!" exulted a Republican friend of mine. It was not a condescending comment, not intended humor. It was a statement of sincere admiration.

Never in American history has a former chief executive worked harder or more selflessly for his country after leaving office.

Jimmy Carter's stature, like that of Harry Truman, seems to rise with every month that separates him from the White House.

In Fort Worth Friday to install Jake Schrum as president of Texas Wesleyan University, President Carter spoke with some of us about his brainchild project, Habitat for Humanity.

While providing the inspiration, Carter gives personal services as basic as carpentry to assist low-income families to acquire affordable homes. His self-help housing projects have sprung up in far-flung sites at home and abroad. But the former president reserves his most persistent effort for his adopted hometown of Atlanta.

It is Jimmy Carter's dream, aided by an army of volunteers, to transform that city's twenty poorest and most crime-ridden neighborhoods into model communities.

Listening to him speak, one is reminded of the refrain from an old hymn: "Brighten the corner where you are."

That is the first thing to understand about this remarkable specimen of American Southern culture. He is sincerely religious. It isn't ceremonial religiosity or wordy faith without works. It's simple conviction.

"The Bible says it's wrong to charge poor people interest," Jimmy Carter reminded me some months ago when we were in Haiti together. All Habitat for Humanity loans negotiated by Carter are interest-free.

Other beneficiaries of the former president's unquenchable thirst for service are the Middle East, Latin America, and underdevel-

With President Jimmy Carter.
OFFICIAL WHITE HOUSE PHOTO, APRIL 25, 1980.

oped countries with an impulse for democracy.

Under Carter's tutelage, a collection of former elected officials offer their services to monitor elections in countries struggling to come out of the crippling cocoon of dictatorships.

Concerning fair elections, the Carter name is a worldwide synonym for integrity.

Several personal characteristics distinguish Jimmy Carter as a breed apart. He has, among other things, a populist streak and a quaint strain of puritanism.

Long before it became fashionable to inveigh against the perks of power in Washington, Jimmy Carter was carrying his own luggage and riding in tourist-class seats on airplanes. He substituted middle-priced four-door cars for limousines in the executive agencies. He sold the presidential yacht, the *Sequoia*, which many of us considered a mistake.

Sparing in his personal tastes, Jimmy Carter banished hard

liquor from White House receptions and greatly reduced the number of once-obligatory social functions.

More than one Carter speechwriter quit after watching the president blue pencil his best, most quotable phrases like a gardener determined to tear out the most colorful flowers from the landscape.

But he can have fun. He is friendly, personable, and polite, almost to a fault. He is articulate, bright, keen-witted, and competent. He has a sense of humor.

Jimmy Carter is a consummate self-improvement bug. He's one of the most thoroughly self-disciplined persons I've ever known. While president, he regularly jogged, played tennis, heard classical music, read philosophy, studied Spanish, and completed a fast reading course.

President Carter once told me that he still had the same waist size as when he was a cadet at the Naval Academy. It was thirty-two inches. "When my trousers begin to feel tight, Rosalyn tells me I ought to buy a larger size," he remarked. "I don't do it. I just eat a little less and get more exercise."

Still, he is capable of great compassion and is fearless in the courage of his convictions. Because he believed them right, Jimmy Carter doggedly took on unpopular issues in the White House and persevered until they became realities. Amnesty for draft evaders of the Vietnam era and the Panama Canal Treaty come instantly to mind. They got few kudos from the American public. But in Carter's book, they were right.

Above all, Jimmy Carter is a peacemaker in a world that glorifies war makers. His patient, persistent, hands-on approach produced the Camp David agreement. That accord has more profoundly and benignly affected the Middle East than all the jingoistic wars with which the so-called "civilized" world has afflicted the region.

Once President Carter and I spent an hour at lunch talking of our respective fathers. It was during his dad's terminal illness that the young naval officer decided to leave military service and go back to Plains. "I decided that my father, who had never been many miles

Aboard Air Force 1, enroute to funeral of Egyptian President Anwar Sadat. From left: Jim Wright, Senate Foreign Relations Chairman Claiborne Pell, Mrs. Rosalyn Carter, House Foreign Affairs Chairman Clement Zablocki, and former President Jimmy Carter, October, 1981.
OFFICIAL WHITE HOUSE PHOTO, OCTOBER 1981.

from that homestead," Carter said, "had done more good for humanity than I could achieve if I stayed in the Navy for an entire career and became Chief of Naval Operations."

Another of Carter's heroes was gruff Admiral Hyman Rickover, whom few others of us ever found very endearing. Carter tells the story of their first meeting. Grilling him about his career at the academy, Rickover suddenly asked, "Did you always do your best?" The young naval officer replied honestly that, no, he really hadn't always. "Why not?" demanded Rickover, abruptly ending the interview.

That question seems to have haunted Jimmy Carter. It became the title of his short autobiography, *Why Not the Best?* And that, I think, is exactly what he has been giving ever since: his best.

Agree with him or not, one can't really ask for more.

*Fort Worth Star-Telegram*, April 26, 1992

## Johnson and Kennedy Ran All the Way to the Convention Finishing Line

THE LACK OF SUSPENSE in the presidential nominating conventions this year makes some yearn for an earlier time when things were not over until the delegates convened.

In 1960, along with others from Texas, I campaigned for Lyndon Johnson. As Senate Majority Leader, Johnson sent surrogates, disdaining personal appearances, on the primary trail.

He thought people would appreciate his staying at his post of duty, deftly managing the affairs of state.

But throughout that spring and early summer, John Kennedy campaigned hard for the nomination, racking up delegates in state after state.

Early that year, believing we could capture the top prize for Johnson, I suggested to Lyndon that Kennedy would be an attractive vice presidential nominee. A newsman raised that possibility in an interview. Kennedy grinned and said, "Let's not talk about vice. I'm against vice in any form."

When the Wisconsin primary went for Kennedy over neighbor Hubert Humphrey, everyone realized Jack Kennedy was a contender. A few weeks later, he dealt a crushing coup to the Minnesota senator's aspirations by trouncing Humphrey in the West Virginia primary.

If the downtrodden dirt farmers and unemployed coal miners of that hard-bitten rural state could identify with a wealthy Boston politician, everyone sensed that Jack Kennedy had a real chance to capture the nomination.

In a little West Virginia mountain town, Kennedy confessed that he'd never been poor. A grizzled miner sought to console him.

"Don't let that worry you none, Senator. You ain't missed a damn thing!"

Many were the jokes, good-humored and snide, about the wealth of the senator's father, Joseph P. Kennedy. At a Washington Gridiron Club dinner, one skit lampooned Kennedy about his father's lavish spending in behalf of his nomination bid. On stage, an actor portrayed the senator singing, "Just send the bill to Daddy."

In his remarks immediately after the skit, Kennedy ad libbed: "I have just received this telegram from my generous daddy: 'Dear Jack: Don't buy a single vote more than you need. I'm damned if I'll pay for a landslide!'"

By convention time in Los Angeles, the Massachusetts senator had garnered almost but not quite enough votes to sew up the nomination. In a last-ditch move to derail the runaway train, Johnson challenged Kennedy to meet him in a nationally televised debate.

Before Kennedy could respond, Johnson reserved a room in the Biltmore, set a specific time for the event that very afternoon, and invited the Texas and Massachusetts delegations along with a huge battery of news people.

Texans filed into the small auditorium thirty minutes in advance, feeling very smug about our candidate's maneuver. "Lyndon has bear-trapped him," said George Nokes of Waco.

Kennedy faced a dilemma: if he showed up, he would dignify Johnson's candidacy and run the greater risk of losing support to the wily Texan if he didn't perform well in the debate. But if he failed to appear, people would say he was afraid of the one-on-one comparison.

Nobody knew whether Kennedy would take up Johnson's challenge. Inside the room, we Texans waited as the clock ticked off the minutes. Three or four minutes before the scheduled hour of the televised debate, a door opened at the rear of the room and a smiling Jack Kennedy walked in, accompanied by only three others.

Where was the Massachusetts delegation? I thought about the old story of the Texas Ranger who appeared all alone in a strange town to put down a riot. Asked why there weren't more Rangers, he said, "There's only one riot." Texans had to admire Jack Kennedy for his boldness.

Lyndon spoke first. In polite, accepted style, he refrained from mentioning his opponent's name. "What is at stake here is the greatest responsibility within the power of the American people to grant," Johnson began. "When the people sent the two of us to the United States Senate, they did not expect us to abandon our Senate responsibilities simply to seek another office, any more than they'd expect a soldier to abandon his post of duty!"

Then Johnson closed in.

"Certainly the American people do not expect to give the most fatefully responsible job on earth to someone who, given one responsibility by the people, was absent and not voting on seventy-six of the last seventy-nine roll call votes in the Senate!"

It was powerful stuff. Everyone knew Johnson was making a telling argument. He had stayed on the job. Kennedy had spent full time seeking delegate votes while important issues were being decided in the Senate.

Then it was Kennedy's time to speak. He walked to the podium, flashed that infectious grin, and began, "Since Lyndon mentioned no names, I'm sure nobody was talking about me!"

Caught completely off-guard by the humor and the sheer audacity of our guest, the Texans roared with laughter. The spell of Johnson's logic was broken.

Kennedy spoke for seven or eight minutes. He talked of our country and our party and our opportunity to "get things moving again in America." He complimented Lyndon.

Kennedy said absolutely nothing about his own record of Senate absenteeism. When he finished, he waved and walked out of the room to our applause. He had faced the Johnson challenge.

He had not won our first ballot votes, but he'd won our admiration.

*Fort Worth Star-Telegram,* July 5, 1992

## Big Faith, Big Flaws, a Big Man

SAM HOUSTON, born two hundred years ago today, was bigger than life, his story more fascinating than fiction.

No other person in American history has been governor of two states, president of a republic, US representative, senator, ambassador of an Indian nation, and general of an army.

Houston's boldly mottled personality both startles and inspires.

He was as unorthodox as a beer party in church. He also could be as unexpectedly devout as a prayer in a saloon.

Sam Houston was about six feet three inches tall and of striking appearance. He was sentimental, generous, and hot-blooded, sometimes violent, and often contrite. He was three times wounded in battle. Indifferent to public opinion, he followed his own drummer.

The conventional moralist can find a lot to criticize. Like everything else about this remarkable giant, his behavioral transgressions were king-sized.

He swore profanely, so much that the Mexicans called him Señor Goddamn. He drank excessively, seemed at one point on the verge of drowning his future in alcohol. The Cherokees named him Big Drunk. Mentioned in his mid-thirties as a bright prospect for the presidency, Houston threw away a promising political career and resigned the governorship of Tennessee under a cloud of suspicion.

He married three times, once without the benefit of clergy unless you count Cherokee tribal customs. He fought duels in violation of the law, and on one occasion was censured by the US House of Representatives for publicly thrashing a member who insulted his honor.

Baptized by immersion in an icy stream at age sixty-one, he was told, "All your sins are washed away." Houston replied, "God help the poor fish!"

But Sam Houston had enormous redeeming virtues. If his faults were bigger than life-size, so was his faith. If his crudeness was colossal, so was his basic integrity.

For fifty years, he wore a ring given to him by his mother. Engraved on the underside, next to his skin, was one word: honor.

Houston strode into the pages of enduring history on April 21, 1836. He was forty-three, and at that point in life a celebrated failure.

On that day, under his command, a hastily assembled and only partially trained contingent of fewer than eight hundred volunteers routed and put to flight the flower and elite of a military empire led by a self-professed military genius who called himself "the Napoleon of the West."

General Houston paused before entering the battleground and spoke briefly. He offered his followers a choice: "If there are any here who shrink from the issue, they need not cross the bayou. Some must perish, but victory is as certain as God reigns. Trust in the God of the just and fear not."

They crossed. Houston ordered the bridge burned behind them to seal off retreat. The odds seemed insuperable. But the God of the just was worthy of their trust. Against the Texan casualties of eight dead and twenty-seven wounded, the elite corps of the Mexican army lost six hundred and thirty killed and seven hundred and thirty prisoners. Santa Anna was among the captured.

The Houston legacy does not belong to Texans alone. It is the story of the invincible spirit of free men and women.

Sam Houston was born in Virginia, left home at fifteen, and lived for three years with the Indians. He gained his first military experience under Andrew Jackson in what is now Alabama.

He began, and for a time ended, his political career in Tennessee. Thereafter he wandered aimlessly for many months and was reported drunk on a Mississippi River boat; finally he turned up in the Oklahoma Indian Territory living again with the Cherokees.

Sam Houston came to Texas on a special mission for President

Jackson, the one man whom Houston idolized.

He was at different times a citizen of four nations: the United States, the Cherokee Nation (which he once served as its ambassador to Washington), the Republic of Mexico, and the Republic of Texas, which he served as president. Through it all, however, his real loyalty was to the United States and to statehood.

Sam Houston was never a citizen of the Confederacy. With all his heart, he believed secession to be treason. He vacated the governorship of Texas rather than swear allegiance to an entity that made war upon his nation. So unpopular was this view that Sam Houston died reviled and rejected by the state that now claims him as its patron saint.

Twice governor of two different states, he twice relinquished the position rather than compromise a conviction. Personal honor was to him more valuable than public office.

The problem that caused Houston to leave the Tennessee governor's chair and the state involved his young first wife, Eliza Allen. She left him after only a few weeks of marriage, giving no reason. Rumors floated, accusing Houston of drunkenness and infidelity.

When his supporters pleaded with him to make some sort of statement, he would say only, "She is blameless." Asked to think of his career, he replied, "Whatever the price of silence, I will pay it." He resigned as governor and left Tennessee, vowing to return and kill any man who spoke ill against Eliza.

A few years later, Houston was sent by the Cherokee Nation to Washington as its ambassador. A representative from Ohio named William Stanberry implied that Houston and President Jackson had profited personally from government contracts to supply Indian rations.

Houston encountered Stanberry on Pennsylvania Avenue and demanded satisfaction. Stanberry pulled a pistol, but it misfired. Houston manhandled him rather brutally.

Stanberry, invoking the law of congressional immunity, demanded that Houston, a former member, be tried and punished by the House. Houston appeared in his own defense, humble and contrite.

"I stand before this House," he said, "branded as a man of broken fortune and blasted reputation. Never can I forget that reputation, however limited, is the high boon of heaven. Though the plowshare of ruin has been driven over me and laid waste my brightest hopes, I have only to say, with the poet Byron:

*I seek no sympathies, nor need;*
*The thorns which I have reaped are of the tree I planted;*
*They have torn me and I bleed.*

And so, on May 9, 1832, Sam Houston was officially reprimanded by the House.

All of this happened before Texas, before San Jacinto, before his presidency of the Republic, before his brilliant battle for statehood, his service in the Senate, his brave but futile fight to save the Union. Those came later, catapulting this warmhearted, impetuous man to a form of immortality.

A motto for his life might well be the words he spoke on the eve of San Jacinto: "Trust in the God of the just, and fear not." When his reputation was in tatters, his honor was intact.

Sam Houston's faults were big, but his faith was bigger. Perhaps in that there is hope for the rest of us.

*Fort Worth Star-Telegram,* March 2, 1993

## Tip O'Neill Was a Big Man with a Big Heart to Match

THOMAS P. O'NEILL JR. That's the way his stationery reads. To his friends he was "Tip." And friends abounded. I have never known a politician with fewer enemies.

For ten years—longer than any predecessor had served continuously as Speaker of the House of Representatives—O'Neill imprinted his personality on national policy.

During those years, as Tip's understudy, I learned a lot about leadership, about personal warmth and human kindness. Tip O'Neill never bore a grudge.

At 285 pounds, abundant white hair cresting his ample frame like snow on a mountain top, Tip would amble through the corridors of the Capitol like an amiable polar bear.

He was accessible. On the House floor, O'Neill frequently turned the gavel over to another and took a seat where he'd be available to members. They would line up six and seven abreast awaiting a turn for a personal conversation.

Like a congenial parish priest, Tip would take their questions by the hour, sympathize with their problems, try to help with their projects. Maybe sometimes he even gave one a penance to perform.

O'Neill's philosophy was really fairly simple. He summed it up as "work and wages." Tip believed there should be a job for everybody who wanted one, adequate wages, a livable home for every family, and a college education within financial reach of the humblest youngster.

He clashed with President Reagan on almost every domestic policy issue, but he didn't let that sour their personal relations. Both were gregarious raconteurs. They'd save up funny stories with which to regale one another.

O'Neill was never mean spirited. He never used his power to punish an opponent and had rich contempt for the new breed of

Conversing over coffee with Jimmy Carter and Tip O'Neill.
OFFICIAL WHITE HOUSE PHOTO, JANUARY 11, 1980.

politics that thrives on character assassination.

The angriest I ever saw him was when Representatives Newt Gingrich of Georgia and Bob Walker of Pennsylvania would wait until the day's business was finished and everyone had gone home and then make speeches to an empty House attacking the reputation of colleagues.

Tip never forgot his roots. He told me of an earlier time in Boston when working people were systemically denied access to voting. Polls opened at 10:00 a.m. and closed at 4:00 p.m. Tip's father had led the fight to end that cruel hoax.

The big Irishman's tastes were modest. Until he became Speaker, wife Millie O'Neill and the children lived in Boston, and Tip shared a small Washington apartment with fellow Massachusetts Democrat Eddie Boland.

He never amassed any personal wealth until after he left office. "Geez, Jimmy," he'd say, "you and I must be the two poorest fellows in the House." Later, a book contract and substantial fees for TV commercials brought the aging former Speaker some money that he promptly put into a fund for his grandchildren's education.

Once, at a dinner in his honor, I sang him a parody to the tune of "Mother Machree": "Sure, we love the dear silver that shines in Tip's hair/and the cigars he smokes which befoul the pure air." Tip loved it.

From his youth, as captain of Boston College's basketball team, O'Neill was a sportsmanlike competitor. He hated to lose but would not take unfair advantage to win. At eighty, after two cancer operations and plagued by arthritis, he still loved golf. After playing eighteen holes in Florida last winter, he groaned, "Geez, Jimmy, everything hurts." He paused. "And what doesn't hurt doesn't work!"

On Tuesday mornings during Jimmy Carter's presidency, a small group would meet at the White House for breakfast. I usually sat beside Tip. Once the waiter brought a steaming platter of grits and asked if the Speaker would like some. Tip, whose New England tastes ran to seafood, potatoes, and corned beef, looked balefully at the grits and said, "I'll try one."

Carter, an inveterate Baptist Sunday school teacher, always called on some member of our group to open the meeting with prayer. Tip once marveled to Carter at the capacity of Protestant laymen to pray extemporaneously. Carter, not wanting to slight the Roman Catholics, asked Tip how many of his faith there were in our group. "Just Danny and I," said Tip.

On the eve of the following Tuesday, it dawned on Tip that the president probably would call on Danny Rostenkowski for the next day's invocation. Frantically, he called to give Dan advance warning.

Sure enough, the first words out of Carter's mouth were, "Danny, will you say our prayer today?" There issued forth a stream of eloquence that might have been written by the archbishop of Canterbury. Tip beamed, elbowed me in the ribs and said, "Didn't think he could do it, did you?"

*Fort Worth Star-Telegram,* January 9, 1994

## A Good Side of Nixon

RICHARD M. NIXON WAS A REMARKABLE MAN, little understood and insufficiently appreciated.

Unlike more gregarious predecessors in office, Nixon often withdrew behind an almost glacial reserve. Even some who worked closely with him considered him as enigmatic as a cross between the Sphinx and Whistler's mother. Yet I always had the feeling that, behind the façade of controlled emotions and sometimes contrived conviviality, there lived a warm person eager to be known.

His political career was a collection of paradoxes. It began when he answered a newspaper ad seeking a young war veteran to oppose Representative Jerry Voorhies, soared to a level of professionalism seldom matched, and ended twenty-eight years later in his gut-wrenching resignation from the presidency on August 9, 1974.

Catapulted up the political ladder by appeals to the nation's fear of communism, Nixon actually did more than any other post-World War II president to thaw relations with the Soviet Union and China and to end the Cold War. His international initiatives were acts of remarkable vision and daring.

Richard Nixon never lacked political courage. Nor were his convictions mere figments of convenience. He played political hardball and had an instinct for the jugular in the political arena. To fight hard was part of his character.

I accompanied President Nixon to the 1969 Texas-Arkansas football game for the mythical national championship. Nixon made no secret of favoring Texas. On the return flight, we discussed our favorite athletes. The president said of one tennis player, "He does not play to win; he plays not to lose." Almost contemptuously, he added, "I don't believe in playing not to lose!"

But he also knew when to subordinate partisanship to patriotism.

After the 1960 presidential election, when a razor-thin margin in several states barely tilted the balance to John F. Kennedy, there were several reports of vote fraud and pleas by prominent Republicans that Nixon, the GOP standard-bearer, demand a recount. Nixon refused. Earl Mazo of the *New York Herald Tribune* began a series of articles questioning the election results. But Nixon personally persuaded the writer to desist.

"Our country can't afford the agony of a constitutional crisis," Nixon told him, "and I damn well will not be a party to creating one."

A decade later, as chief executive, he was inextricably caught up in such a crisis. Perhaps no other president, except for Abraham Lincoln, had a harder task of holding the nation together in the face of internally combustible divisions. Widening domestic polarization about our involvement in Vietnam rocked the White House repeatedly and shattered all hope of the new president's success in his first announced goal: "To bring the American people together."

Nixon's plan was to extricate US troops from Southeast Asia while preserving South Vietnam's right to political independence. He wanted a gradual disengagement by training South Vietnamese to assume responsibility for their self-defense while appealing to the North Vietnamese for a negotiated settlement. But try as he might, he never could persuade anti-war protesters at home to give his plan a chance.

Once, near desperation, he pleaded at the White House with hardline congressional opponents to give him "just one month" without publicly criticizing his Vietnam policy, "so that I can speak to Hanoi without being drowned out."

Nixon insisted that the "silent majority" of Americans were with him, but that their support was being distorted by excessive media coverage of the protesters. This, he believed, gave North Vietnamese leaders encouragement to hold out because they were convinced that public support in America was collapsing.

To counter this impression, on my initiative, the House passed, 333-55, a resolution expressing bipartisan support for the president's appeal to Hanoi for a settlement based on free elections. But the media gave this action scant coverage, and it made little impression on Ho Chi Minh's followers.

It did make an impression, however, on Richard Nixon. He repeatedly went out of his way to show me his appreciation. Last July, after seeing him briefly at the funeral of former Texas Governor John Connally, I got a handwritten letter from our former president reminding me of that occasion twenty-four years earlier.

"While you and I were on the opposite sides of the aisle politically," he wrote, "we were always on the same side personally and patriotically."

Richard Nixon and I became friends. Initially skeptical, I came to appreciate him as a person of intense and dependable loyalty, combative by nature, purposeful and relentless in pursuit of his own principles. The serious side, so dominant in Nixon's character, sometimes made it hard for him to communicate effectively with journalists. He had a hard time laughing at himself, and the media never seemed to appreciate the depth of Nixon's commitment to causes.

He pronounced his principal presidential aim to "create a new structure of peace in the world." Nixon and I discovered our common admiration for Woodrow Wilson, whose sometimes taciturn temperament Nixon's resembled. Nixon's view of world order, like that of Wilson, was moralistic.

When I told him our country was violating the spirit of our agreement with Mexico by inundating Mexican farmlands with large quantities of crop-destructive minerals leached from US soil by the Colorado River, Nixon unequivocally said, "We must do something to correct that."

We did.

A president of my party would have been pilloried mercilessly by the right wing had he attempted Nixon's bold overture of detente with the Soviet Union and China. Precisely because of his fierce anti-Communist reputation, Richard Nixon was able to put in place the

Discussing Vietnam peace initiatives with President Richard Nixon.
OFFICIAL WHITE HOUSE PHOTO, DECEMBER 1969.

first Strategic Arms Limitation Treaty. Primarily because of his vision and leadership, a dark cloud of fear has been removed and the world breathes easier.

On Sunday mornings, Nixon would invite a cross section of friends to join his family for worship services in the East Ballroom of the White House. No other American president, to my knowledge, has done this. One Sunday during the last year of his presidency, feeling lonely and besieged, the president arose early and went alone to the Lincoln Memorial. There a group of visiting students discovered the president in the early dawn seeking succor at the foot of the Lincoln statue.

Richard Nixon fought for what he believed. He jealously guarded the powers of the presidency and battled with Congress about constitutional questions like impoundment and executive privilege. As a member of the majority party in Congress, I opposed him vigorously. I campaigned against him in four national elections and actively resisted much of his domestic agenda. But I hurt intensely for him and secretly fought back tears the day he left the White House.

Richard Nixon probably wished at times for the lightning-quick humor of Jack Kennedy or the down-home folksiness of Lyndon Johnson. He was, by nature, a more private person. He felt that the media did not understand him, and he took personally and suffered deeply the unfair treatment he believed he received at their hands. In later years, he may have wished he hadn't given vent to his feelings as he did in 1962 after the race for governor of California when he said, "You won't have Richard Nixon to kick around anymore!" But it must have felt good at the time.

I remember a happier moment, an evening at the Washington Press Club in the mid-1950s. With the curtain drawn, the announcer intoned, "Our mystery guest tonight once served as vice president of the United States, and one of his hobbies is playing the piano." From behind the screen came the unmistakable strains of "The

Missouri Waltz." Everyone was certain it was Harry Truman.

Then the curtains opened to reveal Vice President Richard Nixon stroking the keys, playing the piece quite well. He had fun that night.

Personally, I hope he had a lot more fun in life than most of us saw him having. He deserved to. Beneath the conscious dignity that guarded his emotions, Richard Nixon loved America. From the time he served in the Navy in World War II, he gave fifty years of his life to it.

*Fort Worth Star-Telegram,* April 23, 1994

## I Cannot Speak of All Mothers; I Can Only Speak of Mine— but What a Story I Can Tell

MOTHER'S DAY does not lend itself to generalizations. For each of us it recalls one distinct person, evoking memories distinct and intensely personal.

Marie Louella Lyster Wright was a lady. In a day before political correctness rearranged the language, that noun was her perfect predicate nominative. It fit her like a pair of hose, and she wore it like a tiara.

No boy she raised could fail to respect and appreciate womanhood. The manners on which she insisted, like holding a door for women, removing one's hat in the presence of a lady, or rising when one enters the room, may seem quaint today. But social graces were important to Mother. She called them marks of breeding.

It wasn't that my mother lived a sheltered life, or was unacquainted with toil. She was born in 1894 in the New Mexico Territory. When she was only eighteen months old, her father died. Her widowed mother, then barely twenty and hundreds of miles from home with an infant to raise, took a job running a retail store.

Later the two returned to Weatherford, where my grandmother managed a hotel. Among the recurring guests were troupes of actors and actresses who came four times a year to perform plays at the Opera House. The actresses would let the fascinated little girl with the big brown eyes try on their costumes—fancy shoes, large-brimmed hats, and feathered boas. Mother developed a strong yen to be an actress.

Her very proper family squelched that ambition. The acting profession, they insisted, was not altogether respectable. Being an actress was not, in their word, ladylike, a quality to which they attached ultimate importance. Their objections did not extend to being a teacher, however, even if one spent her hours teaching acting to others. So after completing school, Mother taught drama, poetry reading, and English literature.

She and my father married in 1916 in Valentine, Texas. Dad commanded a company of the National Guard, sent there to protect the border from incursions by Pancho Villa's forces. The marriage was an attraction of opposites. She was, by training and practice, aristocratic; Dad was egalitarian and had been a professional boxer until he saved enough to buy a business in Weatherford.

Both were romantics and bibliophiles, sharing a love of language and a penchant for poetry, which they encouraged their children to recite at the dinner table. They had a marvelous bond of mutual reinforcement. My mother's praise of him made me regard my father as a hero. And he told me repeatedly how fortunate we were to have her example.

Three objects I shall always associate with my mother: her sewing machine, her piano, and her books. On the first she made most of my sisters' dresses, more fashionable than we could have bought. The day I graduated from high school, I wore a shirt of her craftsmanship. When her grandchildren came, she turned her sewing talents to teddy bears, Raggedy Ann dolls, and lavishly dressed stuffed animals.

Once when I was in the fourth grade, Mother made me a book satchel out of blue denim. The first serious fight I can remember was with a boy named Jack Burkhart, who called it a sissy-looking satchel. To let anyone disparage my mother's work would have been as unthinkable as spitting on the flag. I grew up eating every morsel on my plate, because Dad said that doing less would reflect on Mother's cooking.

On evenings after supper, we often would gather around the piano. Mother would play, and the rest of us would sing—popular tunes, church songs, Irish ballads of which my father was fond. Mother never permitted a disparaging comment about another's performance, however imperfect. The sharpest reprimand I recall

Wright's mother and father, Marie Lyster and James Claude Wright, Sr.
SPEAKER JIM WRIGHT COLLECTION, SPECIAL COLLECTIONS, MARY COUTS BURNETT LIBRARY, TCU.

followed a facetious remark I once made about a younger sister's singing. Our mother wanted nothing to stifle or discourage the creativity of her offspring.

Mother rejected the idea that children should be seen and not heard. She had read John Dewey and every essay she could find on modern education. She insisted that each child participate in dinner-table conversation and was especially keen on originality. She had self-esteem figured out two generations before the term came into usage.

But it was books that Mother passionately loved. Every night she read to the younger children. If you love reading, she proclaimed, no knowledge on earth is beyond your reach. And she demanded reverence for the language. A stranger may not discover whether you're smart in math or geography, she'd say, but people can tell in two minutes whether you use proper English!

In demand as a book reviewer, Mother relished the exercise. Doing a lively review of a current book before an appreciative audience, she must have secretly fulfilled that childhood wish to be an actress. Most of her other satisfactions were vicarious—pride in her husband's and children's accomplishments.

If we were ever poor, we didn't know it. In Mother's view, to think or act or talk as though we were was unacceptable. In the depth of the Depression, when we owned no house and no car—even that year when we had to sell the piano—I always thought we were well off, more fortunate than almost anyone. Mother had a way of making us feel like nobility. With that, we were rich!

*Fort Worth Star-Telegram,* May 8, 1994

## Father's Day: My Father's Act Is a Tough One to Follow

MY FATHER was the greatest inspiration in my life. Largely self-educated and a voracious reader, he burned with ambition to give his children the benefits he had been denied. In the process of doing that, he challenged us to the peak of our capacities.

"Unless you do better than I have done," Dad would tell me, "then I'll have failed. The whole idea of posterity is for each generation to improve upon its predecessors." What a relentless admonition!

James Claude Wright was born in 1890, the youngest of four brothers. His father soon died and his mother was stricken with polio, confined to a wheelchair. Dad had to leave school and find work at about age ten, chopping cotton and firing a brick kiln.

Yet he never felt sorry for himself. Gifted with self-confidence and a sense of humor, my father had a way with words that made ideas embed themselves in my mind inextricably. Once Dad won a slogan-writing contest for the Dr Pepper Company. His entry, "Drink a Bite to Eat," was used for years.

At twenty, Dad became a professional boxer. Jack Johnson was heavyweight champion, and there was money for anyone who looked like a "white hope." My father stayed with that trade until he saved enough to buy a tailor shop and a cleaning establishment in Weatherford.

He also was company commander of the local National Guard unit. In 1914, the unit was federalized and sent to protect the Mexican border. In World War I, Dad served in France. He had a big cleft in his chin, and a stray piece of shrapnel gave him a permanent dimple in his left cheek.

Dad exalted ambition. He believed emphatically in self-improvement and in America's limitless promise. "You can do anything in the world you want to do," he would tell me, "if you want to do it

Baby Wright with his father.
SPEAKER JIM WRIGHT COLLECTION, SPECIAL COLLECTIONS, MARY COUTS BURNETT LIBRARY, TCU.

strongly enough and are willing to pay the price."

My father's first effort to create a nationwide company ended in failure. Eventually, however, Dad's firm would have more than a hundred thousand clients in two thousand communities in forty-two states.

He was a salesman. His stock in trade was ideas. "Armies cannot kill an idea," he would say. "Only a better idea can do that." Another of his oft-recited dicta was that words are more powerful weapons than fists or guns.

Reading is fun, Dad insisted. He gave me, at age seven, my first Tarzan book. Within a year, I had devoured seven sequels. When I was thirteen, Dad gave me the complete works of O. Henry.

"Read these short stories with a pencil in your hand," he instructed. "Each time you come upon a new word, underline it. When you've finished the story, look up the unfamiliar words. Then use each one at least five times in sentences during the next week. That way you'll own those words. They will be part of your arsenal!" Today, I'm still looking up words.

For a high school graduation present, he gave me a fifty-dollar pocket watch, with one caveat. Each time I looked upon its face, I was to think of the words I'd find inscribed inside the back cover. They were these: *Lead us not into temptation but deliver us from evil.*

Dad also believed in tolerance. Returning from World War I, he actively opposed efforts to revive the Ku Klux Klan. Exposed to the wider world, he said he had observed that all the races and religions were composed of people who "wanted the same things, felt the same hurts, and bled the same color."

Once, at age eight or nine, I said Pentecostal religionists were "crazy" because they thought they heard God talking to them.

"What makes you so certain they do not?" my father asked.

"Gee, Dad, if God had said anything, I'd have heard him for sure!"

Dad switched on a radio set. A vocalist was singing. "Hear that?" he asked. I said I did. As abruptly, he turned it off. "Hear it now?" I admitted I could not. "Do you think he's quit singing?"

That example stressed the folly of hastening to criticize others. I just might not be tuned in to their frequency. Once in the days of segregation, Dad asked me to imagine just how I'd feel if there were separate water fountains for red-haired boys.

My father was an ecumenicist before I ever heard that word. He once compared the world's religions to the spokes in a wheel, with

God as the hub. "Suppose you and I are two red ants on separate spokes," he suggested. "Notice that the farther we are from God, out here on the rim, the farther we are from each other. And the nearer we get to one another, the closer we are to God."

"The best way to defeat an enemy," he said on another occasion, "is to turn him into a friend." That advice served me well many times during my political career.

Once economically secure, Dad helped numerous youngsters through college. I don't know how many. He practiced the scriptural injunction about giving alms in private. A rugged individualist, he wouldn't buy a car with an automatic gearshift. He said he didn't need some mechanic in Detroit telling him when to shift gears.

*Fort Worth Star-Telegram,* June 19, 1994

## Truman, Two Young Men, Photos, and a Bygone Era

AS I FLEW south along the Potomac toward Washington last week, the Virginia shoreline shimmered in the summer haze like a Monet painting. My mind drifted back to a time of innocence and wonder.

Right there, upstream from Roosevelt Island, was where we were driving that day in 1956 when my six-year-old daughter, Ginger, noticed that recent rains had swollen the stream.

"I'll bet ol' George Washington couldn't throw a dollar bill across that river today!" she exclaimed.

"It wasn't a dollar bill," ten-year-old Jimmy corrected her. "It was a silver dollar."

"Actually, I think it was another river," I added.

"Anyhow," said Jimmy, "everybody says a dollar won't go as far as it used to go. Why won't it, Daddy?"

My top aide in those days was Craig Raupe. Before coming to Washington with me, he taught history at Weatherford College. He was twenty-nine. Craig had written his master's thesis on President Harry Truman's 1948 victory over Thomas E. Dewey. Truman was Craig's hero.

One day Craig read in the newspaper that the former president was in town for a few days and would be staying at the Mayflower Hotel. That thesis might be an excuse to meet Truman, he decided—maybe even get a picture of himself handing a copy of that document to his idol.

Craig called the hotel and asked for the former president's room. Truman answered. "Sure," he said, "I'd love to have it! Why don't you bring it by tomorrow morning about eight o'clock?"

Floating on euphoria, Craig called his closest friend, Larry L. King. King, who would later become a noted author and playwright (*The Best Little Whorehouse in Texas* and others), was then twenty-six. He had come to Washington only the year before to assist newly elected Representative J. T. Rutherford of Odessa.

"King," Craig announced, "you and I are gonna see Harry S. Truman! In person! Tomorrow! You bring that big Crown Graphic camera from your office, and you can take my picture giving him a copy of my thesis!"

At an indecent hour on Saturday morning, the two rookies from Texas—washed, polished, shined, and combed—drove into downtown Washington babbling over their adventure like a tree full of grackles. In the lobby, Craig picked up the house phone, stammered through a brief conversation, and grinned. Punching King's arm, he announced, "That was Truman his own personal self!"

The former president answered the door in shirtsleeves and bow tie, beaming that friendly smile. "You boys like some coffee?" When it came, Mrs. Truman joined the group and poured.

As King remembers it, he fiddled nervously with his camera and flashbulbs, wary of doing or saying something wrong, while Craig babbled nervously about elections and Truman looked on in tolerant amusement.

King shot four pictures, Craig and Truman smiling broadly at each other. The flash went off each time. Craig was trying to take leave when King interrupted, "Wait a minute, Craig! Now take a couple of me and President Truman." This done, the two departed.

Craig was happier and higher than an airplane a mile over Denver. He dropped King off and rushed immediately to a photo shop to get his precious trophies developed. Craig waited for the shop to open and then stayed to see the results.

An hour later, Craig burst into King's office, mad enough to eat horseshoes. According to King, Raupe cursed for fifteen minutes. The pictures he had taken of Truman and King were perfect. Those that King took of him and the president were blank. Black as Tahiti at midnight! King muses that he must have had buck fever and forgot to pull a protective plate at the rear of the camera. He swears that he used his whole vocabulary of apologies several times over.

At 3:45 a.m. the next day, the telephone awakened King from a sound sleep. It was Craig. In a deadly calm voice, he said: "King, get up and shave and dress. We're gonna go see Harry Truman again. He takes a walk real early every day. We're gonna be outside the Mayflower when he comes out. You're gonna have your camera in hand, and this time you're gonna pull those damn plates!" Five minutes later, King vows, his phone rang a second time. Craig wanted to be sure he hadn't gone back to sleep.

Truman, by King's account, came out for his walk scant minutes after 5:30 a.m. The two were waiting. Craig explained the embarrassing blunder, the need to take the pictures again. Truman laughed and said, "Let's go upstairs and get the thesis." As Craig and the former president posed together the second day in a row, King insists, Craig spouted running instructions: "Don't forget to pull the plate, damn it . . . screw the flashbulb in tight . . . did you get it? . . . take another one!"

Truman, King remembers, chuckled in amusement, "while I felt like the fifth-place jackass at the county fair."

The young Texans rushed to the photographer's studio. It was Sunday morning. Craig had called the photographer the night before and made a deal to meet him there. The pictures of Craig and the president were good this time. In a volcanic eruption of joy, Craig pounded King on the back as if they'd each scored a winning touchdown.

Maybe this tells something about Truman. And humility. Perhaps something, too, about how Washington used to be before it was contaminated by the poison gases of mistrust.

*Fort Worth Star-Telegram,* July 3, 1994

## For Her Worth Is Far Above Rubies

TOO LITTLE PRAISED are the wives of men in politics. They give much more than they get. At countless functions, they must pretend to enjoy interminably boring speeches. And smile tolerantly when constituents belabor them with platitudes.

The wife is always on stage but never gets top billing. She must feign amusement at the hundredth telling of her husband's favorite joke and sit in rapt attention, eyes affixed on him, while he utters phrases she could recite by rote.

Much of her life is lived under a microscope. She is expected to dress fashionably but not threateningly, to guard her figure but never turn up her nose at local delicacies prepared by local constituents.

Seated at head tables, she must be conscious of her countenance. Pleasant but not vivacious enough to steal the spotlight. She may never yawn nor glance at her watch, however long the speech or late the hour.

While fawning introducers compare her spouse to Abraham Lincoln or St. Francis, the wife must betray no hint of amusement. On other occasions, when he's unfairly attacked, she suffers alone, in silence. It's harder on her than on him.

If there are children, upon the political wife must fall the greater share of family responsibility. Her husband's time and talents are soaked up like rainfall upon the thirsty desert floor. She makes the home, cares for the kids, hears their troubles, takes them to Girl Scouts and Little League.

If she and her husband are not heirs to great wealth, the political wife sacrifices material comforts to her husband's career. Knowing he could make more money elsewhere, she indulges, often without sharing, his thirst for public service.

If she uses her own time and intelligence to keep the family fortunes from crumbling, as Lady Bird Johnson and Hillary Rodham

Clinton have done, she learns the pain of snide insinuations, whispered if not published, denigrating her worth and implying that whatever she may contribute to the family income results from some subtle graft.

Much of the above applies in one degree or another to women with husbands in other high-profile professions—the clergy, for example—that are dependent on the public's favor. And some, perhaps, to husbands of women in public office.

My particular point of reference is a very special lady named Betty, who became my wife twenty-two years ago yesterday. She is smart, talented, and accomplished. I've often thought that she could have done better for herself.

Early in our marriage, before I was drawn into the congressional leadership, we had some time to play tennis, sample Washington's ethnic restaurants, ride our bikes together along the towpath of the C&O Canal. On some weekends, we'd drive to quaint historic places like Harper's Ferry or Berkeley Springs, West Virginia, where George Washington used to go for baths.

As I assumed additional responsibilities in Congress, our time together was more and more compressed. Our weekend trips were increasingly business-related.

In an effort to remedy this, I proposed one January that we arrange our weekends in sequences of three: the first for speeches and visiting constituents in our Texas district, and the second for appearances with colleagues in their districts. Every third weekend we would reserve for ourselves! By September, Betty reminded me that this third weekend had come around in actual practice only four times.

The Old Testament words of Ruth speak of the wife of a public man: "Whither thou goest I will go . . . thy people shall be my people, and thy God, my God." (Never mind that Ruth was speaking to her mother-in-law.)

Betty, it happens, was a city girl. She's from St. Louis. Much as I hate to confess it, she wasn't brought up on Mexican food. Betty was ill prepared for Fourth of July barbecues in the park, sitting among bales of hay, discovering midway through the program that the hay was infested with red ants. But she's a trooper.

At one big celebration in Fort Worth's North Side, Betty was placed on a high-stepping parade horse. It never occurred to the event's planners that she had never been on a horse. As that proud steed pranced and danced on those slippery, timeworn cobblestones, Betty began to wish that she was sitting on the hay with the red ants.

Once I agreed to compete with other representatives in a highly publicized chili cook-off. Judges were ambassadors from Ireland, Iran, and some other country little known for chili. As the day approached, I was up to my eyeballs in crises. No time to cook chili. You guessed it: Betty had to prepare the delicacy that bore my banner.

Thanks to her culinary skill, my entry won. Immediately, I was besieged by newspeople demanding my recipe. I hadn't a clue. From the corner of my eye, I could see Betty, thoroughly enjoying my discomfort. After veiled references to secret ingredients, I finally told a *New York Times* reporter that I had used one large diced leaf of the Maguey plant, one pint of tequila, and two cups of powdered mesquite blossoms.

That recipe appeared in the *Times*, and I wondered vaguely if I could be sued. For malpractice, I mean. If someone tried it and got sick. Betty might sue me for plagiarism, except that a wife can't testify against her husband. Besides, the statute of limitations has taken effect.

*Fort Worth Star-Telegram,* November 13, 1994

## Uncommon Compassion: Princess Diana and Mother Teresa

A THREAD OF UNCOMMON COMPASSION connects the lives of the two very different women whose deaths have commanded such overpowering attention during the past two weeks. Princess Diana and Mother Teresa shared an obsessive sympathy, a compulsion to touch and heal and comfort victims of the world's assorted cruelties.

They had little else in common. Their lives are a study in contrasts. One died young, at thirty-six, in a violent accident; the other worked doggedly to age eighty-seven, when her heart simply wore out. Diana was tall, with stately grace and comely countenance. At four feet eleven inches, Mother Teresa seemed almost dwarfish, her face deeply lined, with skin roughened by toil and exposure.

The princess was born to a life of luxury and social prominence. The nun spent her existence in the company of society's outcasts, people poor and sick and devoid of hope. Yet they shared a love for the unloved and unlovable that moved each to see, to touch, to feel, to caress the earth's most miserably afflicted.

Of what is such love born? Goodness? Gratitude? Guilt? One psychological treatise contends that most of us develop, early in life, one of two unconscious self-identifications. Those who consider themselves overpaid, by whatever good fortune, spend their lives trying to pay for their debt. Others, regarding themselves as underpaid, devote their life's energies to getting even.

Mother Teresa gave herself early to a life of menial service. Diana's brother, Charles, believes that his sister, amid all the glamour and controversy, remained "a very insecure person at heart, almost childlike in her desire to do good for others so she could release herself from deep feelings of unworthiness." Diana herself said, "I'm much closer to the people at the bottom than the people at the top, and the latter won't forgive me for it." She attributed this empathy to her father's preachment to treat everyone as an equal.

It's easy to embrace that concept philosophically, at an intellectual level. But that's quite different from performing deeds that make it live. We give at church and to United Way. We buy ourselves a measure of relief. Our consciences are assuaged, if temporarily. But how many go to homeless shelters, volunteer to tend the sick, or serve food to indigent shut-ins? Can we see ourselves washing the lacerated feet of barefoot urchins?

Would we walk with Teresa through germ-infested slums to comfort and care for those dying of starvation and a host of contagious maladies? Or go with Diana to visit lepers condemned to physical isolation? Or minister to people terminally ill with AIDS?

Most of us do not. *Star-Telegram* reporter Jeff Guinn, who chose to live the life of a homeless person for a week, was astounded to discover how many people deliberately avert their eyes while walking past ill-clad homeless people who stand beside employment centers hoping someone will come and offer them a day's work. Almost nobody speaks, or nods encouragement, or acknowledges the presence of such people, Guinn reports. It is as though we're embarrassed by their presence. We look the other way. Like the priest and the Levite in the parable of the good Samaritan, we pass by on the other side.

In my youth I tried to imagine why a priest would reflect that trait in human character. Was his mind preoccupied with the text of a sermon? The Levite saw the wounded man lying near death, suffering the anguish of his wounds and the indignity of his nakedness. According to that ancient story, he "came and looked upon him." Then, like so many on the busy streets of today's crowded cities, he walked away, swiftly making distance between himself and the unnerving scene. Neither of the two figures was willing to get involved.

There are still good Samaritans, of course. A man named Bill

Wilson, on finding sobriety, spent the rest of his life helping victims of alcohol addiction conquer its deadly attraction. William Booth felt such empathy for the down-and-out that he founded the Salvation Army. People in cities everywhere, overcoming their reluctance to be involved, have created shelters and programs of practical help for battered children and physically abused women. My friend Brooks Harrington left a lucrative law practice for several years to devote full time and energy to serving a small church in an economically disadvantaged neighborhood.

A congressional colleague of mine named Mickey Leland felt an obsession with the desperate plight of hopeless, homeless, famine-smitten children in Africa whose parents had fled starvation, walking many miles over burning desert seeking only food. Leland died on a mission of mercy, trying to fly in a food shipment to an encampment where, weeks before, a fleshless child had died in his arms from malnutrition.

This week in our community, United Way is attempting to meet its goal. We can contribute. What we give is part of the dues we pay in gratitude for our own relatively more abundant lives. In giving to this and similar endeavors, we can vicariously feed the hungry and clothe the naked and visit the widows and orphans in their affliction. This we can do joyously.

There are a few who find such vicarious participation insufficient. They would do more. Do not begrudge, therefore, the attention heaped upon the princess and the saintly nun. They are the leaven in humanity's loaf.

*Fort Worth Star-Telegram,* September 14, 1997

## Óscar Arias:
## Blessed Are the Peacemakers

FORMER COSTA RICAN PRESIDENT Óscar Arias, who will speak February 16 at Texas Christian University, is celebrated throughout much of the hemisphere as the political "conscience" of Latin America. He is renowned worldwide for his sure-footed leadership in settling the series of fratricidal wars that bathed Central America in blood throughout the 1980s.

Before the Arias peace plan came into effect, those wars claimed an estimated two hundred thousand lives. To appreciate the magnitude of the tragedy, and the value of Arias's contribution in stopping it, try measuring the number of fatalities as a percentage of population. In a region the size of Central America, those wars made a gory impact similar to a loss of two million people in our country. That may be more violent deaths than we have suffered in all of our wars combined.

Like Jimmy Carter, Arias seems to have grown in retirement. If anything, he has escalated the pace of his relentless activities since leaving public office in 1990. Given the Nobel Peace Prize in 1987, the quiet Costa Rican used the monetary award to establish his Foundation for Peace and Human Progress. Under its auspices, Arias has extended his peacekeeping mission beyond Central America to help resolve long-smoldering border conflicts among such South American countries as Colombia, Bolivia, Venezuela, Peru, and Argentina.

He also has been a major influence in persuading Latin American neighbors to replace oligarchies and military dictatorships with fair and free elections, and increasing the public emphasis upon raising living standards for the common people. At present, Arias is trying to prevail upon all the heads of state to establish a continent-wide arms limitation agreement. As a starter, he wants a two-year moratorium on the purchase of high-tech weapons. So far, twenty-four national leaders have signed that pledge.

Soft-spoken and scholarly, the popular former University of Costa Rica professor impresses audiences with a peculiar brand of understated eloquence. His unpretentious demeanor, the pensive immobility of his facial features, and his utter lack of theatrical flourishes infuse his appeal with an unmistakable sincerity that captivated the US Congress when he addressed us in 1987 enroute to the Nobel ceremony.

On that occasion, the audience was responsive, lawmakers eager to break in with applause but restrained by his simple straightforward message delivered in flawless English. The very absence of jingoistic slogans and artfully contrived applause lines lent authenticity to Arias's words.

Probably no other leader has a better understanding of Central and South American history, culture, and ingrained tradition. After that 1987 speech, Arias held a private question-and-answer session for interested members. He shared precious insights into the thinking of Latin Americans, predicting that free and fair elections would be honored by the controlling Sandinistas in Nicaragua (as agreed in the regional accord over which he had presided the previous month at Esquipulas) and that, in such elections, the people would replace the Sandinista leadership with a moderate government. It turned out that he was right on both counts.

Now, for the first time in history—thanks in no small part to Arias's insistence upon empowering the people of each country with ballots and exposing them to education and a free press—every country in our hemisphere except for Cuba has embraced a democratic system of government. This doesn't mean they've perfected the arts of democratic governance or managed to spread real economic opportunity among the masses of ordinary people.

All the more precious, then, is Costa Rica's enlightened example. It has the highest literacy rate, the lowest unemployment, the best standard of living, and the lowest incidence of crime in the hemisphere. There is no army (it was disbanded fifty years ago last

With Costa Rican President Óscar Arias.
SPEAKER JIM WRIGHT COLLECTION, SPECIAL COLLECTIONS, MARY COUTS BURNETT LIBRARY, TCU.

December), no secret service protection for public officials, and no need for either. The little country that produced José Figueres and Óscar Arias gives meaning to the term *civility*.

Fort Worth enjoys a blossoming friendship with Costa Rica. American Airlines operates daily nonstop flights of about four hours between DFW Airport and San Jose. Several local firms do business there. It was current President José Maria Figueres, son of the legendary post-World War II leader considered the father of modern Costa Rica, who came to our city two years ago to receive the Botanical Research Institute of Texas award for his contributions to the environment. An enthusiastic local delegation of naturalists makes an annual pilgrimage to Costa Rica's celebrated rain forest, which claims, among other things, the world's greatest variety of birds and its most numerous butterflies.

It's an open question whether Jimmy Carter or Óscar Arias would qualify as the hemisphere's most prodigious peacemaker. Ben Franklin once quipped that he'd never known a peace made that wasn't "censured as inadequate and the makers condemned as injudicious or corrupt." Peacemakers, he jocularly supposed, were meant to be honored "in the other world, for in this [one] they are frequently cursed."

Somebody, somewhere, may be cursing Óscar Arias. If so, I've never heard it.

*Fort Worth Star-Telegram,* February 8, 1998

## LBJ's Tapes Reveal Human Side of Presidency

THE LYNDON JOHNSON White House tapes, available in book or audiocassette, offer the most revealing view into the mind of a president that Americans are likely ever to have.

Here, in Johnson's unrehearsed words, one hears the jubilation of a proud, persuasive man as he alternately flatters, cajoles, begs, and bullies his way to astounding legislative triumphs. We also feel Johnson's profound frustrations when blacks and whites balk at his calls for racial tolerance and the jaws of Vietnam tighten with the seeming foreordination of a Greek tragedy.

Only Johnson and Richard Nixon kept such unforgiving proof of their personal White House conversations. After what Nixon's tapes did to his presidency, no successor has dared to allow his in-house conversations to be recorded. It's doubtful that any future president ever will.

These first published Johnson tapes (*Taking Charge,* edited by historian Michael R. Beschloss) cover the early months in LBJ's presidency, between the numbing assassination of President Kennedy in November 1963 and Johnson's landslide victory the next year. They help round out our portrait of Johnson the human being, in his own spontaneously flowing words, as he grapples with crises big and little.

Johnson was the last twentieth-century president to have a huge, romantic vision of what this nation should be and a passion to goad and guide two hundred million fellow countrymen to fulfill that vision. An activist in the tradition of the two Roosevelts and Woodrow Wilson, he saw government as the agency and the embodiment of all that a nation can be and do when it acts together.

Yet the very grandiosity of Johnson's ambition for the nation tended to exacerbate a nagging inner sense of personal limitation. Johnson was obsessed with forebodings of his own mortality. He told

Shaking hands with President Lyndon B. Johnson.
SPEAKER JIM WRIGHT COLLECTION, SPECIAL COLLECTIONS, MARY COUTS BURNETT LIBRARY, TCU.

me more than once that every male in his family had died young. There was so much to do, and so little time.

The defining blueprint of Johnson's grand hopes for America may have been best expressed in his "Great Society" speech at Ann Arbor, Michigan: "Not only the rich society and the powerful society" but one that shared its bounty with the humblest.

He worked and pleaded tirelessly until he passed a civil rights bill that nobody thought achievable, and forced through a poverty bill that raised new hopes and blazed new trails for America's working poor ("my number one bill," he told Congress).

On May 8, 1964, the president returned from a sixteen-stop tour of Appalachia crowned by what Beschloss calls "courageous, bravura" civil rights speeches in the South. In Atlanta, throngs cheered Johnson after he told Georgia legislators, "I will never feel that I have done justice to my high office until every section of this country is linked in single purpose . . . to bring an end to injustice [and] poverty."

The famous "LBJ treatment" is repeatedly evident, as in his May 13 call to Senate Republican leader Everett Dirksen "to tell you that I admire you." Johnson coaxes Dirksen to help pass the civil rights bill. He doesn't want just "a Democratic bill," Johnson pleads, but "an American bill."

Then, to the Illinois Republican: "You're worthy of the land of Lincoln. The man from Illinois is going to pass the bill, and I'll see that you get proper attention."

To Sargent Shriver, deeply reluctant to take on management of the newly created poverty program, a determined Johnson put it in terms that the other could not refuse, virtually as a test of Shriver's patriotism.

Still, not even the celebrated Texas charm could crack North Vietnam's nationalistic resolve or make America's races feel one another's pain.

Johnson suffered periods of self-pity. He felt that the press treated him shabbily. When journalists harped on his family's broadcasting station and wrote crude stories about tenants on Alabama farms owned by Lady Bird's family, Johnson became depressed. He suspected an informal conspiracy among Ivy Leaguers to belittle him. He chafed angrily at "pistol-packing, shotgun, night riders" in Mississippi who gunned down civil rights workers. And he was bewildered by blacks who set off two nights of rioting in Harlem after he'd stuck his neck out further than any predecessor in their behalf. These acts Johnson took as personal affronts. He entered a stage of despondency.

The presidency, as these tapes show, can be the world's most awesome taskmaster. It can take a man in the prime of his mental and emotional power and squeeze him dry like a lemon.

On August 25, the eve of the 1964 Democratic National Convention, Johnson planned to withdraw as a presidential candidate. He prepared a statement. "The times require leadership that all parties and sections and colors can follow," he read to press secretary George Reedy. "I've learned, after trying very hard, that I am not . . . that leader."

When Reedy and Lady Bird remonstrated, Johnson replied: "I cannot lead the South and the North . . . the Negroes will not listen to me. . . . I don't think a white Southerner is the man to unite this nation. . . . I've learned it after thirty-three years." Later that day, his spirits revived.

All this is prelude to Johnson's astounding 1964 electoral victory and the breathtaking four years of domestic policy triumphs that followed. For students of American democracy, these tapes hold surprises and ceaseless fascination. One can't help wondering how many presidents have suffered such secret moments of despair.

*Fort Worth Star-Telegram,* March 29, 1998

## Goldwater Knew How to Salute the Uniform

BARRY GOLDWATER UNDERSTOOD partisanship, and its limits. He also knew the meaning of patriotism. Nobody had to tell him where one left off and the other took over. An outspoken political conservative and a Cold War hawk, Goldwater could have taught useful lessons to the current breed of Democrats and Republicans who are so full of themselves and so committed to the triumph of their own causes that they scorn both moderation and manners.

The first of those lessons is an old military dictum about saluting the uniform. It goes like this: If you don't respect your commanding officer enough to salute him sincerely, then salute the uniform he's wearing. Extend to him the courtesy and consideration that is owed to the office he holds.

This goes for presidents, obviously—our commanders in chief—and for certain other people in life. How the current breed of congressmen, most without military service of any sort, need to master that simple rule!

Goldwater, like most members of Congress in that earlier generation, was a veteran of World War II. We had shared, as citizen soldiers, a common mortal endeavor on which our national survival depended. We wished our leaders' plans well. Our lives depended upon their success. We could grouse about those leaders, but deliberately sabotaging them was never an option. The habit grooves of that experience remain, carved deeply into our psyches.

In the years after that titanic experience that altered the course of so many lives, many legislators of both parties kept their commissions in the reserve forces against the possibility of being needed again for military service. We would go on active duty three weeks each year.

Every Wednesday morning on Capitol Hill, members of the

9999th Air Force reserve squadron met for briefings on the world situation and military readiness. The commander of our unit was Brigadier General Barry Goldwater.

Democrats among us saw nothing amiss in this relationship. We knew the metes and bounds of our respective military and civilian duties. Secretary of Defense Robert McNamara thought otherwise, however, and in 1961 he disbanded the reserve military units involving members of the legislative branch of our government. Goldwater, along with the rest of us, accepted that verdict.

The Arizona conservative was, in some ways, like Harry Truman. Plainspoken to a fault, he never hesitated to disagree with presidents of either party when he thought one of them wrong on public policy. He publicly faulted Richard Nixon over Watergate and Ronald Reagan over Iran-Contra, for examples.

But in spite of domestic political disagreements, he rallied to Lyndon B. Johnson's side in August 1964 when North Vietnamese PT boats fired repeatedly on the USS *Maddox* in the Tonkin Gulf, and the president ordered them and their supply base destroyed. Goldwater, Johnson's opponent in that year's presidential election, was the first person Johnson called, and the old soldier rallied to the embattled president's side. Whatever their differences, he wanted no partisan sniping to distract an American president from his duties at a moment of international crisis.

Later that year, although trailing Johnson in the polls and desperately needing a political break, Goldwater steadfastly refused to pounce on the personal tragedy of one of Johnson's aides caught in a highly publicized homosexual liaison. The GOP candidate harshly chastised one adviser who was goading him to take partisan advantage of the incident.

And years later, with Jerry Falwell tastelessly trying to equate right-wing political policy with the Christian religion, Goldwater said that Falwell deserved a "kick in the ass." In the senator's old-fashioned scale of interpersonal values, now ignored by so many, some things were simply off base. One was perverting religion to political advantage.

Another was attacking an opponent's patriotism or personal character. Among the worst, we might infer, would be to let partisan considerations interfere with the loyalty that each of us owes the institutions of our government and the sometimes flawed human beings charged with protecting those institutions.

When it became belatedly clear in April 1984 that the CIA had illegally invaded international waters, mined Nicaraguan harbors, and covered the deed with a fabric of lies, Goldwater was incensed. He made no secret of his angst. Governments, ours included, had to play by the rules. The administration, then headed by a member of Goldwater's party, was derelict in tolerating so flagrant an abuse of international law, he said forcefully to those responsible.

Yet when the Iran-Contra scheme emerged, revealing a blatant disregard for at least six laws and setting up "impeachment" whispers and a clamor for Reagan's scalp, calm heads prevailed. The last thing America needed, I felt, was a frontal assault on the president's personal character.

By January 1987, I had been installed as Speaker of the House. Reagan had begun the last two years of his presidency. I knew his dislike of detail, his occasional forgetfulness, his habit of delegating broad responsibilities to others. I deliberately chose to believe Reagan's vow that he hadn't condoned the flouting of laws and couldn't remember ever being told of the elaborate scheme.

As a Democrat, I disagreed with Reagan on many issues. But I took him at his word. He was President. I never wanted him personally embarrassed. Then the country would be embarrassed, focus and energy drained from great national goals. Reagan needed all his credibility to negotiate effectively with the Soviet Union.

Some don't understand that. Maybe they've never saluted a uniform.

*Fort Worth Star-Telegram*, June 7, 1998

## Ford Embodied All That Was Good and Decent

JERRY FORD WAS A GOOD AND DECENT MAN—humble, truthful, gentle, generous, and genuine. In his own wholly unpretentious way, he was remarkably courageous. In relations with those of us in the opposite party, he was trusting and trustworthy.

Ford never expected, nor aspired, to be president. The role once thrust upon him, his thoughts were of responsibility, not popularity. His pardon of Richard Nixon for any possible criminal charges was a stroke of instinctive kindness that calmed a gathering public storm and let the sorely abraded nation heal.

Vastly unpopular among many at the time—just as Ford surely knew it might be—that act of simple human decency kept the country from being torn apart in a welter of savage, recriminatory litigation. Ford's wisdom, then widely scorned, is seen now as Lincolnian.

He came to the presidency at an ugly moment of national outrage and disillusionment over the series of Watergate revelations that had resulted in the resignation of President Nixon.

For that transient moment in time, when everyone for America's sake wished the hapless successor well, the nation needed a calm voice and a healing hand. Nobody could have better provided these than Gerald Ford.

Hardly anyone, just days earlier, had anticipated this turn of events. No American president had ever resigned. No prior vice president, now president, had come to office absent the benefit of nationwide public election. Our ship of state was sailing in unknown waters.

No such likelihood had entered my mind that day months earlier, in the summer of 1973, when I'd been unexpectedly called off the House floor and into the cloakroom for a call from the White House. It was President Nixon.

Vice President Spiro Agnew had resigned, facing charges of

From left: Gerald Ford, Jimmy Carter, Jim Wright, and Richard Nixon.
OFFICIAL WHITE HOUSE PHOTO, OCTOBER 1981.

bribery and tax evasion. Under the new succession law, the president must send a name to Congress, where both houses then would have to ratify the selection of a new vice president.

"I'm considering two men," Nixon told me, "and you know them both. I am thinking of Jerry Ford and John Connally." He said he'd like my opinion.

Stunned at the question, and surprised at being asked, I confirmed that I was friends with both and considered either one highly qualified to be vice president.

Nixon pressed me. "Which of the two would you choose if you were I?"

It depended, I said, on where he thought he most needed help.

Nixon at the moment was facing formidable problems with the press and with Congress.

Connally might help him more with the media, I suggested, but Ford would be more helpful with Congress.

This was before the Saturday Night Massacre and the televised House Judiciary Committee hearings. But I think I told the president right. If anyone could salvage Nixon's tattered relations with Congress, it would be Ford, who was widely liked and didn't have a serious enemy in either party.

Jerry Ford was as nearly nonpartisan as a congressional party leader could be, and as open and friendly to members on the opposing side of the aisle.

As president, he openly acknowledged errors of his own party's agents and appointees. He instructed the FBI and the IRS against using their offices to punish or embarrass any citizen for political disagreements. And he reemphasized the limits of the powers of the CIA.

I didn't always agree with President Ford on political policy questions. He vetoed lots of bills, including several key anti-recession measures when a failing economy was reeling from the first Arab oil embargo. Congress overrode some of these vetoes.

But we never found him unwilling to talk, or reason, or listen. He was, as president, the same friendly, fraternal fellow we'd known as a colleague.

In the summer of 1969, before going off to college, my daughter Kay decided that she'd like to get some work experience on Capitol Hill. The nepotism law forbade my hiring or even recommending her.

Undeterred, Kay applied at the nonpartisan placement office and returned to tell me she had landed a part-time job. Working where, I asked her.

"Working for Mr. Ford at the minority leader's office."

Did they know she was my daughter? No, she said. They didn't ask.

I had wild visions of Ford's GOP colleagues being up in arms, maybe even accusing Kay of being a planted spy. Or being, at the least, resentful. After all, some of them had daughters who might want a summer job.

But when I went to explain Kay's identity to Jerry Ford, he said, "That's fine with me, Jim. I don't have any problem with that. I'll trust her not to be telling you any of our Republican secrets." The last with a grin.

That's the way things were back then. And that's the kind of person Gerald Ford was. Upon becoming president, he said, "Our long national nightmare is over."

He also said, "Let brotherly love calm the waters of suspicion and hate."

That's the kind of person he was. A family man. A true all-American. And one sweet guy.

*Fort Worth Star-Telegram,* December 31, 2006

# II

# Domestic Policy

With one foot on a rooftop, Wright, with the mayor and the district engineer, examines flood damage in North Richland Hills, Texas, 1957.
SPEAKER JIM WRIGHT COLLECTION, SPECIAL COLLECTIONS, MARY COUTS BURNETT LIBRARY, TCU.

## Clean Water

EDITOR'S NOTE: *When he was in Congress, Jim Wright was once chairman of the Watershed Development Subcommittee. He was a leading sponsor of legislation to clean up the nation's polluted streams. This newsletter, written in 1966, is largely excerpted from material contained in Wright's book,* THE COMING WATER FAMINE.

*And if from man's vile arts I flee and drink pure water*
*from the pump;*
*I gulp down infusoria, and quarts of raw bacteria,*
*And hideous rotatorae, and wiggling polygastricae,*
*And slimy distomacae, and various animalculae*
*Of middle, high, and low degree.*
—William Juniper, "The True Drunkard's Delight"

AT LEAST twenty billion gallons of water a day are being wasted in this country by pollution. This is water that could be used and reused, if treated properly. It is ravaged water which is a menace to the health of everyone who has contact with it. It offends the nose and eyes of all who come near it, and flows uselessly past water-hungry communities on its way to an indifferent sea.

This wasted water amounts to about 6 percent of the total needs of the nation. It is a very significant 6 percent, however, since it constitutes better than one-fourth of the country's *pure* water needs, and its loss adversely affects the lives, the economy, the health, and the pleasure of far more than half of our population.

The nation used about *forty billion* gallons of water a day in

1900. We are using *three hundred and sixty billion* gallons daily in 1966. The rate of consumption will continue to go up steadily. Increased uses for industry and irrigation couple with the shiny appurtenances of our affluent society. Automatic dishwashers, lawn sprinklers, the instant carwash, the laundromat, backyard swimming pools, and massive household demands for electric energy all represent new and growing uses. This is our way of life. We sweat to pay for it. We're not about to give it up. Even with harsh restrictions in the middle of last summer's drought, New York City's eight million people used at least three times as much water daily as London's seven million—and *wasted* almost as much as Londoners used.

There is no more water on the earth today than there was in the time of Adam. And despite the fact that our demands on the supply are infinitely greater than they ever have been, the amount is sufficient to sustain us—*if* we can learn to use it and reuse it properly. On an average day in the United States, a volume of almost five trillion gallons of water splashes on our land in the form of rain, hail, dew, snow, or sleet. Three-fourths of this rises again by evaporation, unused, into the heavens from whence it comes. The rest either settles into the earth or runs with our rivers.

Pollution is caused by man's carelessness, indifference, and callousness. It is ironic that law enforcement authorities impose sizable fines upon anyone who litters up a roadside, a picnic area, or a beach, but very rarely bother anyone who litters up a stream.

How dangerous is a contaminated stream? Recently a cupful of water taken at random from the Connecticut River near Hartford was found to contain twenty-six different infectious bacteria, including typhoid, paratyphoid, cholera, salmonellosis, tuberculosis, anthrax, tetanus, and all the known viruses, including polio. The broad Hudson River, which runs sluggishly through New York City, could have saved the Northeast from the 1965 drought. But it could not be used. Its waters were too foul to drink. George Washington, in fact, almost died as a youth after drinking from the muddy Potomac.

Even underground water tables are subject to pollution. Largely unknown to the public, an epidemic in Riverside, California in the summer of 1965 afflicted *eighteen thousand citizens* with violent attacks of vomiting and extremely high temperatures. At least three died as a result. Ultimately, bacteriologists traced the source to the city's water supply, which for seventy-five years had been safe and pure since it came from thirty deep wells. Suddenly, due to a subterranean contamination, death and debilitating disease lurked in the water taps of the city.

Lake Erie can be accurately described as "dying." In 1964, experts carried out a series of oxygen tests of the lake basin. The central core of Lake Erie was found to be for all purposes a dead body of water, so lacking in oxygen that any marine life entering the area is doomed. It is a vast underwater "desert." Daily this "dead" area spreads. Already it measures two thousand six hundred square miles, more than one-fourth of the huge reservoir's entire surface.

Nor is Erie the only one of the Great Lakes beset with decay. It is merely the most advanced case. By 1965, the water level in all five of the lakes had dropped to the lowest point in recorded history. Both Erie and Huron are fully five feet lower than they were a dozen years ago. Michigan and Ontario show similar depletion. Just how significant is all this? A one-foot drop in the water level of the Great Lakes chain results in a loss of 2.75 *trillion* cubic feet of water. At our present rate of consumption, this loss is equivalent to an eighty-day supply for the entire nation.

During the first eight years of our national Anti-Pollution Program, it directly encouraged the building of 5,994 modern purification plants in communities throughout the country. Approximately $500 million in federal grants stimulated local investments of more than $3 billion in water purity.

Impressive as this is, it still isn't enough. The rapid proliferation of increasing contamination of our streams has been halted, but, from the standpoint of the pollution level, we are just about standing still. The infection has ceased to spread dangerously throughout the body of our nation's rivers, but the *degree* of infection is just about the same. While we were eradicating old sources of pollution, new sources were springing up through the growth of industry and population density. We may have begun to hold our own. We are not making appreciable headway on a national basis.

The federal government is investing a little more than $150 million a year in water cleanliness. With just under two hundred million Americans, this comes to about seventy-five cents per citizen annually—the cost of a couple of packages of cigarettes—to protect the purity of our most basic resource, without which no citizen could live.

There is absolutely no such thing as *new* water; nor is there any conceivable limit to the number of times it can be used. Science tells us that the first glass of water you drank this morning contained some tiny molecules that fell in the flood of Noah, some that floated fishing craft in the Sea of Galilee two thousand years ago, and some that washed blood from the beaches of Normandy on D-day, 1944.

An unending cosmic rotation steadily moves man's life-giving liquid by gravity through the flow of streams to the great reservoirs of our oceans, draws it skyward by the sun's attraction to be purified anew, conveys it by cloud and wind, and returns it by rain to refresh the thirsty earth and renew man's lease on life . . . ad infinitum. It is an ever-recurring miracle, the most wondrous natural marvel of a wondrous universe.

Science can comprehend it, but never quite duplicate it. Man cannot change it. He can locally and temporarily befoul the process and bring death. Or he can form a sort of divine partnership with nature, help it along, and preserve life. This is his choice.

from *The Coming Water Famine*
(Coward, McCann, 1966)

## The Coming Water Famine

EDITOR'S NOTE: *Fighting to preserve an abundance of clean water has been a passion with Wright. As mayor of a Texas town experiencing a seven-year drought, he fought for a new fresh lake and new waste treatment facility. In Congress, he cosponsored clean water legislation and helped override a presidential veto. This is another article from his 1966 book of the same title.*

SINCE TIME BEGAN, water and life have been synonymous. Water is the cheapest, yet the most priceless, of all commodities. Since the dawn of history it has given respite to the traveler, solace to the sick, succor to the land, reflection to the philosopher—and to the earth itself a never-ending renewal. No life can exist without it.

Water is twentieth-century man's most necessary servant, and we use it in copious quantities. In the United States today it takes three hundred gallons of the indispensable fluid to produce a single loaf of bread. To grow a pound of beef and to get it to your dinner table requires at least one thousand gallons of water. About one hundred thousand gallons go into the manufacture of each automobile. Almost everything we do reflects its use.

The harsh truth is that in the midst of unprecedented plenty, America is running out of usable water—not slowly, but rapidly. No imaginable crisis could present a bleaker prospect.

Twenty-one years ago a remarkable conservation farmer named Frank White of Azle, Texas, stirred my interest in the subject. He foresaw, long before the hot hand of drought closed a fist upon America's East Coast, what could happen to our cities. I spent many hours in the fields with him, studying the behavior of water upon the land. He was, in the Old Testament sense, a prophet.

My friend and mentor Conrad Russell taught me the meaning of water to the life of a town. He showed me in the lean years of Texas's seven-year dry spell how easily it can be wasted and how good management can husband it, purify it, and develop every available source.

James Dillet Freeman saw beyond the prosaic uses of water to its essential character. He said it well:

> *Water never resists, yet it wears away the most resistant things. Water fits itself to conditions, takes the shape of any bowl it is poured into. Yet nothing shapes more things than water; the continents have the shape it gives them. Water does work, but is never busy. It may turn a mill or light a city, but not by trying. Water lets itself be used. Water has learned humility. It is colorless, yet what is a rainbow but water? It is tasteless, yet what is there better to drink? It always seeks the lowest place. But those in high places come to drink of it.*

Sam Rayburn understood this and talked with me about it. So do my colleagues Bob Jones and John Blatnik and Ed Edmondson, who have discussed the subject of our water crisis with me in depth on many occasions. So does the League of Women Voters, an organization that has been crying in the wilderness for years, begging someone to listen.

If water famine comes, it is your children who will suffer. It then will be too late for reflections upon what we *should* have done. There'll be no comfort in hindsight, no satisfaction in placing blame. It's your country whose future is at stake.

from *The Coming Water Famine*
(Coward, McCann, 1966)

## On Protest and Patriotism

TODAY I WANT TO SAY some things about protest and patriotism. There is a disturbing tendency in the United States today to confuse the right of dissent with a right to disrupt.

There is a growing tendency to speak of "civil disobedience" as though it were some inalienable right protected by the Constitution. So let us have some very plain words about the difference between rights and riots, and the difference between peaceful protest and deliberate disobedience to lawful authority.

Let me make it clear that I am a defender of the right to protest and of the right to dissent—I believe in the right to advocate, the right to petition, the right even to be wrong on matters of opinion.

I agree with Voltaire who said, "I disapprove of what you say, but I will defend to the death your right to say it."

These rights are inseparably American. They form the safety valve that prevents our government from becoming tyrannical and oppressive.

But the very protection of these rights implies a clear obligation to accept the determination of the majority once it has been made and not to engage in deliberate frustration of the rights of others.

The Constitution recognizes no such thing as a right to "civil disobedience." If widely permitted, it would make all law meaningless and reduce democracy to anarchy.

And emphatically there is no right under the Constitution or anywhere else to give assistance to the enemies of this country.

We hear much these days about the so-called "campus revolution." There has always been in each generation a certain spirit of rebellion against the mores and standards of its predecessor. This is a healthy sign—up to a point.

It is an admirable exercise of academic freedom for students to express themselves on public policies, even in silly ways if they wish.

But it is not admirable—nor is it an expression of academic freedom—when student pickets try physically to block the entrance to a building so that other students may not be permitted to have interviews with air force recruiters.

This is no expression of freedom. This is a denial of freedom to others.

It is an expression of freedom—whether right or wrong—for students to express their disapproval of the manufacture of napalm.

But it is not an expression of freedom for students at various universities to stage a sit-in which physically prevents job recruiters from the Dow Chemical Company from being able to talk with other students about career opportunities in chemistry. This is a deliberate frustration of freedom.

So far as I'm concerned, students at the University of California and at Stanford are perfectly within their rights to express their opinions against this country's policies in Vietnam. But they are absolutely not within their rights when they seek to prevent Americans with another viewpoint from being heard and attempt to shout down officials of the United States government appearing on campus. This is the very opposite of freedom!

I am not so old that I have forgotten the crusading zeal and restlessness of youth. Very well do I remember how, as editor of the college paper in 1940, I wrote a series of stinging editorials against the first peacetime draft while it was being debated in Congress. I called it "an insult to the patriotism of American youth" and said that if our country were ever in sufficient danger to need young Americans on the battlefield, all of us would volunteer and go without being called, and that the government should not conscript us in time of peace. With all the idealism of my eighteen years, I believed passionately in every word that I wrote.

The fact that I did volunteer, leaving the university to enlist in the air force within two weeks after Pearl Harbor, does not minimize the fact that I was wrong—dead wrong in my judgment. And I shudder to think what would have happened if all of us had waited until Pearl Harbor, and it had caught us without any substantial number of trained men.

Even the fact that I was wrong did not alter my right to be wrong. I said my say and I lost out. Wiser heads prevailed. The First Amendment and tolerant school administrators kept me from being kicked out of school. And when the draft was officially voted, I bowed to the will of the majority.

Just so do those on campus today have the right to express their views. But they have no right to frustrate the policies of the majority once those policies have been lawfully determined.

College enrollment in this country will increase by 49 percent in the next decade—four times the rate of increase for the general population. Ten years from now nine million youngsters will be in our colleges. They will benefit from the right of free speech—from the rights of questing, seeking, disagreeing—yes, protesting.

But if our country is to have a future, they also will be learning—while learning the courage to express dissent—the necessity to abide by the determinations of the majority once they have been made.

For if we do not teach them that, then freedom will become anarchy, and anarchy is the opposite of freedom.

Today the United States is engaged in a terribly difficult and no doubt unpopular undertaking in Asia. People have a right to disagree with what is being done, although I wish their disagreement could express itself in constructive alternatives rather than mere negative slogans.

But the price of preserving rights is the willingness to impose self-restraint. And the right to criticize our efforts in Vietnam should stop short of the point at which it encourages the enemies of the United States to continue their aggression.

We are winning that war, slowly and relentlessly. Battlefield casualties are running eight-to-one in our favor. While that war is costing only about 4 percent of our Gross National Product, it is costing at least 40 percent of North Vietnam's. Why, then, does the enemy persist?

There really can be no doubt that Ho Chi Minh and his advisers in Hanoi are emboldened to continue what has been for them a hopelessly losing battle by the mistaken belief that we in the United States are just about to cave in and quit.

There is no doubt that this calculation is encouraged by sensationalized news of the protests in our country. Nor can there be doubt that this misreading of American sentiment, by prolonging the war, is taking a tragic toll in the lives of American servicemen as well as Vietnamese.

And the right of peaceful protest has become something else indeed when a group of people will wave flags of the enemy, shout obscene imprecations against the leaders of our country, and try, however futilely and absurdly, to storm the Pentagon.

If this is not treason, it is so close to it as to be almost indistinguishable.

Dissent from the opinions of the majority is a precious right. Deliberate disruption of the orderly will of the majority is emphatically not a right.

Speech before the Downtown Rotary Club,
Fort Worth, Texas, October 27, 1967

## The Constitution Has Steadied Our Course

ON SEPTEMBER 17, the Constitution of the United States will be 205 years old. Though that event may not be widely noted, it deserves to be.

A few years ago, a prime minister of Ireland, addressing our Congress, reminded us that the United States is the oldest republic on Earth. That fact has its roots in our Constitution.

The fifty-five delegates who met in Philadelphia to write that document faced a monumental task. Things were in chaos. The Articles of Confederation had broken down. States taxed one another's goods. Nobody paid taxes to the central government. Deeply in debt, unable to maintain a standing military force, it borrowed money from private citizens and could not pay them back.

The British blockaded our ports. Merchant seamen who ran the blockade were captured by Barbary pirates and sold into slavery. There was an armed revolt in New England.

The national debt was so bad that talk arose of trying to sell some of the former colonies. Spain owned Florida and was interested in buying the Carolinas. That was America, a thin ribbon of settlement stretched along the Eastern Seaboard, in 1787.

The wonder is that the Constitution's drafters were able to bring it off at all. Several times they came near to despairing. Deep suspicions lurked between the small and larger states, between abolitionists and slave owners, between northern manufacturers and southern planters.

What things have made their work endure? Here are a few, I think, that gave it tensile strength.

First, the founders were careful to give the Constitution flexibility. They didn't burden it with details that soon would be outmoded. They wanted a garment with enough elasticity to stretch as the nation grew and accommodate changes then unforeseeable.

Isn't it a marvel that in two full centuries, the Constitution has been amended only twenty-six times? Excluding the first ten amendments, which were necessary to its ratification, and omitting the eighteenth and twenty-first, the Constitution actually has taken on only fourteen modifications in the last two hundred years.

Contrast this with the Texas Constitution, a veritable crazy quilt of patches on patches, which bore four hundred and seventy-four amendments the last time I counted.

There've been temptations aplenty. Every year members of Congress file scores of proposed amendments, each designed to carry out some popular wish.

That amendments haven't encrusted the ship of state like barnacles is testimony to the wisdom of the founders in making the amending process difficult, and to that of Congress in resisting temptations to encumber it while pandering to popular whims.

Maybe we should think of this the next time we become so agitated about the folly or dishonor of fallible buffoons, such as flag burners, for example, that we want to amend the Constitution to put them in their place!

No doubt the system has lasted also because of the careful balance of powers by which the Constitution checkmates any who would accumulate too much authority.

The government was to be a tripod, like an old-fashioned three-legged milking stool. Each branch of government was subject to checks by the other two.

The president should propose, but Congress must dispose. If either went too far, the court would curb them. Within this framework, real power has flowed back and forth with the popularity of some presidents and the assertiveness of certain legislative leaders. But in all these years, it has never once gotten wholly out of hand.

Those who would make radical changes in the finely tuned balance between the branches of our government should pause to ponder the inestimable value of a legislature that may be led but never driven and a chief executive that Congress may influence but never intimidate.

Finally, the system most surely mandates, and must rest upon, a climate of toleration. Some of the early colonies had official state churches, but the United States would not.

Everyone might have an opinion; nobody could force his upon unwilling others. Everyone could have his say; to none went the right to get his way.

Thomas Jefferson, whose brilliant mind and illustrious career were bright beacons in the dim early dawn of our republic's life, asked to be remembered for only three things. Not that he was a talented architect, inventor, agronomist, and writer. Not that he was president, vice president, and secretary of state.

The simple monument that marks Jefferson's resting place, faithful to his request, memorializes him simply as author of the Declaration of Independence and the Virginia Statute of Religious Toleration, and as founder of the University of Virginia.

The latter he dedicated, in his own inimitable phrase, to the illimitable freedom of the human mind. We needed no legal barricades against wrong opinions. Truth, he said, is the sufficient adversary to falsehood. And error of opinion is tolerable so long as truth is free to combat it.

The Canadian Supreme Court a few days ago overturned a lower court's conviction of a man named Ernst Zundel, found guilty of spreading false news against the public interest.

Zundel, an offensive anti-Semite, has been spouting off to all who would listen that the Holocaust under Hitler is a fiction and never really happened. The man, of course, is absolutely wrong on the indisputably documented historical facts.

The high court ruled, nevertheless, that Canada was not so weak nor Canadians so feebleminded that they needed a law to protect them from the rantings of every errant fool who comes along spouting factual inaccuracies and spurious doctrine.

Jefferson, along with most of the founders, would have agreed with that.

*Fort Worth Star-Telegram,* September 6, 1992

## What Is the Value of a Ballot?

HERE'S A THOUGHT TO PONDER, and a question to answer, as Election Day approaches.

What is your one vote worth? What would you sell it for? Suppose we just gave up the right. That's what we do, in effect, when we fail to vote.

It shames me that people in emerging countries, with far less material reason to be grateful for democracy's blessings, appreciate the ballot more than we do. A substantially higher percentage of their citizens, when given the opportunity, exercise its privilege.

During the past several years, I've witnessed elections in El Salvador, Nicaragua, Haiti, and Panama—all wretchedly poor by our standards. In each of these, approximately 80 percent of all voting-age citizens turned out to vote.

On Election Day in August in Mexico, I visited sixteen different polling precincts—in urban slums, affluent suburbs, remote mountain villages—as fully 70 percent of adult Mexicans cast votes.

Here at home, some observers predict that Texas will register a turnout of less than 50 percent on November 8.

And ours is supposed to be the world's leading democracy—the exemplar, the pacesetter. We are the ones on whose model countries in Eastern Europe and elsewhere are supposed to pattern their shiny new democratic orders emerging like butterflies from the cocoons of long political oppression.

Americans did not always value the vote so lightly. It is what the Revolutionary War was all about. Our forebears believed that taxation without representation was tyranny.

A modern Congress-basher might quip: "If they thought that was so bad, they oughta try taxation *with* representation!" A cute joke—until we compare our lot with that of any dictatorship in the world.

It wasn't always so easy to vote, even here in America. The nearly universal access to the ballot which our people enjoy today has evolved slowly over the years.

In early Virginia and elsewhere among the original thirteen states, voting was confined to the propertied elite. A voter had to own property rendered for taxation. Thomas Jefferson led the fight for what was called "universal manhood suffrage."

Those who today would sniff at that term as an expression of male chauvinism should remember that this was a major democratizing reform at the time. The power structure considered it dangerously radical. One newspaper editorially predicted: "The republic is in the last stages of imbecility because the atheist from Virginia is in the White House."

Still, not all men were allowed to vote. Not until the Civil War was the privilege extended, even in theory, to black men. Not until our century were women permitted the vote. Not until World War II was the infamous "white man's primary" declared unconstitutional. And not until the Voting Rights Act of 1965 were notoriously well-established patterns of discrimination ended in practice.

It was here in Fort Worth, in President Lyndon B. Johnson's May 1968 commencement speech at Texas Christian University, that an American chief executive first advocated lowering the voting age to eighteen. Eighteen-year-olds, Johnson reminded us, were dying for our country in Vietnam.

This year, students in my class at TCU are promised a three-point bonus on the final semester grade for voting, and additional points if they volunteer at least eight hours of work for any congressional or senatorial candidate. Still, some pass up the privilege.

Is it in the natural order of things that the beneficiaries of evolutionary progress scorn the most valuable legacies of their own inheritance? Must one have suffered tyranny to appreciate freedom?

El Salvador, through four hundred years of history, enjoyed sporadic efforts at democracy. But no elected president was permitted to serve out his term. Each was overthrown by a military junta. Finally, in 1982 and again in 1984, successive elections allowed for peaceful change. I watched long lines of people, dressed in their Sunday best, standing for hours in the hot sun without complaint, waiting to vote. I saw people who had walked to the polls for ten miles over mountain trails. One woman that day gave birth to an infant while waiting in line to vote.

In Haiti that December, when a spontaneous celebration broke out in the streets after the election of Jean Bertrand Aristide, a Haitian explained the joyous mood of his people. "You have a real election every two years," he told me. "We have had one every two centuries."

Maybe that's it. Could it be we've had so much democracy that we're sated? Are you tired of the whole gaudy panoply? Wish it were over so the media could get back onto something more interesting, or more entertaining?

Sam Rayburn once observed that freedom is not something we work for once and win forever. "It's like an insurance policy," he said. "Its premium must be kept up to date."

Some tell me that they are disgusted with all the negative campaign ads, turned off by the mudslinging. Good! But don't use that as a cop-out. Express yourself. Find a candidate who doesn't attack the opponent and cast a vote for that person.

Feel miniscule and powerless? Think your vote won't count? Stop and reflect. There's only one way it won't count. That's if you don't cast it.

*Fort Worth Star-Telegram,* October 30, 1994

## An Old Wolf Fears for the Pack

EDITOR'S NOTE: *Better, perhaps, than any other single entry, this piece encapsulates the life and legislative struggles of the author and other progressives of his generation.*

AS ONE WHO CAST HIS FIRST VOTE for Franklin Roosevelt and joyously shared Lyndon Johnson's dream of a Great Society, I sometimes identify these days with an endangered timber wolf who watches warily from a hill as the habitat of his youth is systematically denuded by an alien culture.

Trees, grasses, and vegetative cover that meant provender and benign protection to the pack for which the old wolf shared responsibility now give way, mile by mile, to a hostile environment paved over with concrete. What the eager perpetrators of that landscape hail as progress is to the wolf desecration. In his view, they are the predators.

From the time of my youth, the things that set our country apart from all others were our progress in building an upwardly mobile society without class distinctions, and a constantly expanding middle-income sector characterized by rising home ownership, rising educational standards, more family buying power, and shrinking levels of unemployment. Through all this ran a strong strain of sympathy for the underdog, a desire to lift him up into the mainstream. This, we told ourselves, was America! To promote these ends was the business of government.

We said America didn't have, thank God, the hideous extremes of poverty and wealth that were to us so striking in most other countries we visited. No professional beggars, no homeless underclasses here. Ours was a democracy, after all!

Even if this self-image was distorted by rose-tinted glasses, we knew at least where we wanted to go. Sure, blacks and Hispanics had been mistreated, but we were out to cure that. Where earlier generations had been economically shut out from college, we'd make that option universal. The Depression had left ugly scars, but our enlightened generation knew how to create here in this blessed country the bases for a self-perpetuating prosperity. That's what we told ourselves.

Today, a new band of Visigoths is at the gate with bulldozers and wrecking balls, gleefully preparing to tear down our temples and uproot the trees we planted. What gets me, I think, is not simply that they have a different vision of how to get where we were heading. They have an entirely different destination in mind. Their vision is not an egalitarian society but a laissez-faire society whose rewards are survival of the fittest. The devil takes the hindmost. And the business of government: stay out of the way.

The direction in which the new conservatives want to lead us portends an ever-wider spread between the richest and the poorest, with a steady diminution of the once-broad middle-income sector. The radical change in income distribution during the 1980s, so chillingly documented by Kevin Phillips in his book *The Politics of Rich and Poor*, provides merely a prelude to what is coming if Senator Trent Lott and Representatives Newt Gingrich, Dick Armey, and Bill Archer have their way. The rich will get richer; the poor will get poorer; there'll be fewer of us in the middle.

These men do not think of that eventuality as either greedy or cruel. They see it as the dynamic fruition of the natural laws of economics. Cheaper American labor will help us compete abroad, they reason. Private orphanages will care for indigent children. But if we follow this new leadership, entranced by its harsh rhetoric against welfare and its seductive promise of what they call "middle-class" tax cuts, the income gap will grow, median wage-earners' paychecks will buy less, retirees will have a harder time, and kids of average means will find college education less affordable.

Admittedly, some welfare programs haven't been effective, and the system needs a careful overhaul. But anybody who tells you that the budget can be balanced just by cutting welfare is either uninformed or is planning to reduce Social Security and Medicare substantially. Outside those two programs, which most folks don't consider "welfare," eliminating all social spending entirely would not wipe out the annual deficit. Dick Armey has been candid, at least. He advocates abolishing Social Security.

And look carefully at who wins and who loses before going overboard for a Republican tax cut. Conservative theorists soon to be in charge describe their goal as taxing consumption rather than profits. That may sound benign, but it really means more taxes from poor people who have to spend their entire incomes on essential consumer goods and less from those who make enough to set aside substantial savings. Maybe a national sales tax. We worked for decades to perfect a tax system based on *ability to pay*. The new theory is based on *inability to escape*.

There's a sweet-sounding ring to the promise of "tax vouchers" to promote "freedom of choice" in education. But this means that people of modest income whose children go to our public schools will have some of their own taxes given to relatively more affluent families with children in private schools. This might help create an upper-caste educated elite, if that's our country's goal, but it won't do much for average American kids.

The whole thing tilts toward elitism and away from equality. It runs directly counter to our country's historic evolution of social principles. It will hurt rather than help hard-working, middle-income families. Thoughts such as these I've expressed might get you branded in some quarters as a "liberal." But don't let that make you afraid to think them. Our ancestors weren't.

*Fort Worth Star-Telegram*, December 11, 1994

## Liberty and Security

SINCE EARLY IN AMERICAN HISTORY, the greatest threats to people's freedom have risen from the tendency to overreact, sometimes hysterically, when confronted with perceived, and often greatly exaggerated, dangers.

During the Communist scare of the 1950s, movie actors, college professors, radio and television broadcasters, and even army officers were threatened with loss of their jobs and reputations (some lost both) because Wisconsin Senator Joseph McCarthy, or some other self-appointed fearmonger, accused them of being secret Communists.

It was in that period that Arthur Miller wrote his famous play, *The Crucible,* based on the early colonial "witchcraft" trials of Salem, Massachusetts, where innocent people were burned to death at the stake because of a hysterical fear of witchery and the suspicion that these accused citizens might be witches. Miller's play helped American audiences recognize how foolishly some of us were currently behaving toward fellow Americans while trashing our sense of fair play, and without helping our country one iota in the Cold War competition with Russia.

This is not to suggest that we are now in danger of repeating those particular errors. Surely we have better sense. But the speed with which Congress passed the USA PATRIOT Act, the alacrity with which President Bush now wants to expand it—even the very title, which suggests not at all subtly that anyone is unpatriotic to question its contents—all of these call for caution.

Let's stop and look calmly at changes of this profundity before plunging ahead at full speed.

The PATRIOT Act, coming on the heels of 9/11, sailed swiftly through Congress with little debate. It increased government enforcement and investigative powers and freed Justice Department agents from certain normal legal restraints.

Homeland Security legislation, meanwhile, substantially expanded the president's power over civil service employees, allowing him to rearrange government agencies and to reclassify, reassign, and change existing rules of employment and compensation. It could be used to reverse some reform provisions of the original Civil Service Act, which threw out the spoils system, or of the Hatch Act, which depoliticized the professional workforce. Whether this is good or bad can depend on how it's administered.

Now the administration wants the right to examine library files to see what individual citizens are reading and break into internet communications to see which citizens are visiting which websites.

Such powers, if abused, could play havoc with individual privacy rights.

Government lawyers want the right to search private premises without getting a court order and without informing the citizens whose homes or offices they inspect. Their justification, of course, is that this right is intended to facilitate the hunt for terrorists.

Nothing tests the character of a democratic society like a clash of two values and the priorities its people attach to each. Individual liberty and national security are two such values.

These two fundamental policy goals can collide in times of war or national crisis. There's always a temptation to subordinate our Constitution's guaranteed freedoms to the immediate task of subduing an "enemy" either real or perceived.

As a twenty-one-year-old lieutenant in the Army Air Corps, I was shocked in 1944 to hear a respected elder in my home community suggest that our country should just simply suspend all elections for the duration of the war.

That year, the Supreme Court upheld a 1942 executive order by President Roosevelt incarcerating thousands of Japanese-descended American citizens in internment camps for fear they might be agents of sabotage. A later court, in the calm of peacetime, reversed that ruling.

Nor did World War II mark our first aberration from the straight and narrow paths of Constitutional freedom. During President John Adams's administration, when the Constitution was young, Congress passed an anti-dissent abomination called the Alien and Sedition Act. Under that vanguard of super-patriotism, spurred by an irrational fear of "Jacobinism," the government seized printing presses and shut down publishers whose expressed opinions made them somehow suspect.

And those of us who virtually deify the memory and inspiration of Abraham Lincoln owe it to others to acknowledge that it was our ideological icon who unilaterally suspended the rights of habeas corpus during the Civil War.

So maybe we can understand, if not applaud, the impulse behind the PATRIOT Act and the president's proposed expansions of it. But, perturbed though we are at terrorists, we'd be fools to forget that freedoms, once forfeited, might be hard to reclaim.

October 12, 2003 (unpublished)

Between Dallas and Fort Worth, 1976. CongressmanWright had ushered a bill through Congress to help pay for the completion of Loop 820.

SPEAKER JIM WRIGHT COLLECTION, SPECIAL COLLECTIONS, MARY COUTS BURNETT LIBRARY, TCU.

## A Tale of Two Cities, One Airport, and One Pesky Amendment

EDITOR'S NOTE: *A heretofore unpublished account of the creation of the Dallas/Fort Worth International Airport and efforts to fulfill its purpose.*

DURING NEARLY THIRTY-FIVE years in Congress, I long ago lost count of the number of sundry amendments I've offered to various bills. Surely more than a hundred of them became law. But these days whenever people in Texas ask me to explain "the Wright Amendment," I know the one they mean.

That law was an effort in 1979 to keep faith with the people of Fort Worth and Dallas, whose cities had acted in unison to build—with the help of some $96 million from the federal government—a truly world-class airport.

Our government had granted that money and its official sanction on the clearly stated condition that both cities adopt legal ordinances permanently closing Love Field in Dallas and Meacham Field in Fort Worth to all commercial passenger traffic.

Both city councils had done precisely that. Wanting something far better, safer, more modern, and more serviceable for all the people of our region, they formally shut down the two old nearby airports to all but private flights.

Greater Southwest (GSW), an earlier attempt to popularize a midway airport for the two cities, would be subsumed as a sort of southerly appendage to DFW, and it of course would no longer independently originate any commercial passenger flights.

The Federal Aviation Administration (FAA) correctly foresaw the growth of long-distance, even international travel, requiring larger and larger aircraft with longer radius-of-maneuver requirements that would create dangerously overlapping takeoff and landing patterns if both DFW and Love were initializing passenger flights in large aircraft.

Concerned for safety and fearful of aerial traffic jams, they demanded wider separation than the close physical proximity of Love and DFW runways.

Agency spokesmen insisted, before signing off on the ambitious development plans for DFW, that passenger service at Love, Meacham, and GSW be terminated altogether.

Those conditions having been met by the closing of the two old commercial airports, bonds were sold, guaranteeing their purchasers, in writing, on the good faith and credit of the two cities, that there would be no commercial passenger flights at Love, GSW, or Meacham field.

In 1974, citizens of our two largest cities and other nearby towns celebrated together the grand opening of DFW airport. It was a triumph of reason over greed, we told one another. It proved we'd outgrown our childish feuds and finally buried our hatchets, elsewhere than in one another's skulls.

Progressive leadership in both towns hailed the dawn of cooperation to drive away the long night of feuding.

That old rivalry had fed for over a century on a colorful if flinty-hearted past.

In the days when wagon trains were bringing settlers westward, Dallas merchants would regale west-bound migrants with lurid tales of mortal danger and/or lethal boredom that lay in wait to devour them if they ventured as far west as Fort Worth.

They'd either be scalped by Indians, eaten alive by wild animals, or condemned to terminal stagnation. Fort Worth, aside from being dangerous, was described as already dead itself—so sleepy, according to one warning, that panthers had sometimes been seen dozing languidly in the middle of Main Street.

To counter this verbal roadblock, Fort Worth organized teams of outriders to intercept the wagon trains east of Dallas and escort them to Fort Worth by a circuitous route that skirted any sight of the rival village. Both towns whetted their competitive skills and reveled overly long in the two-way surfeit of one-upmanship.

When Dallas in 1936 hosted a year-long exposition in honor of the Texas Centennial, Fort Worth countered with a gaudy Frontier Exposition of its own.

"Come to Dallas for culture," Fort Worth sloganeered, "but come to Fort Worth for fun."

An earlier attempt to operate a mutual airport had faltered in the late 1940s and early '50s. Runways had been located meticulously halfway between Fort Worth's Hotel Texas corner and the Adolphus Hotel corner in Dallas. Then Dallas discovered that the terminal building would face west from the centerline toward Fort Worth, and the deal was off!

Legend says that Fort Worth's number-one booster, publishing icon Amon G. Carter, carried his lunch in a paper sack when going to Dallas to avoid patronizing any Dallas eatery. And Dallas merchant prince Stanley Marcus refused to order merchandise from any company whose salesman had flown into the midway airport, known variously as "Greater Southwest Regional Airport" and as "Amon Carter Field."

But now in 1974, we all mutually rejoiced that we were, at last, singing from the same hymnbook and working together!

In this euphoric spirit, things rested—until the intercession of a state agency known as the Texas Aeronautics Commission (TAC). That commission, now defunct, on being petitioned by Southwest Airlines, ordered the City of Dallas to reopen Love Field for use by Southwest, which then was headed by Lamar Muse.

The state commission's edict had to be obeyed by the cited city, but had no jurisdiction outside Texas.

If Southwest had wanted to establish out-of-state schedules, it could quite well have done so by flying from DFW, just as all the other airlines were doing. At the time, however, Southwest was principally interested in launching flights linking Dallas, Houston, and San Antonio.

Meanwhile, freed from certain landing fees that helped pay off the DFW bonds, Southwest adopted "no frill" service, advertised low rates, and began to flourish. Its owners began to dream of interstate flights. All its Love Field destinations were in Texas. Invited to use DFW, the management expressed disinterest.

Then came 1978 and 1979. A movement quietly supported by the economically dominant airlines and a group of laissez-faire economists had been gathering steam to deregulate American aviation.

From the birth of the federally subsidized industry, scheduled passenger flights and fares had been approved and closely monitored in the interest of the flying public by the Civil Aeronautics Board (CAB), just as safety matters were monitored by the FAA. The CAB saw to it that all markets were served, fares were reasonable, and that no airline was allowed to monopolize service.

Now President Carter somewhat surprisingly endorsed the concept of deregulation. A bill swept through the House to effectively abolish the work of the CAB. Suddenly, prevailing aviation laws would expire and we'd simply let any airline fly from and to wherever it wished and charge whatever fares it might choose.

Civic leaders, frequent travelers, mayors, and city councilmen from Fort Worth and Dallas saw this as a potential danger to DFW's contractual agreements.

If any company could fly anywhere it wanted out of reopened Love Field, this could easily renew all the old cutthroat battles the international airport had been created to settle. This group of concerned citizens came to me in 1979 for help.

My original amendment, the one that initially passed the House, would have prohibited any interstate commercial passenger flights to or from any airport within a twenty-mile radius of DFW airport. It was enthusiastically supported by the official leadership of both Fort Worth and Dallas.

It set off, however, a massive lobbying effort in the Senate, which rejected the amendment as written and called for a conference committee to resolve differences.

It was at this point that my office participated in discussions with every party at interest, seeking a solution that everyone would recognize as fair.

It was through these negotiations that we ultimately reached an agreement which all parties embraced. It allowed Love Field to serve interstate traffic limited to turnaround service between Love and the contiguous states—Louisiana, Arkansas, Oklahoma, and New Mexico. This restriction applied equally to Southwest and all airlines.

Southwest was not singled out in any way.

Herb Kelleher, founder, legal counsel, and longtime leader of Southwest, expressed satisfaction. He'd won a significant victory. And he was welcome, even overtly encouraged, to expand into other states with longer-range flights into and out of DFW Airport.

Southwest is still welcome there. That Southwest has chosen not to accept the invitation has been entirely of its own volition.

That's about all there is to the "Wright Amendment."

This compromise was designed to be in perpetuity, to settle once and for all this very divisive issue.

Although I was not personally involved in all of the negotiations with the parties, which included Dallas and Fort Worth City Councils, affected airlines, and federal agency representatives, my office was represented in all of them.

It was well understood by each and every party, including Southwest Airlines, that this was an agreement which was to put this issue to rest once and for all, and that all of the parties would abide by it and none would attempt to unravel it.

At least, this was my understanding.

My friend, Herb Kelleher, remembers it somewhat differently. Herb is, in my view, a thoroughly honorable person. Who is to say that I am right and he is wrong?

I've no hostility toward Southwest. It's a splendid airline—well run, on time, reasonably priced. If its investors want to inaugurate long, cross-country flights from our market, that's fine with me. Just let them fly, like all the others, out of and into the airport our region's taxpayers, and others, built for that precise purpose. Let them charge

Delivering a speech at the opening of the Dallas/Fort Worth International Airport, 1973.
SPEAKER JIM WRIGHT COLLECTION, SPECIAL COLLECTIONS, MARY COUTS BURNETT LIBRARY, TCU.

whatever fares they wish, be just as competitive as they can.

But we shouldn't need to pay for two international airports, nor have to compromise regional passenger safety by overlapping takeoff and landing patterns.

Besides, a deal is a deal. And this one was a good deal. A guy named Jim Wright has no proprietary ownership of this agreement. It was a compromise hammered out by a lot of people. Equally fair to everyone, it treats all airline carriers alike.

I don't have a current figure on just how much has been invested in DFW airport—but I'll assure you of this: it's well into the billions. And I can't tell you how much, exactly, it has brought to the economies of our neighboring countries, but this is certain: it's in the multiple billions!

Every citizen in North Texas has a big investment in DFW airport and both a financial and civic interest in its future.

Sometimes I wish I were as wise as Solomon. Then maybe I'd know how to make everybody happy with our human efforts to compromise and get along. Unfortunately, Solomon was not on the faculty at either Weatherford College or the University of Texas when I was a student at those institutions. Who knows? Even if I had enrolled in his course, I might have flunked it.

June 26, 2005 (unpublished)

# III

# Politics: Raw, Medium Rare, and Well Done

Astride a Brahma bull on the steps of the US Capitol building.
SPEAKER JIM WRIGHT COLLECTION, SPECIAL COLLECTIONS, MARY COUTS BURNETT LIBRARY, TCU.

## Keeping Free Enterprise Free

### Part I

SOME TIME AGO I told a friend in Austin that I was playing around with the notion of writing something on the subject of "Keeping Free Enterprise Free," and right away he suggested that a better title would be "Keeping Laissez-Faire Fair." When I made what to my mind was the obvious reply that too many folks don't know what laissez-faire means, he said "Well, how many know what 'free enterprise' means?"

I suppose it is true that the definitions for free enterprise are as many and varied as the colors in a rainbow. Some are inclined to regard it as merely another phrase for the survival of the fittest, with a dog-eat-dog connotation. There are those who talk of free enterprise as though it meant a form of anarchy where no protection is to be afforded anyone from the unscrupulous operator.

To most of us, free enterprise has probably meant that a fellow can go into business for himself, render a good service at a price the public is able to pay, employ others at a fair wage, and keep a reasonable profit for himself. It would mean further, I think, that by hard work and honest and ethical dealing this small businessman can have a fair chance of expanding his business, employing more people, and becoming more prosperous himself.

It means that he doesn't have to buy the concession to be an independent businessman from anyone in either the political world or the business world. That the government will not favor any particular firm over and against its competitors but will serve as an impartial referee to enforce the rules of fair play and see that everyone gets the same break. That the humblest youngster in the land, born of the most improvident circumstances, will be assured as his birthright a decent chance of success in business without having to deposit his self-determination with some guy who controls the gates of opportunity.

It means something for the consumer, too. For him it gives assurance that free competition and high production will bring him more of the commodities he needs at a price he can pay. Under free enterprise a fellow gets rich not by selling a few articles at high profit margins but by selling lots and lots of stuff as cheap as he can. Eric Johnson ought to know a lot about free enterprise, and he says that "ever lower units of profit and an ever higher volume of sales" is bound to be its inevitable policy.

This in turn means more folks can buy more things than under a non-competitive economy. So when free enterprise is really free, a higher standard of living for all is the natural result.

At least this is my conception of free enterprise, and to me there is something very sacred about it.

Those of us who believe that free enterprise offers the fairest and most efficient economic system in the world are naturally disturbed when we realize that our ideal is threatened by rampant practices which even now are gnawing, cancer-like, at their very heart. There are those abroad in the land today who, while mouthing loud paeans of praise to the competitive system of free enterprise, are using every artful dodge to circumvent the law and every conceivable craft to prevent and stifle that very competition upon which our business system is based.

We come now, as inevitably we must, to the word "monopoly," which is the direct antithesis of the phrase "free enterprise."

First, let's bring a few monopoly practices under the microscope. Let's fieldstrip a few seedling monopolies close at hand and examine their effects.

I live in Weatherford, a county-seat town with an oak-shaded courthouse lawn and close to ten thousand inhabitants, where until very recently the tempo of life rose and fell with the annual watermelon crop. You wouldn't expect to find a monopoly in these pastoral surroundings, would you?

Last summer there were two different ice plants in Weatherford. This summer they have both been bought out by the TPU. Now you'd think that a big corporation like that could satisfy itself with a lower margin of profit, and since it is guaranteed the business of the entire town and doesn't have to get by on just part of the sales with a competitor taking some of them away, you'd just suppose they could make the customer a little better price, wouldn't you?

Well, last summer ice was forty cents per hundred. This summer it is sixty cents. This is an increase of exactly 50 percent. And yet the overhead cost per unit sale is considerably lower that it was for either of the plants last year.

The TPU also sells ice on a sort of wholesale arrangement to a few little filling stations around town. Last week I talked with a fellow who runs one of these filling stations. He had thought sixty cents was more than the ice was worth and was cutting down his own margin of profit to let the public have it a little cheaper. A representative of the TPU had just been by to tell him that unless he raised his price to sixty cents, he wouldn't get any more ice to sell.

Well, there you have effect number one of all monopolies: higher prices and poorer service to the customers.

In Dallas last summer, there was an agreement among the ice plants. Each of them put up some good-faith money and deposited it with the treasurer of their association, and each week a little of it was returned to those who had not manufactured more ice than their allowable quota. This was to discourage any independent cuss who might manufacture more than he could sell at the inordinately high prices and who might then be tempted to lower his prices in order to unload it, thereby spoiling the racket for everyone else.

So hand in hand with higher prices and poorer services goes artificially restricted production in counting the effects of monopoly. The Dallas ice plants were just minnows, but they had learned their game from the whales. And it is just this same game of production restricting and price fixing, played on a grand national scale, which prevents the small or middle-sized retail merchant in your hometown from having enough merchandise on his shelves and which is making it hard for him to sell this merchandise at a price you can pay.

I don't mean to imply that this small, independent merchant is a co-conspirator in such a plot, because he is not. On the contrary, he wants more merchandise, and he is probably selling what he has just as cheaply as the prices he is obliged to pay will permit. There is much evidence to indicate that he is the victim of restricted production tactics much nearer the mouth of production, and administered in a manner similar to the Dallas ice plant scheme.

Part II

EARLY LAST YEAR, the National Association of Manufacturers (NAM) was running full-page ads in the newspapers of the nation saying that full production was essential to a healthy economy and a prosperous country. The workers in some of NAM's factories were on strike, and NAM was pointing out that strikes prevented full production. A good deal of what they said made a certain amount of sense—as far as it went.

But talk about a sit-down strike! Along with a few others in Congress, Wright Patman, chairman of the Small Business Committee in the House, was telling everybody who'd listen that his committee had found evidence that some of the country's biggest manufacturers and wholesalers were engaging in a sit-down strike all their own, methodically stockpiling goods waiting for higher prices, while empty shelves yawned in every small retail store in America!

Free enterprise . . . is supposed to respond to the law of supply and demand. Yet in many important lines of business we have reached a point where the mammoths of monopoly can actually manufacture and control supply and demand. They can turn it on and off like a faucet.

Here in Parker County we are mighty proud of our young and growing dairy industry. Several hundred families in my own county earn their livelihood by keeping and milking small herds of dairy cows. Practically all the milk they produce is sold to a handful of distributing plants in Fort Worth and Dallas, who in turn market the product throughout North Central Texas. I may as well name them: Tennessee, Borden, Boswell, Metzger, and Alta Vista.

Until sometime in May these companies were paying our small dairymen the standard price of $5.30 per hundred pounds with no restriction whatever upon the amount of milk they produced. In fact, last winter the demand was so great that certain distributors were actually paying an incentive premium for all milk the farmers would produce in excess of their normal production levels. As a consequence, numbers of my dairyman friends, feeling that milk was vitally needed, enlarged their herds at a time when this meant a considerable outlay, as practically all the feed was to be bought in the winter. And, brother, it's high!

In May, however, these same companies set for each dairy farmer in my county an arbitrary quota considerably below his normal production. In some cases, a man's quota was only 35 or 40 percent of the milk he was producing, and for all milk in excess of this quota, the milk plants announced that they would pay only $3.20 per hundred pounds. In this way, as you can see, the dairy farmer had imposed upon him a 40 percent reduction in the price he could get for much of the work of his head and his hands.

Caught in this vice, the average farmer was virtually helpless. He could not market his milk directly to the public because he lacked the bottling and transportation facilities. The milk plants were his only outlet. It would avail him little to transfer his account to another plant, because strangely enough all the plants had announced the production-restricting program simultaneously. And those dairy farmers who did try to switch from one plant to another where they thought they might get a little better treatment were told that a "gentleman's agreement" existed between the "rival" distributing companies, and that one plant simply could not take a producer away from another one.

The mammoth distributing plants tried to explain away their production-restricting program by declaring that there was just not sufficient market to take all the milk the farmers were producing. Yet investigation disclosed that many retail grocers in Fort Worth and Dallas were not supplied enough milk by the distributors to meet the consumer demand, even at the prevailing prices of twenty cents a quart, which was and is an all-time high. Certain grocers in Fort Worth said they were selling their entire daily allowable quota before noon each day.

And even assuming all the milk could not be sold at prevailing prices, is it not boldly evident that the distributors could have had a much larger market simply by lowering their price to the retail grocer, so that he in turn might offer Texas housewives the benefit of cheaper milk for their children? This would certainly be the logical course for free, competitive enterprise.

In late August the milk-plant combine abandoned its arbitrary quota system, and, again acting in unison, the major companies reluctantly agreed to pay the standard price for all milk produced. But only after the attorney general's office had taken reams of testimony on their monopolistic price-fixing practices, and the irate farmers had begun making plans to bottle and market their own milk if relief was not forthcoming from the costly quota imposition.

I am not indiscriminately criticizing all big corporations simply because they are big. That would be childish and absurd since many of them are conducting honest and ethical business. Bigness is not a sin. But neither is it a virtue!

If anyone actually believes that monopolies try to give the public a break in the way of better products or lower prices, he has only to look to a well-known monopoly combination—the major oil companies operating in Texas. There are 3,300 oil producers listed with the Railroad Commission, yet last year thirteen of them produced more than half the oil that came out of Texas soil. Really, the majority of the total production is traceable to only eight different concerns at the most, because at least six of these big thirteen are all subsidiaries of Standard Oil.

Now that we're satisfied a monopoly exists, let's see how well this monopoly is passing on its profits to the public in the way of reasonable prices.

On January 31, the *Wall Street Journal* published an interesting article on oil company earnings. It revealed that 1946 profits had been 25 percent above those of 1945 for all the nation's leading oil companies. Last year, the article said, had been the most profitable year in over a decade for the petroleum industry. And 1947 earnings were foreseen as at least 15 percent above those of last year, assuming that retail prices would stay exactly the same.

But what was the disposition of these monopolists after devouring such heady nectar? Did they pass on a bit of their good fortune by reducing the price of gasoline and oil so as to sacrifice unit profit for a bigger volume of sales and thus let more people buy more gasoline? Unfortunately not! Retail gasoline prices today are two cents a gallon higher than last year, and the attorney general of Texas has been moved to look into the "coincidence" of the last five uniform price increases. The major oil companies had taken identical action within a twenty-four hour period a short while back, the attorney general disclosed.

If another depression comes, it will be because of just such me-first combinations which are busily brewing the ingredients of an economic collapse such as the one which struck like a tornado two decades ago and left a broken economy in its wake. By strangling small business and then drying up all competition, by keeping prices inordinately high and siphoning off buying power, by restricting production and holding back the developments that make for a higher standard of living, monopolistic combinations today are following the well-worn paths that led to the catastrophe of 1929.

## Part III

NOW THAT WE UNDERSTAND exactly what a monopoly is and the exact manner in which it represses free enterprise, let's try to appraise just how strong a grip it has on our national economy. Today that grip can almost be described as a stranglehold. Some of the facts involved are absolutely appalling, and yet somehow they do not seem to have made a very big ripple upon the surface of public opinion. Perhaps this is because they are not sufficiently well known.

For example, figures available in the Bureau of Internal Revenue of the United States Treasury Department show that 455 gargantuan corporations, constituting less than one-eighth of 1 percent of the total number of corporations in the United States, own outright in their own names more than half of all the corporate assets in the country. And through certain well-known monopoly devices, they control a great deal more of the nation's economy than is shown under their actual ownership.

One of these devices is known as the interlocking directorate. These gigantic economic organisms had a total of 3,544 directors at the time Berle and Means wrote their book *The Modern Corporation and Private Property.* This was an average of about sixteen directors apiece. Yet frequently the same men were found occupying the directorates for several of the giants. One man served as director for nine of them at the same time. Each of three men has served on eight of their directorates, and each of six has served for seven of the corporations at one time.

Another favorite device has been intercorporate stock holding. Still another dodge is the development of corporate interest groups. A number of corporations with similar business interests will form an interest group to see that they all stay in line and nobody starts cutting prices or improving services in such a way as to force the rest of them to meet competition. And then there are interest groups which control interest groups. The Morgan group, in controlling forty separate and distinct interest groups, controlled the assets of almost one through three of the two hundred largest, or in other words about 15 percent of the corporate wealth of the country.

Well, if those are the conditions today, what can we expect in the future? Are we heading in the direction of more monopoly or less monopoly?

For years there have been four fields of enterprise which have steadfastly resisted monopoly control to hold out the last remaining hopes for those who want to live and do business in a free-enterprise economy. They are: agriculture, retail trade, the service enterprises, and construction.

Yet today the grasping tentacles of monopoly are reaching into these surviving strongholds of free enterprise. In agriculture, the family-size farm is slowly disappearing as the size of the average farm steadily increases and absentee ownership grows. Even in retail business monopoly is on the march. In 1915, less than 15 percent of the retail trade was done by chains. In 1945, these organizations made 32 percent of all retail sales. One large grocery chain sold 14 percent of all the groceries sold in the United States last year.

Now that we see the direction in which we are heading, one is prompted to ask, where is it all likely to end? Dr. Walter Prescott Webb of the University of Texas declares that if the trend of the past seventy-five years is continued, another seventy-five years will see all business done by a few large corporations.

It seems to me that there is yet time to save the system which we are pleased to call free enterprise from the fates that are predicted, by taking bold and resolute action to turn the tide away from big business collectivism toward freedom of opportunity. While no single panacea is at hand, there are several things which we as a free people can still do to make it increasingly more difficult for giant organisms to evade competition.

1. First off, we can start at the top and legislate to prohibit the participation of American business enterprises in international cartels.

2. We can make for more adequate enforcement of the Sherman and Clayton antitrust laws by increasing the penalties to a level such that it is no longer profitable for a monopoly to transgress the law with impunity, secure in the knowledge that the fine will be less than the profit.

3. We must mend the loopholes in the statutes and insist that Congress enact legislation such as the O'Mahony-Kefauver bill of the recent session to prohibit monopoly merger by assets as well as by stock.

4. We can prevent monopolistic abuses of patent rights by demanding that a United States patent must be put to use within a reasonable time to turn out better and less expensive products, and not simply held off the market, or else it should become null and void.

5. We in the southern and western states can follow Georgia's lead in bringing court action to eliminate discriminatory freight rates which militate against the success of infant independent industry in the South and the West.

6. If we value free enterprise, we must jealously guard Congressional appropriations for the Justice Department's Antitrust Division and see that this all-important function of government is not burnt upon the altar to the god of false economy.

7. The states must stop relying completely upon the federal government and must begin to institute vigorous antitrust enforcement of their own. In Texas, Attorney General Price Daniel's probe of monopolistic price-fixing practices is a good start in the right direction. It is certainly the duty of every Texas citizen, whether he voted for Price Daniel or not, to let him know that we appreciate these efforts and that we

are expecting him to follow through with indictments and prosecutions.

It is later than we think. But, there is still time—if we are willing to act—to keep free enterprise free.

*The Texas Spectator,* September 1947

## An Open Letter to Mr. Amon G. Carter and the *Fort Worth Star-Telegram*

EDITOR'S NOTE: *In the 1954 elections for the US House of Representatives, the* Fort Worth Star-Telegram, *founded and owned by Amon G. Carter Sr., steadfastly opposed candidate Jim Wright in favor of his opponent, the incumbent Wingate Lucas. Carter also owned the first radio and TV stations in Texas, and was a powerful force in the district and state. In the last two days of his campaign—his first run for the US House—Wright concluded that the only way he could get positive coverage from the local paper was to purchase a full-page ad. The story goes that when Wright's copy was presented to Mr. Carter before the paper went to press, he asked how much Wright paid for the space. Told that it was more than nine hundred dollars, Carter told his staff to run it. Wright won the election, and true to his father's advice, he soon secured the elder Carter's friendship.*

Dear Mr. Carter,

This is hurriedly written to meet your deadline, which comes right on the heels of the appearance of your yesterday afternoon paper and its front page editorial.

Therefore, it won't be well written . . . but the facts will be here!

The $974.40 for this ad is coming out of my own pocket and it's going to be worth it to me . . . even if it overdraws my savings account.

For you have at last met a man, Mr. Carter, who is not afraid of you . . . who will not bow his knee to you . . . and come running like a simpering pup at your beck and call.

I expected you to editorialize against me, Mr. Carter . . . in spite of my many good friends and supporters among the working and writing staff of your paper.

But I didn't expect you to engage in misrepresentation. I thought you were a bigger man than that! I still think you are, and that you will retract it.

You say in your editorial that I have given no formula, no "well-defined ideas" for bringing about the things I've discussed as the goals of this nation . . . such as winning the cold war for the minds of men and women, preserving our freedoms, and avoiding atomic warfare.

You say that I have not commented on the farm program, taxation, federal spending, etc.

But I have, Mr. Carter . . . and your editorial writers KNOW that I have. In my very first announcement speech over your TV station . . . in subsequent speeches . . . and notably on May 14th at the barbecue dinner attended by more than one thousand people . . . I went into considerably greater detail on my stand on these issues than your private errand-boy congressman has ever done.

You say that I have kept my feelings on these things "well concealed." Let's tell the truth, Mr. Carter. YOU and your personal newspaper have kept them well concealed!

You had reporters at the May 14th barbecue . . . two of them. They wrote good stories . . . the type the huge attendance and the positions I took would have justified. And then somebody in your organization KILLED the most important facts in those stories. The biggest political dinner in the recent history of Fort Worth, and you gave it less space than an obituary of some tourist from Seattle who once passed through Fort Worth!

Yes, I have commented publicly on the issues, Mr. Carter, I have spoken out against socialized medicine . . . on how to reduce foreign aid by increasing trade through reciprocal trade agreements and the lowering of tariffs . . . against the proposed sales tax . . . against the "hard money" policy . . . I have gone into detail in my speeches on the farm program and the changes I would recommend . . . and I have devoted an entire TV program to how best we can clean up "the mess" in Washington and restore dignity to the sacred calling of free government . . . I devoted half a TV speech last Monday noon to how to solve the critical water-supply problem for our area.

None of these things has been quoted in your paper. Am I to blame for that? In most cases . . . in fact, every case, I believe . . . I went to some pains to see that your paper had a copy.

Is this how you have controlled Fort Worth so long? By printing only that which you WANTED the people to read? By refusing to quote a man in your paper when he does take a stand and then running a front-page editorial saying he has not taken any stand?

The people know only what they read in the papers. For that reason, a newspaper has a sacred obligation.

"Ye shall know the truth and the truth shall make you free" is a holy promise. But how are we going to know the truth when it is suppressed by the papers?

Your personal ownership of the TV station, too, has been a part of this campaign. In late March, your TV lawyers first approved my original announcement script, then called it back after conferences to delete my request that the public share in the costs of the campaign. "Against FCC rules," they said. I didn't complain. But less than two weeks later, a congressional candidate made the same identical request unchallenged over the Dallas station which is required to abide by the same FCC requirements.

And Governor Shivers was permitted to make such a request over YOUR station.

You have permitted ads intended to cast aspersions upon my business, Mr. Carter . . . in which the opposition has purported to print an affidavit bearing my signature. But they left out the one significant part of the affidavit . . . the part where it says it is not to be construed as indication that any statute or regulation had been violated.

I respect you, Mr. Carter, and I think, if the truth were only known, you'd respect me much more than you do the people who are always kowtowing and catering to you.

I admire the many wonderful things you have done for Fort Worth and our area. It is because of the inspiration of such "doers" as yourself and others that I have aspired, too, to try to do things for our area and our people.

But it is unhealthy for ANYONE to became TOO powerful . . . TOO influential . . . too dominating. It is not good for Democracy. The people are tired of "one-man rule".

This is a new day. New blood and new minds and new thoughts, fresh from the people themselves, are needed.

On Saturday, Mr. Carter, the PEOPLE are going to vote for me . . . in great numbers, unless I am terribly mistaken. And I mean people of all sorts. And let's not bring in that old "labor leaders" bugaboo that has been used against everyone who has run against the "rubber stamp" boys.

The labor leaders know, just as you know, that they don't control me. I have talked to them just exactly as I am talking to you now.

And if I am your congressman, as I think I am going to be . . . I want you to know I will be delighted to work WITH you . . . not FOR you . . . in building a greater America, a greater Southwest, and a greater Fort Worth area.

I will be YOUR congressman, just as I will be EVERYONE'S congressman . . . not your personal, private congressman . . . but a congressman for ALL the people!

Very sincerely yours,
Jim Wright

*Fort Worth Star-Telegram*, July 23, 1954

## The Responsibility of Elected Officials

EDITOR'S NOTE: *This speech was delivered to an audience of Texas city mayors, councilmembers, and other Texas city officials.*

POLITICS IS THE LIFEBLOOD of democracy, the fuel that propels the engine of a free society. To profess love for the democratic form of government but disdain for politics is to pretend to honor the product while despising the process that creates it.

*Webster's* defines politics as "The art and science of government." And this, whether by occupation or avocation, is our profession. More than one hundred and seventy-five years ago, Andrew Oliver said in Boston:

> *Politics is the most hazardous of all professions. There is not another in which a man can hope to do so much good to his fellow creatures; neither is there any in which by a mere loss of nerve he may do such widespread harm; nor is there another in which he may so easily lose his own soul; nor is there another in which a positive and strict veracity is so difficult. But danger is the inseparable companion of honor. With all the temptations and degradations that beset it, politics is still the noblest career any man can choose.*

The attributes of an ideal public servant could be as many as we'd care to enumerate. I'll not even attempt to cover the list. At the risk of oversimplification, I'd like to highlight three basic responsibilities of every elected public official.

I. Accessibility

THE FIRST IS, quite simply, accessibility. It can be unnerving. It is often frustrating and frequently exhausting. But it is the price we pay—and should pay gladly—for the privilege of public service.

It is the genius of our peculiarly American system that the politician may never be a lordly creature aloof and remote from the clamoring throng, but must of necessity be "a people's man," drawing his inspiration from the public itself.

When you come right down to it, if you don't genuinely like people—with all their human foibles, eccentricities, personal predilections, and sometimes impossible schemes—you really have no business in elective office.

Wise old Sam Rayburn volunteered one word of advice to Presidents Truman, Eisenhower, and Kennedy as each assumed the splendid misery of that most fateful public office on earth.

"Don't let them isolate you," Mr. Rayburn implored. "Your well-meaning friends and associates, if you aren't careful, will surround you with a layer of protection so thick that the people can't get through to you. Don't let that happen."

It was during an experience as mayor of Weatherford that I learned an indispensable lesson of public servants: that the very surest way to dissipate the foggy mist of unfounded rumor, and to eradicate the germ colony of myths which breed and proliferate wherever sunlight doesn't penetrate, was to throw the doors completely open, at all times, on all questions of public administration and policy.

A weekly press conference was instituted. No holds were barred, no questions disallowed, none answered with a "no comment." Where I didn't have a factual answer at the tip of my tongue, we'd bring in the books and records and find it together. Once fully realizing that there were no secrets at city hall, the public responded beyond my most sanguine hopes, passing necessary bond issues by votes of better than nine to one.

Democracy—whether in a city, a state, or a great nation—rests upon the assumption that the people, given the accurate and unvarnished facts, will do the right thing. If you can't believe that, you're in trouble before you begin.

II. Leadership

THE SECOND GREAT responsibility of the elected official is that of leadership.

And here we see the other side of the coin whose face reads "accessibility." For accessibility, even in a public servant, must not become servility.

To be no more than a sounding board of public fancy or a carbon copy of the electorate embodied in one personality is not in itself to be leader. A leader is one who, having divined the path, persuades the people to follow him on it.

James A. Garfield, then a member of Congress, confided to his diary on February 19, 1872: "It is a terrible thing to live in fear of the constituents to the extent which many members do. I would rather be defeated every day in the year than suffer such fear."

And tough old Harry Truman, who had no patience with the public man who fears to make the hard political decisions, often advised his fellow politicians: "If you can't stand the heat, then get out of the kitchen!"

Sam Rayburn was convinced that any congressman worth his salt could lead his district. It was, in his seasoned judgment, the duty of an elected official not only to reflect public opinion, but to mold it; not to imitate but to initiate; not only to react but to create.

And so in the midst of the turmoil of our days, there has to be a budgeting of our time so that occasionally we may draw away from the tumult and the shouting to think creatively.

The curse of our hurried existence seems to be that a public official must do his thinking "on the run." Somewhere within our harried, hurried, activistic schedules of receiving constituents, hearing their problems, invading their precincts, shaking their hands, bombarding their ears with the spoken word, we must find time to think. And this, in the turmoil of our times, is not easy.

So there must be a further balance. We must make time and opportunity not only to listen; we must make time and opportunity to *think*—and then, on the basis of this to, *act.*

III. Integrity

IN ADDITION TO THE QUALITIES of accessibility and leadership, the public official owes to his constituency—and to himself—a third ingredient which can be expressed no more simply than in the word *integrity.*

Integrity is not merely a matter of financial honesty or moral behavior, although surely nobody would deny the necessity of these attributes.

While embracing them, integrity encompasses a concept far broader still. *Webster's Collegiate Dictionary* assigns to the word the following meaning: "The state or quality of being complete, undivided, or unbroken; entirety."

Integrity, then, is first and foremost the condition of being one's self. Shakespeare distinguished it as man's first duty: "This above all, to thine own self be true, / And it must follow as the night the day, / Thou canst not then be false to any man."

No other can pronounce with certainty whether your public career has been a faithful extension of yourself and what you most truly believe—or the extent to which you may have temporized with eternal truth, made a god of popularity, muted your message, or defiled your dream.

Nobody has to tell you. You know. In the quiet recesses of your soul, a still, small voice repeats the verdict in almost deafening tones. And no clamorous overplay of noisy self-justification can silence it.

Wright on the phone, busy at his desk.
PHOTO BY DEV O'NEIL.

The tragedies of public service are not written in the histories of lost elections or unfulfilled careers. The tragedies are the unfulfilled pages which waited, clean and bright with promise, for each of us to write something distinctly his own and thus make the unique contribution of himself.

Speech before the Texas Municipal League Annual Conference, Fort Worth, Texas, November 15, 1966

## Clean Money for Congress

NO FACET OF AMERICAN LIFE cries out more loudly for reform than the dingy gray area of political campaign financing, which casts a lengthening shadow across all else we do in our elective public institutions.

As a veteran of seven successful campaigns for the US House of Representatives and one losing race for the Senate, I've experienced firsthand the skyrocketing cost of politics. It is now, in fact, nearly impossible in most states for men of modest means to seek high elective office—unless they are willing wards of the wealthy.

The price of campaigning has risen so high that it actually imperils the integrity of our political institutions. Big contributors more and more hold the keys to the gates of public service. This is choking off the wellsprings of fresh, new thought and severely limiting the field of choice available to the public. I am convinced, moreover, that the intellectual *quality* of political campaigns is deteriorating as a result.

One curious by-product of big money in politics is the slick, shallow, public-relations approach with its nauseating emphasis on "image" at the expense of substance. In the arenas where Lincoln and Douglas once debated great issues, advertising agencies last year hawked candidates like soap flakes.

So far as my own case goes, I've been luckier than most politicians. When I made my first run for Congress, I had enough money of my own to pick up the tab personally for half (about $8,000) of the campaign cost. Since the beginning, I've made it an unvarying rule never to accept more than a one-hundred-dollar contribution from any individual. The average over the years has been around ten dollars. This preserves my independence from personal obligation. I wouldn't want it otherwise. A congressman can get by this way if he's fortunate—as I am—in having a very understanding constituency.

But this formula is impossible for a statewide contest, as I discovered in my 1961 try for the Senate. In that race, two balloons of fantasy exploded in my face. The first was the notion that if I announced my candidacy early, I would frighten off other prospective aspirants. Instead, seventy-one would-be candidates threw their hats in the ring, creating the biggest field of entries in the history of Texas politics. If this raised some doubts as to my ability to intimidate opposition, I argue that it should have established me as a *leader of men*, since never before had so many followed the example of one.

My second and more serious fallacy was the assumption that a determined man in good health could make up by prodigious personal effort what he lacked in finances. I would simply campaign harder than anyone else in the race.

In the ensuing four months, I traveled twenty-seven thousand miles, made six hundred and seventy-eight speeches, slept an average of four and a half hours a night, and worked off eighteen pounds. During one week, I averaged eleven speeches a day in as many different localities. But it was like trying to siphon off the Gulf of Mexico with an eyedropper. For there were then ten million people in Texas; if I worked sixteen hours a day and wasted no time, it would have taken me some twenty-eight years to talk for one minute with every citizen in the state. I had four months.

The upshot was that I came close, but not close enough. Out of the seventy-two entries, I barely missed the second spot, which would have put me in the runoff with John Tower, the sole Republican. Tower subsequently won, over airline executive Bill Blakley, who had nosed me out of the number-two position. Each of these two men had spent on billboard, newspaper, and radio advertising at least three times the amount I'd been able to put together.

I planned to make the race again in 1966 when Senator Tower would be up for reelection. But as the time drew near, the problem of money again loomed large. I could not bring myself to initiate alliances with those who could provide the wherewithal in big chunks. This is, alas, the accepted way in Texas, and probably in most states. Nor, with a son in college and two daughters almost ready to enter, could I mortgage their futures on another underfinanced race which might leave me owing $100,000 or more and out of a job.

In a last-ditch effort to find a broad base of campaign financing, I bought $10,000 worth of television time for one statewide broadcast. I told the audience exactly what it costs to run a statewide campaign in Texas, and said that I would become a candidate for the Senate if twenty-five thousand individual Texans who agreed with my views would participate to the extent of contributing ten dollars each.

The response was good. I received nearly seven thousand letters —a bona fide expression of grassroots support. But contributions and precise pledges totaled only $48,828.50—far less than the $250,000 I had considered a minimum base.

I am convinced that I could have won with sufficient public exposure. But to obtain it I would have had either to make a beggar of myself in repeated telecasts, or to meet privately with affluent individuals and organized groups to discuss what I could do for them, primarily, rather than for the United States. I'm not temperamentally suited for the former role nor conscientiously fitted for the latter.

So there was nothing to do but return the generous contributions and forget about running for the Senate.

In my opinion, the profligate spending and shallow sloganeering that are becoming commonplace in American politics insult the public's intelligence and do the electorate a grave disservice.

Traditionally, Americans have mistrusted the concentration of power in too few hands. We have steadily democratized the ballot. In the space of one generation, we have sounded the death knell to the "white man's primary," passed civil rights voting laws, swept aside the rotten boroughs of maladjusted districts, and outlawed the poll tax. But of what real effect is all of this if we cannot recruit our elected officials from all levels of our society? Of what value is "one man, one vote" if the real power remains in the hands of the few who provide the money for political campaigns? What real choice does the voter have when only a limited few can afford to get their names on the ballot?

This year Congress will once again consider bills designed to restore decency and sense to political financing. Let us hope that this will be a year of action.

*Harper's Magazine,* April 1967

## Legislation and the Will of God

IN SEPTEMBER 1964, the House was debating the first appropriation of money for the antipoverty program. Advocates recited the stark statistics of grisly want in the midst of affluence. Democratic spokesmen rhapsodized upon our unrivaled opportunity to "heal the gaping sores of economic denial" and "banish poverty from our land!" Some of us were thinking, what a chance to carry out that scriptural mandate to feed the hungry and clothe the naked! To visit widows and fatherless in their affliction! Could anyone doubt we were doing the right thing?

Then Joel Broyhill, Republican congressman from Virginia's Tenth District, entered the debate. Joel is a decent guy—friendly, energetic, hardworking, popular with both constituents and colleagues. But his speech ripped into some of my most cherished assumptions. Broyhill denounced the antipoverty program as the "most flagrant, unabashed vote-buying scheme I have seen in all my years in Congress." He scorned the very idea that the federal government is capable of eliminating poverty. He quoted scripture:

"The Bible says, 'For ye have the poor always with you,' and while I do not wish to make an odious or offensive comparison, I have a good deal more faith in the Bible than I have in some politicians' promises!"

Others in the House elaborated the Broyhill theme. Some expressed deep concern over the increasingly popular fallacy that "the world owes me a living." One voiced the view that anyone who really wants to work can find a job, and another hinted darkly that too easy access to goods without work was "destroying the moral fiber" of the American people. Someone charged that multiple welfare payments were encouraging illegitimate births—and darn near proved it. A southern Democrat, leaning on the back railing of the House chamber, peered over his glasses and grunted to a colleague:

"The Bible says if you don't work you don't eat!"

A couple of days later, the *Washington Post* editorially excoriated Broyhill. In scathing sarcasm, the *Post* editorial described the Virginia Congressman as that "noted theological and Biblical commentator," recounted his use of the scripture, and concluded:

> *Mr. Broyhill has piously reconciled himself to his fat and fortunate lot, and he expects the children of the poor to reconcile themselves with equal piety to their thin and miserable one. We await with great interest Mr. Broyhill's next sermon which, according to a current rumor, will take as its text Matthew 19:24. As we remember it, no doubt imprecisely, the verse warns, "It is easier for a camel to go through the eye of a needle, than for a smug and complacent real estate operator with political connections to enter the kingdom of God." If only the same rule of admission were enforced in the halls of Congress.*

The tarbrush portrait, if unkind, was recognizable. Joel's family is prominent in real estate. And financially successful. Fat? Well, things are relative, you know. Pots and kettles and all that. Let's just say Joel outweighs me by ten pounds or so. (No need to mention he's at least a half inch taller . . . )

But if I'm tempted to pass moral judgment on either Joel Broyhill or the *Post* editorial writer for a lack of Christian charity in this case, they both might well report: "Who the heck is Jim Wright to be so confounded self-righteous? We haven't heard *him* making any speeches against the *oil depletion allowance*! Did you know he took a political contribution from some truckers? And whatever else we need, we don't need some balding, bushy-eyebrowed Texas Democrat to lecture us on our moral responsibilities!"

And, much as I hate to say it, they'd have a point there. (It would be nicer, though, if they referred to me as "red-haired" instead of "balding." And as for my bushy—I mean my dramatic, forceful eyebrows—well, that just shows how prone some people are to abandon the issues and deal in cheap personalities.)

SEVERAL THINGS need to be clear before we really try to get into the question of how a lawmaker can ascertain the divine will. Maybe the little story I've just recited illustrates a few of them. The first is that men of goodwill and sincere purpose often disagree. And this can happen without either antagonist being a sycophant, a demagogue, or a rascal. Or even stupid, for that matter. None of us is given an exclusive franchise on God's truth, and we indulge a powerful presumption when we try to create God in our own images.

The second thing we need to recognize is that Congressmen are, after all, just people. The Congress is *of* the people. It is in one sense their mirror, and it reflects the aggregate strengths and weaknesses of the electorate. Its membership might include just about the same percentage of saints and sinners, fools and geniuses, rogues and heroes as does the general populace. The typical Congressman is a fairly average American—a bit better educated, a little more gregarious, and considerably harder working than the norm, but still rather generally "representative." And this, after all, is his title as well as his description.

In sum, Congress is a collection of ordinary Americans grappling with extraordinary problems.

It is the problems that make our function unique—the almost infinite range and variety of them, the enormity of their consequences, and their sometimes baffling complexity. It is absolutely impossible for anyone to be a sufficient current authority on even most, let alone all, of the ever-changing issues with which Congress must deal—the intricacies of the monetary system, the explosive uncertainties of the ghettos, the dilemmas of American agriculture, the volatile currents in the Middle East, the shifting patterns of power in Europe, the newest mood in the Kremlin, the brooding undertones of Southeast Asia, to name but a few. As soon as we think we've come to grips with one of these basic situations, the facts change in a cataclysmic and unexpected way, revealing the inadequacy of our knowledge and deflating our finest theories.

Yet we ordinary Americans must bring our very finite knowledge and fallible judgments to bear upon these problems. That is our job. The problems will not yield to simple, one-sentence solutions. Where are the clear moral absolutes and how do they apply? Often there is truth on both sides. We can't just ponder and pontificate; we must vote! Two thousand bills will come before us in an average session. All have some importance. Perhaps one hundred are of major national consequence. Debate concluded, the clerk will call the roll. Often we'd like more time, more information. Sometimes we wish that we might answer, "Yes, but . . ." or "No, if . . ." But as the roll is called, each congressman's individual response must come as one unequivocal monosyllable. It is either "Yea" or "Nay," and that's that. Afterward, we hope that we were right.

What I'm saying is that if any group of people ever stood in need of the superhuman insights of divine revelation, it is we.

The third thing to know is that most Congressmen earnestly want to do the right thing. Few are theologians and fewer still are mystics, but most do have religious conviction. Cartoonists and jokesmiths to the contrary, a very appreciable number of legislators were inspired by idealism when they first decided to seek the office. It is a naïve politician perhaps who thinks he can change the course of the world dramatically, but most members were convinced that they could add something of value to the total political achievement of the nation. In my own case, I decided as a sophomore in high school that I wanted someday to serve in the Congress and to help create the foundations of a peaceful world.

Perhaps my case is revealing if not altogether typical. In my youth I was very certain in my vision of the road to world peace and of what I conceived to be my "mission in life." Like Moses, I would lead people from the bondage of war and oppression into Isaiah's promised day when men would "beat their swords into plowshares, and their spears into pruning hooks" (Isaiah 2:4, KJV). I'd be an architect of Tennyson's Parliament of Man, where war drums throbbed no longer and battle flags were furled. I'd fulfill Woodrow Wilson's Fourteen Points and Franklin Roosevelt's Four Freedoms. It was all extremely heady stuff. I was young.

I was, frankly, intolerant of conflicting views. Though I wouldn't have admitted it and was probably clever enough that it didn't surface too visibly, I had a sort of messiah complex, which, if forgivable in youth, can be insufferably dangerous in a public official. I hadn't yet learned that other people too were smart and could be equally sincere while seeing things another way. I hadn't learned to walk the tightrope between self-righteousness and cynicism. Maybe I still haven't, but really that's the trick.

The next thing we ought to understand—and it has a bearing on what I've been saying—is the realistic limitation on what an individual lawmaker really can expect of himself. There was a time when I felt at one with Saint Paul's assertion, "I can do all things through Christ which strengtheneth me!" (Philippians 4:13, KJV). You know, I still accept that as a sort of philosophical abstraction; I wish I still could feel it as an absolute personal truth. (Maybe my trouble is just that I've had my forty-fifth birthday.)

Actually, about the best that a good Congressman can reasonably hope for is to leave a decent footprint on the sands of progress. If he has done a good job, he will know, when he leaves Washington, that he has helped thousands of his constituents with their individual problems. He will have the satisfaction of realizing that he has accomplished some worthwhile things for his district. Perhaps he will rejoice in the fact that some of his ideas have become a permanent part of a major piece of legislation, even though someone senior to him (or perhaps of the opposite party) has been given the credit.

When the average Congressman completes his tenure of service, he will not really have changed the world much, but he will have seen important changes and will have participated to one extent or another in many of them. Remembering the thousands of individual services he has performed for people, the world leaders he has met, a few really good speeches he may have made on important issues, the hundreds of votes he has cast, the slice of history he personally has witnessed, he certainly will have the feeling that he made some contributions to the democratic process and to the shaping of his time.

No doubt it's just as well that this is so. The gradual dawning of legislative reality and the faint flawing of grandiose dreams can be effective antidotes to the terrible disease of *subucula inflata*, otherwise known as the stuffed shirt. It is, in fact, a terrible affliction, and politicians are peculiarly susceptible. Let me try to explain how.

A political career in a way is like the medieval ordeals which once were supposed to test the inner worth of an individual. Elective officialdom subjects its practitioner to a long series of subtle trials which have the capacity to bend and change his very character and to reveal its imperfections.

Many people, as I've said, enter the legislative arena impelled by some basic conviction of service to fellow man. Whether the individual's vision of a better world be true or false, clear and right, or foggy and mistaken, is not the point right here. The point is that he *has* such a vision, worthy in his own mind of the dedication of a major part of his life.

He wouldn't say this to you, but he sees himself as a potential servant of cosmic forces—at least as an instrument through which good may come to his fellow creatures, perhaps as a possible agent of deity. Our fledgling lawmaker dreams of reforms, laws of his authorship which bring strength, beneficence and a better life to his land. Did he not so dream, why would he seek such an office? It all would be fatuous and empty, devoid of meaning.

Subtly and slowly, however, his dream of bringing off that reform begins to grow faint about the edges, dulled by reality, like the early-morning stars which fade and seem farther as the gray light of dawn appears. Major legislation, the Congressman discovers, is written by committee chairmen. And one gets to be a committee chairman by staying in Congress longer than all the others. But, as the star fades, something else takes its place.

People are constantly coming to our lawmaker for help, for advice, for intercession with administrative agencies of government. They keep telling him what a fine man he is, what a gracious fellow, what a real friend. While awaiting the opportunity to exercise important legislative craftsmanship, he *does* get some things done for his district, some local projects approved, some new jobs created. This is something. It is, after all, service of a sort. Sooner or later, they'll throw an appreciation dinner for him. They'll lionize him. And he'll discover, perhaps to his amazement, that he isn't embarrassed at all. He sort of likes it.

In the bright sunlight of personal acclaim, it's hard to keep the little stars of humility and altruistic service in one's vision. Nevertheless, our legislator rationalizes, if he can just hold on until seniority makes him a committee chairman, *then* he'll be able to make the great dreams come true. Therefore, naturally, it's important that he be reelected. It becomes a bit incongruous, then, to do his alms in private, lest like the flowers in Gray's "Elegy" they waste their sweetness on the desert air.

I recall the first time a public official suggested to me what I might say in introducing him for a speech and my shock at his immodesty. Now, after fourteen years in Congress, I send out mimeographed copies of a biographical summary to program chairmen where I'm slated for a speech. Well, technically, my office staff sends them out. But do you think I haven't read the summary, or that they'd send one of which I disapproved? I blush a little bit to tell you this. But not much. Not enough.

Press releases extolling a Congressman's accomplishments become a way of life. Try keeping your humility as you edit a press release, written about yourself in the third person, careful to give yourself the credit due. First thing you know, you'll start insisting they refer to your eyebrows as "forceful" instead of "bushy." At that point you'll know you have *subucula inflata.* Or—much worse—you'll have it and not know it!

The truth is that public office is just awfully hard on humility. We try to recapture it. We strike poses. We try to convince ourselves that we still possess it. We debate with the still, small voice and sometimes shout it down. Finally convinced that we're humble, we grow very proud of our humility. But feigned humility is worse than none at all. For it isn't only others but ourselves that we deceive.

How does this fit what we're saying? A fellow who has reached this point—and it's easy to do—is terribly vulnerable to one of the twin snares I've mentioned earlier: cynicism and self-righteousness. Either he decides it's all just a gaudy, worldly game after all, or he begins to believe his own propaganda and to invest his private judgments and opinions with a sort of divine infallibility. One can be as bad as the other.

Little need, perhaps, to dwell upon the dangers of political cynicism. If you were guilty of it, you probably wouldn't be reading this book. But let me make this plea: don't become cynical about politics. It is, in one sense, the only game in town!

Ridiculed in public print, satirized by cartoonist and comedian, butt of the street-corner humorist and self-righteous moralist alike, politics nevertheless is as necessary to the functioning of our society as water is to the flow of a river. It does not have to be filthy and corrupted—and neither does the river—for man has the means, if he has the will, to keep them both clean.

Politics is the lifeblood of democracy—the fuel that propels the engine of a free society. To profess love for the democratic form of government but disdain for politics is to pretend to honor the product while despising the process that creates it. The extent to which the political life of our country becomes corrupted is the result almost entirely of the tendency of sincere and decent people to wash their hands of the responsibility, like Pontius Pilate, and abdicate the field to the cynical.

More than one hundred and seventy-five years ago, Andrew Oliver said in Boston:

> *Politics is the most hazardous of all professions. There is not another in which a man can hope to do so much good to his fellow creatures; neither is there any in which by a mere loss of nerve he may do such widespread harm; nor is there another in which he may so easily lose his own soul; nor is there another in which a positive and strict veracity is so difficult. But danger is the inseparable companion of honor. With all the temptations and degradations that beset it, politics is still the noblest career any man can choose.*

I believe that. If I didn't believe it, I'd be doing something else. And I *should* be. So much for the snare of cynicism.

What of the other danger, the danger of self-righteous presumption? History shows us. In almost every age, there have been zealots, fanatics, and pompous egocentrics who claim they have seen the vision of holiness and have been called to enforce it in the political arena. Often they've been completely sincere. Saul of Tarsus, before his conversion, felt a sanctimonious urge to persecute Christians. He went about it with the zeal of a Joe McCarthy hunting Communists. The Crusades, the Spanish Inquisition, the witch burners of early Massachusetts, John Brown—all claimed a religious justification. Perhaps all were convinced they were doing God's will.

The sad and checkered tale of ecclesiastical history in the last two thousand years gives evidence that few tyrannies are worse than that of tyrannical churchmen acting out of a sense of divine, infallible mission. The Jews persecuted the Christians before the Christians suffered martyrdom at the hands of the Roman Empire. After the

Empire was Christianized, the Jewish people endured some twelve hundred years of persecution from devout Christians all over Europe. Catholic officialdom persecuted Protestants, who later persecuted Catholics. Episcopalians and Presbyterians killed one another in bloody battles. Most thought they were doing the will of God.

A friend of mine has a watch his father took from a German soldier in World War I. Its inscription: *Gott mit uns!* The Japanese kamikaze pilots in World War II believed they were ensuring their hereafter by crash-diving their planes into American ships. And, of course, we felt so strongly that God was on *our* side. Or as heavyweight champion Joe Louis put it: "We're on God's side."

But Lincoln recognized in his second inaugural that "Both read the same Bible and pray to the same God, and each invokes His aid against the other. It may seem strange…but let us judge not, that we be not judged." Many Northerners did judge, of course, and so did Southerners.

And if you think self-righteous fanaticism is confined to the hawks of this world, you just don't know the hawkish doves. In March of 1969 a group of self-anointed young men affecting the clerical garb of monks broke into and physically wrecked the offices of the Dow Chemical Company in Washington. They thought of themselves as avenging angels and considered their act of vandalism to be above the law. After all, they were for "Peace"! So no doubt with many who've shouted down speakers, physically intimidated college faculties, and set fire to buildings on university campuses. So just and righteous do they deem their cause that they consider themselves exempt from any responsibility to the restraints of charity, humility, and the forbearance so necessary to the functioning of a free society.

Perhaps these examples seem terribly extreme to have relevance in a dissertation on the moral judgments of Congress. They are necessary to indicate the enormous danger of presumptive moral judgments in the political arena. To become completely convinced of the infallibility of one's personal predilections on a secular political issue is to play God, to assume to oneself the attributes of deity. It cultivates an arrogant intolerance of dissenting viewpoints and thus relegates one's political adversaries to the category of evil per se. In a parliamentary democracy, this attitude can be deadly.

Ben Franklin put it well. Toward the end of the Constitutional Convention in 1787, he told his fellow delegates: "I have experienced many instances of being obliged by better information, or fuller consideration, to change opinions even on important subjects." He pleaded that each delegate "would with me, on this occasion, *doubt a little of his own infallibility. . . .*"

Compromise—not necessarily a dirty word—is the very essence of the legislative process. Henry Clay said, "Do not despise compromise. It is the cement that holds the Union together." Those who scorn the art of conciliation and consider it somehow lacking in principle simply do not understand the business of lawmaking. Absolutists tend to hold compromise in rich contempt. Some even think it cowardly. But I'd warn them that they scoff loftily, if unknowingly, at man's most cherished political compromise—the Constitution of the United States. To condemn compromise is to blaspheme the steadying hands of moderation with which those thirty-eight memorable Americans penned that deed to freedom.

That the framers of the Constitution conciliated and compromised until they found a consensus does not mean that they lacked conviction. To the crucible full of conviction that man ought to be free, they applied the pestle of their collective experience, their fear of too great a central power, their scorn of one too weak. They had lived fretfully through both, and they wanted neither.

One cannot read Madison's *Notes on the Constitutional Convention* nor Elliott's *Debates*, which record the trials of its ratification, without being acutely aware of compromise on every page, conciliation in every paragraph. Who among us now would charge that they violated principle? Instead, we have created shrines to the very principles they evolved: the federal union of states, tripartite central government, and the Bill of Rights . . . a democracy within a republic. They built an instrument of government worthy to endure, and all of it was the product of compromise.

The thought recalls the drama of the fateful afternoon of March 7, 1850, in the Senate of the United States. Daniel Webster, turning aside from his own abolitionist supporters, rose in the chamber and spoke to the hushed audience . . . "not as a Massachusetts man," he said, "nor as a Northern man, but as an American and a member of the Senate of the United States . . . I speak today for the preservation of the Union." Webster then proceeded to give to the Clay Compromise the support of his magnificent talents—and to the nation ten more years of internal peace. What chance he had for his party's presidential nomination fled with the last syllable of that speech.

Is a man less honorable or does he have less courage who, heeding the voices of both extremes, partakes of each and acts for the sake of all? On the contrary, it often requires far greater courage to stand against the howling winds of mob hysteria and refuse to be stampeded by the thundering hooves of an unreasoning conformity.

Few have endured so much contemporaneous abuse from friend and foe alike as Abraham Lincoln; yet few have left their character so clearly etched upon our history. Lincoln was despised alike by the proslavery Southerners and the fanatical abolitionists. He was repudiated by members of his own party. For compromise was the soul of his offering; conciliation was his policy; moderation was his plea. To unite and thus preserve America was his single goal.

It was not that Lincoln loved his party less; it was that he loved his country more. It was not that he lacked conviction, but rather that he had conviction of a higher sort. His heart was too big for hatred, his view too broad for petty argumentation, his philosophy too deep to be confined by any of the glib labels of his day. His one consuming passion was to save the Union.

This is our common heritage. It is the business of democratic government to promote orderly progress, to synthesize a position which will satisfy the wishes of the responsible majority while protecting the rights of the most implacable minority. This must be the responsibility of political leadership. Unless we are constructive, we are of no use. Unless we cultivate a disposition to submerge petty differences and find areas of responsible agreement on which the reasonable and sensible majority can unite, we are impotent. As we fail in this, we fail America.

In the legislator's job, then, it is far more important than in most vocations that we be on guard against self-righteous presumption. The more one becomes an absolutist, the more intractable one is in the positive rightness of his own position, the less likely he is to make any positive contribution to fashioning the workable compromise which is the warp and woof of legislation. Each of us in this business must, it seems to me, reserve in his mind the possibility that there may be some truth on the other side. And if the legislative process is to work, each of us must be ready to acknowledge that sincerity *does* exist on the other side.

How do we reconcile this necessity with the idea of profound moral conviction? Certainly not by abandoning our convictions. Each of us must work as hard as he can and argue as persuasively as he can for the positions he believes to be right. But he must not play God. He must not arrogate to himself the presumption of almighty wisdom. He must be very slow to pass harsh moral judgment upon those whose convictions disagree with his. He must proceed from an assumption that his antagonist is as sincere as he and may indeed have a thought worth considering.

There are people in the Congress with whom I almost always disagree on major legislation. Take James B. Utt of California or H. R. Gross of Iowa. They are Republicans; I am a Democrat. In the glib and superficial labeling which has become current in newspaper practice, they are "conservative," while I guess I am a "progressive" or a "moderate," or something like that. Both Jimmy Utt and H. R. Gross are churchmen. I am not in any position to question the genuineness of their convictions or the sincerity of their moral concern with social issues.

But we do very profoundly disagree. Utt thinks we ought to "get the US out of the UN and the UN out of the US." I regard the UN with all its imperfections as mankind's best existing hope for peace. I get emotionally involved with the future of Latin America and am determined to consider its possibilities hopeful. H. R. Gross believes it's largely a lost cause. Gross actively opposes most social legislation—federal aid to schools, medical care for the elderly, aid to the strife-torn cities, etc. I support this legislation. Certain of my colleagues from the deep South vote for some of these social welfare programs, but vote against civil rights bills while I am voting for them. How do we reconcile our widely varying conceptions of the Christian's social duty?

The idea of revelation is deeply imbedded in Christianity. If the Creator is omnipotent, as we say he is, then the source of infallible judgments must be right here somewhere for us to tap. There has to be a socket into which we can screw our bulbs and show forth the light of perfect truth. Yet, for most of us imperfect creatures it isn't quite that simple.

Is it possible that the Creator in his infinite wisdom makes Utts and Wrights, Goldwaters and Humphreys, internationalists and isolationists, liberals, conservatives, and moderates in the precise electoral proportion to accomplish his will? Could it be that he shows to each of us a part of the truth, and then "stacks the deck," so to speak, so as to achieve the result he foreordains in some mysterious and inexplicable way, on a scale of probabilities and a timetable beyond our mortal comprehension? Is it conceivable that the whole thing resembles a gambling parlor at Las Vegas where—whatever happens on an individual spin—the house is bound to win out in the end? That's a possibility at least. The conclusion may be tempting to some of us Presbyterians—predestination and all that. But somehow I can't quite think it works just that way, either.

For one thing, I just don't believe that God intended for people to hate and kill each other. I don't think he ordained for some to live in misery and pain and want or for any to die of starvation. I can't conceive that he purposes for some to be hounded and persecuted by others. These things just do not square with my conception of a loving Creator. I believe he intends his creatures to work for peace among men, for a just and compassionate social order, for reconciliation of differences between people of different races, different nations, different religions, different social strata, even between men of different generations. "Blessed are the peacemakers" may apply with particular force to members of Congress.

I take quite literally Saint Paul's description of the Almighty as one who created "of one blood all the nations of men for to dwell on all the face of the earth" (Acts 17:26, KJV). I think he intends for us mortal creatures to patch up our differences, to love one another, to banish selfishness and evil, and to see that none of his creatures is mistreated. That is a tall order, and we haven't achieved it, but I think the eternal wisdom purposes that we do so. And I believe these goals are to be attained not only through individual deeds of individual humans but in society as well and in the social structures that we create.

None of this has come to me in a blinding flash of light as to Saint Paul on the road to Damascus or as to Moses in a voice from a burning bush. It just happens to be the way I conceive of the universe and the purposes of God. It is the only logical set of assumptions I can equate with the great commandment to love the Lord thy God and love thy neighbor as thyself.

But how do we go about achieving this perfect state of things with laws which must of necessity bear the frailties and imperfections of their authors? I have some personal ideas about that from time to time, but so do my equally conscientious colleagues. Sometimes our ideas differ. When I start delineating all the specifics of how to achieve these divine ends, I begin to get in trouble.

Even churches get in trouble. They don't always agree with one another. Individual denominations sometimes disagree internally. When a group of denominations bands together and seeks consensus, it—like as not—will encounter opposition from an adversary grouping. The National Council of Churches has offered guidelines on a broad variety of legislative fronts. Now comes a consortium of more fundamentalist denominations, calling itself the American Council of Christian Churches, blasting the NCC as "one of the most dangerous groups in America," accusing it of promoting what the ACC views as the triplet sins of modernism, socialism, and ecumenism.

Do you see what troubles we poor mortal Congressmen confront? At my age maybe I can go along, up to a point, with those who are irritated by modernism, and as a somewhat general matter I am opposed to socialism, but when they start jumping on ecumenism, then I think they have quit preaching and gone to meddling. (Me, I'm an ecumenicist—a *Presbyterian* ecumenicist, of course.)

IN ALL SERIOUSNESS and in total candor, it is no easy matter for a legislative body to be certain of its place in interpreting moral issues. The problem has haunted and hounded mankind almost since the beginning of the race. We have frequently fumbled in our efforts to locate the precise point at which the rights of society begin and those of the individual leave off. This question has challenged the most learned legal and theological minds of all ages.

Laws by their nature contain restraints. That is a primary purpose of law. The truly ideal society would be one in which no legally enacted moral restraint would be necessary. Everybody would do the right thing *voluntarily*. Yet it needs no argument that this sanguine state of affairs has not yet arrived.

So it is the business of law to impose restraints. But what restraints? Nobody will question that society needs to protect its members from injury by such obvious crimes as theft, murder, assault, or kidnapping, for example. A state with no such restrictions based upon commonly accepted moral fundamentals of right and wrong would be anarchy in its rankest form.

By the same token, we surely would find general public agreement today that no one group in our society has any right to force its own particular predilections of morality upon society as a whole, no matter how deeply held its convictions may be. A federal law prohibiting contraception, for example, would provoke open opposition as an attempt to impose the convictions of one ecclesiastical order upon the rest of society. Similarly, most people recognize today that a law would contravene our most basic legal concepts if it sought to prohibit dancing or card playing or movies on Sunday afternoon, although in an earlier time many communities invoked such ordinances because religious people found these practices objectionable.

If a man would protect himself and his family against forceful observance of the moral beliefs of others, must he not then protect others against being legally forced to observe his own? So what is the proper function of society in upholding and defending public morality by legal enactment? The great difficulty always lies in making differentiations between that which is truly harmful and dangerous to society and that which is merely distasteful to ourselves. And the great danger lies in the fact that laws must be written and administered by fallible human beings.

The preponderant majority of public sentiment, for example, will surely agree on the need for some laws to protect the public sensitivity and particularly the unsuspecting young from offensive obscenity. My mail is heavy—and so is that of most Congressmen—with disgusting enclosures which invaded the mailboxes of constituents, sent now to me with expressions of outrage. Yet those who have attempted to write laws defining what is and is not obscene know the difficulty which this task poses. In the end the courts must make a separate determination in each case.

Enforcement of such laws becomes a problem in itself. During my tenure in the Congress, we have four times enacted statutes to impose penalties upon the distribution of lewd and salacious literature and pictorials through the US mails. The most revolting advertisement of such wares had sometimes been sent unsolicited to entire mailing lists of young people. No sooner had the anguished cries of outraged parents reached the enforcement authorities, and mailing privileges of the offending firms been revoked, than the smut merchants had moved to other towns and set up their operations under different names. That the offending publishers would incur such repeated inconveniences and risk heavy fines to pursue so depraved an activity indicates one disturbing fact: financially it was paying off. What can any legislative body do to reform the tastes and morals of the entire citizenry and thus make such nefarious activities unremunerative? The answer, of course, is relatively little.

This has been true since the beginning. Unless people are led to *want* to obey laws, they find ways to evade them. This is true even in a repressive police state with its reprehensible crimes against human dignity. So much more is it true in a free society which rests its case upon a faith in its public and in the assumption that most people will willingly respect and obey laws which are not unduly repressive of their rights.

Some of the earliest attempts at legislating morality stemmed apparently from the belief that it was somehow sinful to indulge oneself in luxuries. Nor can this notion be laid exclusively to Puritanism, or even to Christian ethics. Long before the Christian age, Greeks of the Spartan influence sought to limit legally the type and amount of furniture a man might keep in his house. In the year 215 BC, the Romans passed a law prohibiting women from possessing more than one-half ounce of gold or from wearing dresses of more than one color. And in 161 BC the serving of fowl was prohibited, "except for one hen un-fattened." This body of law, equating austerity with righteousness, came to be known as sumptuary law. If the purpose of these laws was basically economic, at least they were advocated and defended on grounds of morality.

Such taste statutes persisted well into the Christian age, took renewed fervor, and became extensive throughout Europe during the Middle Ages and after. Nürnberg legally regulated extravagant dress, with stringent restrictions against peaks on shoes, which apparently were thought to be provocative of low and base thoughts. One regulation then in vogue might appeal to parents of modern teenagers. It prohibited "any but the customary dances which have come down of old."

An unexpected reverse twist is seen in certain European statutes of the time which sought to regulate—of all things—men's clothing. The particular object of public opprobrium was the shortening of the jacket above the knees. Apparently this offended the taste of some folks then in the same manner as the modern miniskirt or the plunging neckline in women's apparel.

In 1520, three men were actually executed in Switzerland for swearing. The government encouraged people to inform on violators. Sunday laws prohibited card playing but permitted rifle and crossbow practicing. In Zurich, silk borders on bodices were outlawed and legally confiscated, but oddly two classes were specifically exempted—women of aristocratic guilds and "public prostitutes." England outlawed the wearing of furs by women. It hardly needs to be observed that these laws occurred before the day of women's suffrage!

As might be expected, these taste statutes which sought to bring about marked changes in public habits by legislation almost always failed. It is easy enough for us in retrospect to scoff at the now rather apparent futility of such efforts. With the benefit of several hundred years of hindsight and almost two hundred years of experience in religious freedom, we see several obvious flaws.

First of all, we see in them an almost shocking lack of faith in the public and in such civilizing non-governmental influences as the church and the family to provide leadership in such voluntary matters of public taste and morals. Secondly, we might stand astonished at the arrogance and presumption of medieval lawmakers who invoke the name of God in attempting to force their own private tastes upon others. It seems a rather clear case of men attempting to make God in their own image!

Yet it would be well for us to remember that religious freedom as we know it did not spring full blown even in America until after this country had undergone nearly one hundred years of sad and mottled experience with official state churches and the inevitable repressions of freedom which this almost always meant.

It seems ironic that this country, composed largely of people who had fled the tyranny of religious persecutions and wars that had terrorized Europe for nearly two hundred years, did not automatically establish total religious freedom. Yet, humanly enough, once they had settled, most of our forebears fell into the very patterns from which they had fled. Every colony except Pennsylvania and Rhode Island had an officially established state church, and almost without exception the laws of the colonies discriminated against dissenters from that church. Persecution, witch hunts, and heresy hunts began to break out with appalling frequency. Thoughtful men wondered if the blood baths of Europe were going to flame anew on this continent. Fortunately, there was a Thomas Jefferson and enough men of vision and goodwill to follow the leadership he represented.

And so for almost two centuries we as a nation have sought to keep such legal enactments to a necessary minimum.

Ruskin said the strength of a society may be measured by the amount of *persuasion* which can be used as opposed to the amount of *force* that is necessary. The test of a man or of a nation is what he or it will do when not forced to do anything. The English moralist Hobbes put it this way: "To force morality by threat of punishment is to confront the individual with a choice between *two evils*, not a choice between good and evil."

All Americans, and particularly those of us who hold strong convictions, need to be on guard constantly against the ugly temptation to assign impure motives to others who simply disagree with us, thus enthroning our personal opinions and mistaking our own prejudices for holiness. The ultimate blasphemy is to attempt to make oneself God. Judge Learned Hand once said that the spirit of liberty is the spirit which is not too sure that it is right.

Certain general guidelines may be helpful. First of all, the law exists not for the propagation of one set of ideas against another, but rather for the protection of society. Second, the basic purpose of law is not to punish criminals but to prevent crime. It is successful law only insofar as it accomplishes this purpose. Third, the law per se is concerned not with internal attitudes but with external conduct. Motives are not normally the concern of the law; they belong to the individual conscience. Finally, law in the Western tradition is essentially limited. Constitutions exist for the purpose of limiting rather than expanding the application of law.

What, then, are some of the particular areas of proper legal responsibility? We have already mentioned the need to protect the public against the flaunting of unwanted obscenity. Similarly, the nation has determined that all traffic in narcotics must in the public interest be subject to extremely stringent controls. On almost all counts of the definition stated above, forced restraint against traffic in narcotics surely qualifies as a proper area of public enforcement.

In an age of mass merchandising when the public lies largely at the mercy of information and claims disseminated by advertisers, and when those same advertisers to a large extent control the very media of public communication, society has found laws necessary to protect the public against fraudulently misleading and fundamentally untruthful advertising.

Often the mere threat of public censure will serve to make certain industries clean up their own backyards rather than submit to public control. One example is the television industry. All of us were appalled a few years ago to learn that we had been taken in by rigged contests. While there was nothing unlawful about this, surely nobody could contend that it was anything less than fundamentally dishonest. Hearings were conducted by Congressional committees. As a result the television industry voluntarily imposed its own prohibitions against such deception.

I happen to be one of those who feel that television as a whole still exhibits far too much violence to be an altogether healthy influence. Yet, I am free to influence what programs my minor children view over television. Not only am I free to do so, as a parent, I think I have a responsibility to do so.

Television has an unrivaled capacity to become either a great elevator or a great leveler. To overestimate its potential for good or bad would be difficult indeed. But in a free society the control that can properly be exercised by law is limited. Although television and radio, as a collection of licensees using the public airwaves, are properly subject to certain restrictions which do not apply to movies, magazines, and newspapers, any attempt by government to regulate program content would smack of thought control. If the American people made it clear that they did not *want* so much exposure to sex and violence, however, it no longer would be profitable for any of the media to exhibit so much.

The same may be said of books. I am appalled at the apparent belief on the part of writers and publishers that the surest way to have a bestseller is to fill a book with pointless filth. Yet, apparently, there is some basis for that conclusion. As repelled as many of us personally may be by the themes of depravity and perversion contained in some bestsellers, I must say in candor that apparently the most successful way to sell a book is to get it talked about by reviewers, banned in Boston, or challenged in the courts.

As distasteful as this fact is to me, I fear even more deeply the other extreme in which we would set up public censors under the aegis of government to tell the public what it may or may not read. This could lead to the most detestable forms of thought control, moving insidiously and perhaps inevitably from attempted moral censorship into the field of political censorship. If any churchman should be tempted to desire general public censorship of books and periodicals beyond that encompassing only the flagrantly and incontestably obscene, then he ought to recall the fact that history's first and most vigorous attempts to prohibit publishing of the printed word were directed against the publishing of the Holy Scriptures themselves.

What it all comes to is that government by compulsion can only prevent certain overt abuses. Government can and must protect society against clear and unmistakable danger. Yet the fundamental truth remains that morality is not changed by law.

A corollary truth, however, also remains: society *is* changed by morality. This is the fundamental distinction between political action and religious action. The politician may say, "There ought to be a law." But the Christian churchman will say, "There ought to be a change; therefore, let it begin with me."

Hasn't there been a curious omission in this part of our discussion? We have talked almost wholly in terms of the "thou shalt nots." We have hardly mentioned the "thou shalts." Yet morality and social ethics are concerned with both. The law by its very nature is a negative thing in the areas of prohibitions and sanctions and penalties.

Yet Christianity is not a negative thing. It is a positive thing. Its essence is not found in the stale and hidebound prohibitions of the Pharisees. It is not found among the white sepulchres. It is found in the clean fresh air and under the open skies where humanity first breathed the incomparable fragrance of the Sermon on the Mount and felt the harsh and restrictive chains of legal obedience fall away in the new freedom of love for all mankind.

And so it is with a nation and its morality. Its security lies not in mistrust but in faith. Its strength is never founded on fear but on hope. Its power derives not from hate but from love, from charity. We Christians claim to be heirs to the hope of the world. To our safekeeping has been entrusted the mustard seed, the leaven for the loaf. Are we concerned about public morality? Perhaps we might do well to think more in terms of what constructive things we ourselves must do and less in terms of what we would force others not to do. The heart of our faith is that God deals with man in the realm of the unenforceables, that he transforms society through individuals, not individuals through society.

Members of Congress are individuals. It is our job in life to speak and act for a lot of other individuals. But we need ever to be conscious of our limitations. We cannot *create* the ideal society. Perhaps the best we can create is a legal *climate* conducive to its development. We can outlaw obvious evils. We can try to see that no citizen of this land is deprived of his just rights. We can strive by political means to guarantee that every child, created in God's image, shall have a fair and full chance to develop his own potential for good—and the broadest opportunity to express it. By deed and word, as it is given to us to see the truth, we can work for peace among men. And we can hope that our wisdom is not folly.

As has been said by Paul Tillich, we live in two orders. All history tells us that the political order will not really change the spiritual order. But the spiritual order, when its conviction is deep enough and its dedication true enough, will ultimately and immutably and supremely change the political order. This is our hope.

Meanwhile, what do we fellows in Congress do about all this? Well, we just do the best we can. A member of Congress, fallible and mortal, can contribute to the fulfillment of this hope. He can if he will balance the awareness of his power with an awareness of his human limitations. He can if, with Saint Francis, he seeks first to understand rather than to be understood, to love rather than to be loved.

Empowered to determine what others must render unto Caesar, the lawmaker first might ask what he himself may render unto God. For the face of the coin bears Caesar's image, but that of man bears the image of his Creator. The coin performs its intended use only as it serves the will of the power that minted it. And so it is with man.

from *Congress and Conscience*
(Lippincott, 1970)

## Remember the Good, the Bad, and the Lessons of '92

THE WEEK BETWEEN Christmas and New Year's Day is a time for reflective self-indulgence. Maybe this afternoon or tomorrow when kids are enjoying the company of their peers and the decibel level in the house has subsided, we can pause for an unhurried look into the fireplace and relax with our thoughts.

Maybe we'll recall a time of special happiness in the year just past. For me it was an almost leisurely six weeks I spent in Houston undergoing radiation treatments at M. D. Anderson hospital following the removal of a cancer from the base of my tongue.

I'll remember 1992 with personal gratitude as the year I faced the terrifying reality of cancer and learned that it need not be fatal. That very word sounds a note of horror to the minds of most people. Until it strikes us personally, we never reflect on how many thousands, with the miraculous help of modern medicine, have overcome cancer to enjoy many years of health and productive work.

How fortunate was I that this specter did not come to haunt me four years earlier, when I was House Speaker. Preoccupied with work and obsessed with the urgency of each of its minuscule demands, I almost certainly would have put off going for an examination. The stark truth once revealed, I surely would have delayed the surgery until I could find time for it and the recuperation. From that predictable folly a beneficent fate has spared me.

So, as I stare contentedly into the fire today, I give thanks for that peculiar boon of timing and for my good health. For those unto whose lives the terrifying name of *cancer* has not intruded, I offer one word of advice and another of comfort. Don't delay, and don't despair. When detected early, cancer is most often operable. You'll find hundreds who have surmounted it.

Then, maybe, as you lazily ponder those events that swept so swiftly past you this year like pickets in a fence as you hurriedly drove by, some humorous moments may return to lift the corners of your mouth. I recall that warm, drowsy day in Houston . . . Betty and I had brought along our two little white dogs. Mine is a West Highland terrier named Maggie. Betty's GiGi is a Bichon, sweet and complaisant as Maggie is peppery and self-willed. While Betty ran into a shop for a purchase, I chose to sit in the car with Maggie and GiGi and enjoy the somnolent sunshine. I leaned back into a new beaded seat cover. Soon I dozed off.

After some minutes, I became aware of a voice at close range. Someone was talking to me. A man stood beside the car peering in. Both dogs had scrambled between my lap and the steering wheel and were sniffing him through the open window. In the first words I could consciously sort out, this stranger was asking: "Did you get them here in Houston?" Supposing him to be talking about my cuddlesome canines, I stifled a yawn and replied, "No, we got one in Cleburne and the other at the little town of Acton between Cresson and Granbury."

"You didn't get them at the same place!?" There was disbelief in his voice. The question sounded more like a challenge. By now I was fully awake.

"Well, no," I replied. "As you can see, they are not alike. And their personalities are entirely different!" He seemed puzzled, even slightly irritated. If I had been more observant, I might have seen him staring intently at our obviously identical seat covers.

"I was asking," he said, "because I was thinking about buying some." My heart went out to him. Another dog lover!

"Good! You can't go wrong!" I assure him. "If the whole thing turns against you, they'll stick to you like glue!"

At this, he fixed me with an uncomprehending look like that of a newly beached fish. Finally, he asked, "What I really wanted to know is, do they help your back?" Now it was my turn at bewilderment. How on earth would two small dogs be expected to help anyone's back?

After a pause to consider, I replied as thoughtfully as possible. "Well, I suppose they could if it needs limbering up. They do seem to make you bend over a lot."

At this, he muttered something unintelligible and turned to move away. Just then it dawned on me. I shouted at his slowly departing figure. "Hey! You weren't even talking about my dogs!"

He turned. "No, and you weren't talking very sensibly about your seat covers." I hoped he didn't know who I was.

How often in life have we, absorbed in our own thoughts, failed to tune in to what someone was trying to say to us? How frequently do we all, like the inheritors of the Tower of Babel, speak words that simply do not communicate because we don't bother to get on the same wavelength?

So now, as we sit by the fire in passive reflection, caress the good memories, and ponder the hopes of a new year, here is a modest New Year's resolution that shouldn't tax any of us too grievously and might do all of us a little bit of good:

May we resolve that in the year ahead we'll try to enjoy each blessing more gratefully, and listen more attentively with our minds and our hearts to what other people are trying to tell us.

*Fort Worth Star-Telegram,* December 27, 1992

## Wit Helps Make the World Go 'Round a Bit More Smoothly

REVIEWING A VIDEOTAPE of John F. Kennedy's presidential news conferences last week, I was struck anew by the realization that the most valuable asset a public official can have is a sense of humor. It can break the ice, ease tension, lance a boil, dispel gloom, or deflate anger—sometimes all at once. Kennedy was a master at it.

Told that his brother Bobby was too young and inexperienced to be attorney general, Kennedy quipped that he saw no harm in giving the lad some "legal experience before he goes out to practice law."

Once he was asked, considering the difficulties of the president's office, if he would ever recommend it to anyone. The job did have one attractive feature, the president suggested: "You can walk to work."

At Kennedy's first meeting with Nikita Khrushchev, the Russian leader tried some of the same medicine. Kennedy asked if Khrushchev ever admitted a mistake. But certainly, the latter replied. "In a speech to the twentieth party congress, I admitted all of Stalin's mistakes."

Almost on a par with Kennedy in the humor department was President Reagan. More than once, the clever old thespian would destroy the careful arguments of his political opposition with a quick shaft of wit. By 1984, when he ran for reelection, Reagan was the oldest man ever to serve in the presidency. Opponents hinted darkly that senility was creeping up on the chief executive.

During a televised debate with his Democratic opponent, former Vice President Walter Mondale, a reporter asked Reagan if he would care to comment on "the age issue." Feigning shock at the suggestion, Reagan said he just didn't think it would be fair to point out his fifty-six-year-old adversary's youth and inexperience. Even Mondale laughed.

Whenever Reagan addressed Congress, copies of the president's speech would be embargoed until shortly before airtime. Hastily reading a sneak preview one evening, I discovered one statement that seemed to concede a major Democratic point of view. Quickly assembling a few leading Democrats, I pointed out the line in the text and asked them to move swiftly in advance among colleagues and orchestrate a standing applause as soon as the president read that particular sentence. They gleefully fanned out, enlisting scores of eager collaborators.

There we all sat, glued to the script lest we miss the opportunity, as the mellifluous voice intoned speechwriter Peggy Noonan's eloquent cadences. Finally the president came to the one pro-Democratic line in his speech. To his surprise, the chamber erupted with wild applause. Even many Republicans who had been mentally napping, now seeing other members rising to their feet, stood and joined in the enthusiastic ovation.

The demonstration caught Reagan off guard for only a few seconds. He stared briefly in astonishment and then quickly recovered his composure. Grinning broadly, he said: "And all this while I thought you fellows were sitting there reading the newspapers!" This time the laughter was universal. Having deftly turned the spear point in our direction, Reagan calmly resumed his speech.

Sometimes people draw closer by joking together about things that would be taboo in formal society. The trick is knowing with whom to joke and when, and how far to go. This judgment has to be largely intuitive.

Senator Daniel Inouye of Hawaii was the first Japanese-American to serve in Congress, elected to the House in 1960, when Hawaii became a state. Inouye, a decorated military veteran, had lost an arm serving our country in World War II. Arriving in Washington, he went by for a ritual call on Speaker Sam Rayburn and was warmly received.

"You're going to like it here," the venerable Speaker predicted

Alongside then Vice President George H. W. Bush at an address by President Ronald Reagan before a joint session of Congress, 1981.
SPEAKER JIM WRIGHT COLLECTION, SPECIAL COLLECTIONS, MARY COUTS BURNETT LIBRARY, TCU.

affably. "We're all mighty proud to have you. In fact, aside from myself, perhaps, you are probably the most recognizable member of the House."

A surprised Inouye protested that he could not be very recognizable since he had only arrived.

"Danny," the old speaker said with a smile, "just how many one-armed Japs do you think we have in Congress?"

Rather than being offended, Inouye broke up in laughter. He cherishes the episode and recounts it still in convivial settings.

Mo Udall of Arizona, however, claimed to be a more exclusive minority in Congress than even Inouye. After all, several other Japanese-Americans also have served with legislative distinction. "But where, aside from me," Udall would demand, "can you find another one-eyed Mormon Navajo?"

Actually, I always doubted that Mo had any Navajo blood. But he would have gladly taken some by transfusion if he thought it would have improved his joke. He did have a glass eye. After unsuccessfully seeking the presidential nomination, Udall wrote an uproarious book titled *Too Funny to be President.*

In spite of his glass eye, Udall played professional basketball with the Denver Nuggets and managed to get a single-engine pilot's license. He loved to go into the cockpit of a big commercial airliner and look at the magnificent instrument panel. Once, while admiring the new technology, he confided to the airline captain that he was a certified single-engine pilot.

"Well, that's fine, Congressman," said the pilot, "you just go back and strap yourself into your seat, and if we get down to one engine we'll call on you!" Udall loved telling this story.

Being able to enjoy a joke on oneself is an essential ingredient of a healthy disposition. It may be the most useful lubricant to ease the frictions that develop in human relationships.

*Fort Worth Star-Telegram*, July 31, 1994

## Granite-Domed Carnival

THE TEXAS LEGISLATURE was a carnival which came every two years to parade its gaudy entertainments and hawk its lusty wares under the imposing dome of native red granite which rises beyond a spacious lawn at the foot of Austin's Congress Avenue. For legislator and lobbyist whose flocks return like migratory waterfowl in January of every odd-numbered year, it is mecca. The Capitol building's ancient high-ceilinged halls have reverberated to the oratory of giants like Sam Houston and James Stephen Hogg and provided covert crannies for the petty panderings of pygmies. Here the business of what was then the nation's largest state is, for better or worse, transacted.

My first official act was to pay a courtesy call upon outgoing Governor Coke Stevenson. Tall and spare, he sat puffing on his pipe, his well-worn copy of the Texas Constitution the only piece of current business evident upon the top of the ample gubernatorial desk. Stevenson's principal accomplishment was that, during the war years, he had husbanded the state's fiscal resources, subduing every temptation to spend, and now was bequeathing to the incoming legislature a handsome surplus. His primary concern, he told me, was that we should not regard his bequest lightly nor fritter it away on frivolous projects.

There were, among the one hundred and fifty House members and thirty-one state senators that year, a total of ninety-five new members. Even for an institution repeatedly ravaged by turnovers, this was an almost unprecedented crop of freshmen. Everyone I met in those first few weeks was as friendly and accommodating as greeters at the church door. Glad-handing and flattery abounded in head-turning profusion. And none were heartier in their approbation than the retinue of lobbyists eager to ingratiate themselves with each new member. I decided it might be a good idea if lobbyists were required to wear distinctive buttons, the better to assist the neophyte legislators in evaluating the sincerity of their praise.

To describe the Texas legislature of that era as lobby ridden is like saying that a Shetland after ten years in an outdoor pony ring has been slightly child ridden. Members of the Third House, as the lobby came to be known, plied their wiles daily, openly, and with varying degrees of cunning. Their tactics were tailored to the disparate personalities, principles, and peccadilloes of the individual lawmakers they set out to cajole. For some budding politicians the heady wine of flattery was all that was required. Others responded to the lavish hospitality which flourished nightly in various public and private watering spots. An El Paso newspaper characterized the 1947 Austin atmosphere in an editorial entitled "Beefsteak, Bourbon, and Blondes." At least a few fledgling solons later learned to their dismay that indiscreetly committed sins of the flesh could lead to a subtle form of blackmail, with payment expected in the coin of votes on crucial bills.

And, let's face it, there was a certain amount of outright bribery. A shopworn in-house cliché among the lobby defined an honest legislator as "one who'll stay bought."

I cannot forget how appalled I was at the unabashed boast of an otherwise undistinguished third-term member who asked me, early that year, if I'd like to know the secret of his success in the legislature. I could tell he'd had a couple of drinks, but went along cheerfully with his gambit. Sure, I said, what was his success secret?

"It's my overcoat," he smirked.

"Your overcoat?" I repeated. This had to be the lead-in to a new gag, I thought, and waited for the punch line. The only funny thing is that he wasn't joking.

"Yeah," he confided. "I leave it hangin' right there on that same rack in the cloakroom every day." He pointed. There, sure enough, was an overcoat.

"That overcoat has made me more money than anything else I ever owned," he said. My stupefaction must have been apparent. By now, I'd decided he was not propounding a comic riddle.

"First year I was here," he continued confidentially, "I left that coat hangin' there one day. Went to get it later and found a note in the pocket. It said 'Support S. B. 37,' I think it was. There was a fifty-dollar bill attached to the note, and I supported hell out of that bill. Been happenin' ever since, and sometimes it's a hundr'd. Don't know who does it and don't wanna know."

If he expected me to be impressed, I was. In the same way I'd be impressed if the preacher told a vulgar story complete with four-letter words from the pulpit.

"I even carry that coat in the summertime," he snickered.

Then, with a knowing wink as he took his leave: "My advice to any new member is—get yourself an overcoat."

I was aghast! The man certainly didn't *seem* to be joking. But if it were true, would he have volunteered such information to me, a virtual stranger? Could this bawdy tale simply be a form of shock treatment, part of the initiation ritual for new members?

As I observed that particular legislator off and on during the legislative session, I concluded that what he told me probably was the truth. And my eyes opened little by little to other events which were every bit as startling and more consequential, if slightly less crude.

The two issues which produced the most fireworks in the legislature that year involved taxes and labor. A willing protagonist in the taxation fight, I was like a noncombatant struck by a spray of stray gunfire in the hostilities which swirled around the questions of labor policy. Like others before and since who've tried to preserve an objective neutrality, I was drawn involuntarily into the spinning vortex of the labor imbroglio. My first reaction was that of a pedestrian standing at an intersection when a two-ton truck jumps the curb. There was no holding it back nor time to get out of the way.

The bill which created the greatest ruckus was one to impose a statewide ban on closed-shop agreements. Merchandized as the "right-to-work" bill, it carried a basic, simplistic appeal. Would we allow labor barons to erect a toll stile at every gate of employment? Would we take from a person the right to earn wages for his failure to pay union dues? If a common laborer didn't believe in unionism, would we make all his children go hungry? If joining a union was against his religion, must the poor fellow be jobless?

All these pleas and more were summoned in support of the bill. It was huckstered through newspaper ads and editorials, in letter-writing campaigns by trade associations and chambers of commerce, and from not a few pulpits. Members soon were inundated by phone calls and letters from home. There was scarcely any public opposition to the proposal. Only about 10 percent of the Texas work force belonged to closed shops, and less than 30 percent belonged to unions. Joe Belden's poll showed that 41 percent of the state's union members favored the bill, along with about 80 percent of everyone else.

If this was not sufficient overkill, what happened next made it politically suicidal for most members to oppose the measure. A young woman named Ruth Koenig came over from Houston, identified herself as secretary of the Communist Party of Texas, and said she and her fellow Communists were against the bill. She asked to be heard formally by the legislative committees to which the bill had been assigned. To the confounding and embarrassment of the elected leaders of Texas labor organizations, it was her testimony—not theirs—which got all the attention.

It was the most sensational thing that happened at the marble-domed carnival that year. This was the first real, live Communist most Texas legislators had ever seen. They gawked at her as they might at a three-headed calf.

Bravely but feebly, the chosen spokesmen of organized labor tried to explain their opposition to the anti-closed-shop bill with sophisticated arguments. They pointed out that elections were required among all employees before a union could be designated to speak for them. They stressed the subsequent legal responsibilities of unions to represent all within a bargaining unit, on individual grievances as well as on pay and working conditions. But what they said could not be heard above the still-echoing announcement by the strange little woman that the *Communists* opposed the bill. It was whooped through the committees and onto the floors of House and Senate.

The bill whisked through both houses like a sharp knife through warm butter. Sid Gregory of Gatesville, who occupied the desk next to mine, was a former Marine. His wife had been a labor organizer for the garment workers before their marriage. She harassed him like a hair shirt about the "evils" of the bill, but each succeeding day's mail brought a mountain of evidence that Sid's constituents wanted it passed. Weighing the numbers, Sid braved his wife's scorn and voted for it. The beaches of Iwo Jima, Sid concluded, were mild hazards compared with the wrath of the voters. The people of Parker County, like those of Sid's district, clearly wanted the bill, and I too voted for it.

A few days after the House passed this measure, a man named Vance Muse, who published a right wing sheet called *Christian American*, printed a special edition which he mailed throughout the state. It featured a photograph of Ruth Koenig, the lady Communist, at the top of the page with smaller pictures of those few members who had opposed the "right-to-work" bill printed below. A headline proclaimed, "Where She Leads Us We Will Follow." The text of the circular brazenly accused those who had voted "no" of following the dictates of the Communist Party.

Sid Gregory and I, whose votes for the bill blissfully spared us a place on the scandal sheet, agonized over the plight of our colleagues who had risked this sort of calumny to vote their negative convictions. It was hard to tell whether the Communists or the gleeful hatchet men of the Vance Muse stripe constituted the greater danger to free speech.

Both Sid and I subsequently voted against a constitutional amendment that would have incorporated the anti-closed-shop provision into the state constitution. It was my belief that simple statutory law, even a law for which I'd voted, had no place in the Texas Constitution. That document, already weighted down with a patchwork of more than a hundred amendments, was on its way to rivaling the Sears Roebuck catalog in bulk.

Marshall Bell, quarterback of the right-to-work forces, also proposed a constitutional amendment to prohibit Texas from ever voting a state income tax. When the committee considering the proposition amended it by proscribing the levy of a tax only on incomes of less than $10,000, Representative Bell denounced the action and promptly dropped his sponsorship of the measure.

With a growing resentment of the pressure tactics of the antilabor juggernaut, I voted "no" on several other bills whose sole purpose seemed designed to harass and penalize union activity.

In the raging struggle between management and labor it was hard to be objective. With no experience in industrial organization and few predilections, I was trying to measure each proposition by the sweet light of reason. But attempting to rise above the fray on some magic carpet of statesmanship was dream stuff. There was no room in this fight for neutrals or peacemakers. In the frantic dichotomy of the time, every member would be described as either prolabor or antilabor. Trying to remain unbiased was like trying to walk a high wire without a balancing pole. Because I hadn't voted for *all* the restrictions propounded on labor, I would be described as "under the thumb of the union bosses." I vaguely suspected this at the time, but was ill prepared for the cannonading that would come.

My principal legislative effort of the session involved taxes. The scope of my undertaking would have pleased Tycho Brahe, the Danish astronomer who admonished against the making of little plans. I sought to create a vehicle by which the state could raise teachers' salaries, pave rural roads, and increase welfare payments by taxes on the industries that were depleting our most valuable natural resources—oil, gas, and sulfur.

Six of us carefully put together a bill of utopian scale and monumental length, aimed at achieving all these objectives in one bold legislative stroke. Those joining me in sponsoring the ambitious effort were Sid Gregory, Davis Clifton of McKinney, Ed Hughes of Newton, James Spencer of Athens, and Paul Wilson of San Augustine. All of us, except for second-termer Spencer, were freshmen legislators. All were war veterans, and all represented rural sections of Texas.

We were assisted in the bill's drafting by a tousled young lawyer named Bob Eckhardt whom I'd met at the Young Democrats convention. A big fellow with a fondness for seersucker suits, Bob always managed to resemble an unmade bed generously sprinkled with cigar ashes. But the almost studied untidiness of his appearance belied a fastidious legal mind. Bob was practicing law in Austin at the time and drawing the cartoons that appeared weekly on the cover of the *Spectator*. Quite probably he was the brightest of our whole crowd of postwar reformers. He would serve later in the legislature and in Congress.

There is little question that we attacked the state's three most pressing financial needs. Public education in Texas was approaching a crisis. Teachers, attracted by better pay outside the classrooms and frustrated by rising classroom numbers, were leaving the profession in droves. It was getting harder to hire new ones. Fewer students were preparing for teaching careers. Governor Jester in his State of the State message recommended raising teachers' pay to a $2,000 yearly "average." We wanted to make it a $2,000 annual minimum. The current average was somewhere around $1,700 a year.

The rural population, badly in need of more dependable roads, long had been deceived by the illusory promises of politicians. Texas then had some hundred thousand miles of dusty automobile trails which turned into impassable mud ruts when it rained. In some rural areas it was not uncommon for children to miss as many as sixty days of school each year because school buses simply could not negotiate the soggy byways. The intolerable lack of hard-surface roads isolated many thousands of farm homes from medical care during much of the year and caused perishable farm products to rot in the fields while markets lay inaccessible beyond the muddy hollows.

The old age pension for years had been the state's favorite political football. Under the guise of having more for the old folks, the economy lobby two years earlier had sold voters on establishing in the constitution a $35 million annual ceiling. But appropriations never quite came to that figure, and each time a new pensioner was certified onto the rolls, it increased the divisor and lowered the dividend. Our bill would have raised enough money for the state to appropriate the constitutional limit for the elderly, blind, and needy children's programs.

We figured our revenue goal at $26 million more for the schools, $10 million more annually for farm-to-market roads, and an additional $2 million each year to supplement the amount already going into the pension fund. In all, we calculated it would take $38 million a year. That would comport roughly with trying to produce almost $400 million in new state taxes a generation later.

We found what we thought was a way to raise the additional revenue without burdening Texas consumers. We would tax those native endowments of our state which were being piped off in huge quantities to other states, and from which Texas was deriving practically no income at all.

Texas produced more than half the world's supply of sulfur. Dr. Bob Montgomery of the University of Texas declared, in his caustic book *The Brimstone Game*, that production costs by a monopolistic patented process were in the range of $3.50 per long ton. For a full generation, the companies had been selling the sulfur for no less than $18.00 a long ton, and Texas received taxes of $1.27. We proposed to raise that tax to $5.00 per long ton, but to exempt any small producers who were not privy to the patented process.

Natural gas was selling then at about ten cents a thousand cubic feet at the wellhead and was being delivered to out-of-state consumers at anywhere from fifty cents to sixty cents a cubic thousand. We proposed a severance tax of one and one-half cents a thousand cubic feet at the well. But we would keep the cost the same for Texas industrial and residential consumers by repealing a gas utility gross receipts tax, which amounted to about one and one-half cents per thousand.

On oil, we went after the big companies. We didn't want to hurt the small independent wildcatters, who already were scraping bottom on borrowed money looking for the black fluid, with little more than a rig and a rabbit's foot for good luck. Bob Eckhardt discovered that Montana had a graduated tax on the production of metals, the rate depending on the volume mined by each producer, and that some states in the waning days of populism had adopted graduated taxes on chain stores, the rate rising as the number of retail outlets increased.

So we devised a severance tax that would start at 3 percent of the cost per barrel on monthly production up to 175 barrels, 3.5 percent on production up to 750 barrels, and so on until it reached 15 percent on production in excess of six million barrels a month. The bigger the producing company, the more taxes it would pay on each barrel. And the more, we figured, it could afford to pay. There were 3,300 oil producers listed with the Texas Railroad Commission, yet eight big companies in the previous year had produced more than half the oil which came out of Texas soil.

The funniest thing about all this is that our closest estimates on the amount of revenue these taxes actually would have yielded the state were outrageously below the mark. A group of graduate students at the University of Texas haunted the Railroad Commission offices for about a month, ran company-by-company calculations, and came up with a startling revelation. They confided it to us privately several weeks after the bill had been introduced, and our utopian scheme had made a big splash in all the Texas newspapers.

To our total amazement, the bill we'd introduced would have raised not $38 million but almost $500 million a year, and a majority of the oil producers in Texas (the small ones) would have been paying less tax than they already were paying. Texas could have abolished all other state taxes, run the state solely on the revenues from our tax bill, and had money left over to invest in permanent endowments.

Our gross miscalculation was a carefully guarded secret. The big oil companies were certain to have run our plan through their own calculations and discovered the truth, but neither of us ever breathed it outside our respective circles. We hated for anyone to know what sloppy draftsmen we'd been. They probably didn't want anybody to find out how easy it would be to raise that much money from their industry.

With straight faces, we jointly preserved the myth of a $38 million a year tax bill. We never mentioned the mistake to them. They never mentioned it to us. Neither of us mentioned it to the Committee on Revenue & Taxation before whose members we appeared to argue our opposite sides of the question. Soberly, all witnesses referred to the $38 million figure. The six cosponsors agreed among ourselves that, if this bill ever found its way to the House floor, we'd have an amendment ready to scale it back to proper size. We never had to prepare the amendment, as it turned out. The committee, heavily influenced by the very interests whom our measure would tax, doggedly refused all year to report our bill or any other bill to impose a tax on natural resources.

Even though the legislature did not adopt our euphoric view of an all-purpose solution to the state's woes, we did generate enough heat to propel the sluggish engines of Texas government toward some of our objectives.

Probably the outstanding achievement of the fiftieth Texas legislature was its awakening to the crisis of public education. We took a bold upward step in the state's annual apportionment for each scholar in the schools from thirty-six dollars to fifty-five dollars. And this was done over the governor's strong opposition.

Nor did we let other necessities of education go neglected. We increased aid for the rural schools from $28 million in the preceding biennium to $36 million. Support for state institutions of higher learning jumped from $26 million to $45 million. And we almost trebled the appropriation for public junior colleges, although the $1,850,000 we dispensed in our two-year appropriation, which looked so grand at the time, would be pitiful by today's standards. We increased by $1 million the amount for vocational education and raised the appropriation for teaching handicapped children from $300,000 to $700,000. In all, we pledged about $82 million more for educational purposes than our most generous predecessors had done.

In the House, we even passed a bill to tax the gathering of natural gas. This action came in a floor revolt. We voted to take the scaled-down bill away from the Revenue & Taxation Committee and bring it to the floor where, by majority vote, the House approved it. We calculated that it would raise close to $40 million a year, with half pledged to the schools and the rest to rural road construction. For three months our House-approved measure gathered dust in a remote Senate cubbyhole. The Senate committee never even called a public hearing to consider it, and the bill died when the final gavel ended the session.

We did force a moderate increase in funds available to build and pave farm roads. We voted reforms in the state's prison system. The House, at the urging of our reforms bloc, approved a secret ballot law and a long-overdue legislative redistricting bill, but these were killed in the Senate.

The major oil companies were granted a few, but not all, of their requests. They were gratified when the legislature made possible the extension of their leases on public lands without competitive bidding and when the Senate granted them a reprieve on any new taxes. But they were disappointed when the House in its closing days killed their Senate-passed unitization bill, which would have exempted them from the antitrust laws of the state.

Toward the end of the session, I sensed that I was gaining in strength and influence among my colleagues. I wasn't the best-informed or the most productive legislator of the session, but maybe

I was the most eager. Increasingly, others were coming to seek my help for their legislation. At least a dozen asked me to go with them and speak to civic clubs in their hometowns. One of these was crusty old Tom Martin of Fredericksburg, with whom I almost never agreed. Sardonically, Tom described himself as "leader of the House Republican forces." There actually were no Republicans in the fiftieth legislature. Every member was a product of a Democratic primary, but the broad tent of the Texas party covered the spectrum of political philosophies.

In June, the fiftieth legislature adjourned, closing out the books on the first one hundred years of Texas lawmaking. The centennial session had been neither the most inspired nor the most ignominious in the state's history. It had been for me, however, the most fulfilling experience I'd ever known. As its result, the people of Texas had 470 new laws and the option to sew nine new swatches onto our state constitution, which already resembled a patchwork quilt.

On closing day, while awaiting the final gavel, we recited poetry, told funny stories, and sang loudly in the House chamber. There I stood, shoulder to shoulder with political antagonists like Sam Hanna and Tom Martin, giving sentimental voice to an off-key rendition of "Auld Lang Syne."

As the session ended, I felt the heady afterglow of battles well fought. I'd finished stronger than I began. I had made some mistakes and profited from a few, learned the ropes, won some fights, made lots of friends, and earned respect from some of those who'd first held me in contempt. If they didn't agree with me, they could no longer ignore me. That fact, I was to discover, could be a two-edged sword.

ca. 1995 (unpublished)

## The Presidential Race is for the Dogs

THE PRESIDENTIAL CAMPAIGN is finally getting down to a serious issue, and it's reigning dogs and cats.

Candidate Bob Dole has vowed that his schnauzer, Leader, will chase the Clinton family's cat, Socks, off the White House lawn and all the way back to Arkansas.

A heated debate is arising. I can just hear Bill Clinton, in straight-faced indignation à la FDR, proclaiming to the world that his detractors have at last gone too far. "Will they stop at nothing? Not content to vilify my wife, Hillary, not content to criticize our daughter, Chelsea, they now are trying to drag our poor defenseless kitty, Socks, into the fetid gutters of partisan debate!"

It has a nice ring to it. Or he could take the issue head-on. "Presidential politics has been going to the dogs for years. For too long we have decried it. Now its time to do something about it! Down with dogmatism!"

On the other hand, President Clinton may move with stunning speed to co-opt the issue. With characteristic agility, he could get a dog. And not just some nondescript dog. Clinton could get a Great Dane, or maybe a Pyrenees. If a dog lover is what folks want in the White House, Bill Clinton will be a dog lover's dog lover!

This is what the Republicans secretly fear. Every time they think they've found the popular side of an issue, Clinton endorses their position. Worse yet, he *does* something about it.

Take deficits, for example. For years, GOP orators have flayed the annual deficits. Clinton played a dirty trick on them. He not only denounced deficits; he started reducing them. In the past three years, he has cut the annual deficit approximately in half. That's downright unethical.

Or take "bloated government." What a fine thing to rail against! It has launched more speeches than Helen of Troy launched ships.

Visiting with presidential candidate Bill Clinton on the campaign tour in Fort Worth, Texas, September 26, 1996.
PHOTO BY PHOTO-OP, INC., SILVER SPRING, MARYLAND.

What a rotten thing it was for Clinton to announce last January that the days of Big Government are over. Since taking office, he reduced the federal payroll by two hundred thousand people. The bureaucracy is the smallest in thirty years. As a percent of the civilian workforce, it's smaller than it's been since 1933.

Look at how he filched *law and order* and *family values*. The GOP thought they had squatters' rights on those issues, maybe even owned the trademarks. Clinton just moved in and muscled them out of the way, grinning all the while.

So it wouldn't surprise me a bit to see Bill Clinton get a dog. Doing so would drive the Republicans up a tree. And that's where a cat has an advantage.

Think of the presidential race as an allegory. Bill Clinton is a lot like a great big, friendly Saint Bernard puppy. He comes up waggin' his tail and licks you right in the face. And makes you like it.

Then our grumpy neighbor comes by and starts trying to tell us our dog has fleas. He doesn't say much about his own dog; he just keeps talking about our dog.

"Your dog has fleas! Your dog has fleas!" He is stuck on that note. He calls it the *character issue.*

Well, after a while we get sick and tired of hearing this. We begin to get angry. Not angry at our dog; angry at our neighbor. Finally, we say: "Stop telling us that! He doesn't have any more fleas than other dogs. And even if he does, he's a lot better than that old snarly, snapping Doberman of yours. And, furthermore, he's our dog and we're going to keep him!"

That's about the way Bill Clinton hopes this presidential race will play out. Anyway, it is finally on a high note. And a doggone interesting one.

*Fort Worth Star-Telegram,* June 23, 1996

## Elections and Mutual Respect

SOME CONSIDER THIS the most important presidential election in the past generation. It could conceivably influence America's direction for years to come. That doesn't excuse a personally abusive campaign. We mustn't reduce it to a choice of which side can more flagrantly defame or misconstrue the other's position.

"There's real hate out there this year," noted one veteran political observer. Little wonder. Not since Joe McCarthy's era have we seen more deliberate effort expended to foment hate. Nor ever so many millions spent on blatantly negative commercials.

Politics doesn't have to be this way. We shouldn't condone its degeneration to this level of abuse. Some of us have known a better, fairer, more American way.

Last week I had a friendly telephone call from my neighbor, Jim Bradshaw, former Fort Worth city councilman and mayor pro tem. The same Jim Bradshaw who ran against me for Congress in 1980.

Jim's call was no surprise to me. We've talked frequently in recent years. He's an outstandingly constructive citizen, and I count him a good friend. Nor was it strange that he was recommending a book he and his wife, Ouida, had just read. Thinking I'd enjoy it, Jim bought me a copy. He was calling to ascertain that I was at home so he could bring it by.

The book's title: *The Prayer of Jabez.* It's a delightfully incisive meditation that makes its readers think. Jim's guess was right. I have enjoyed and benefited from it.

Bradshaw was, in my retrospective view, the toughest opponent I faced in eighteen congressional elections (1954-88). He was hard working, fully focused, well financed, and aggressive. He made me hustle to hold on to my job. We met head-on in several vigorous debates.

None of this made us dislike each other, question one another's motives, or attack one another's character. Absolutely not. Not then, not now.

Though sometimes vexed by political opponents over the years, I've never hated one, and hope none ever hated me. Nor should I, or any decent person, sink to defaming the good name of an adversary for the sake of winning public office.

Presidential politics need be no different. If anything, that contest should impose an even higher standard of civility.

John Adams and Thomas Jefferson, America's second and third presidents, engaged in a hard-fought, sometimes bitter contest that Jefferson won. But they became fast friends and carried on intense correspondence in their later years. They died on the same day, July 4, 1826. Adams, on his deathbed, is said to have exclaimed, "Thank God Jefferson still lives!"

Jimmy Carter and Gerald Ford fought a close presidential battle in 1976. Yet neither was embittered. Neither made a disparaging personal comment about the other. On numerous recent occasions, these old rivals have jointly sponsored forward-looking projects for the country.

The presidential election of 1912, cited by historians as engendering the "most substantive," issue-oriented debates of all, featured Democrat Woodrow Wilson, Republican William Howard Taft, and Progressive Theodore Roosevelt. When a gunshot wound inflicted by a would-be assassin laid Roosevelt up for two weeks of physical recuperation, the other two candidates—out of personal respect and in the interest of fairness—cancelled all public appearances until their competitor was able to join them.

What a difference today! The old-fashioned name for what crosses our TV screens was "mud slinging." The substances being flung in candidates' faces today are more toxic, more noxious, and more soiling than good, clean mud.

It isn't the presidential candidates themselves who've been so nasty this year. Their third debate seemed quite civil, more presidential, and less given to oversimplifications.

Instead, it's the anonymous gaggle of backstage connivers and "independent expenditures" fat cats who're trying to purchase the elections with big buys of horrifically negative, untrue, and even slanderous claims blackening the reputations of the candidates they oppose and are out to destroy.

The attempts on both sides to besmirch the Vietnam-era military service of both Kerry and Bush, then in their twenties, are in abominable taste and unworthy of a civil society.

Likewise, efforts to flim-flam gullible voters into believing all Godly virtue reposes in one political party and that voting otherwise is committing sin—well, this is the most regrettable anomaly of all, an unconscious mimicry of those fanatical religious zealots abroad who preach that God hates America.

October 17, 2004 (unpublished)

## One Riot, One Mayor, One Jail

CONRAD RUSSELL WAS MY MODEL and mentor as mayor of Weatherford. He had a direct, friendly way with people and often could persuade or cajole even the most contentious into doing what was best for the town—and oft as not for themselves.

Yet in a place like ours, occasions unexpectedly arose that challenged even Conrad's celebrated skill as a peacemaker. One of those occurred on a Friday evening at the most public of places, our community football stadium, during a tensely contested game between Weatherford and Ranger High Schools.

A disputed call by a referee brought strong protests from one of the coaches, resulting in an angry, arm-waving face-off in midfield. Players themselves intruded into the discussion. One exasperated contestant shoved a member of the other team, which brought several members on each side rushing off their respective sideline benches onto the playing field, intent on protecting their teammates.

With the approaching pandemonium midfield, partisan members of the audience began leaping from the stands from both sides of the field to swell the unruly growing crowd on the gridiron.

The situation had become suddenly uncontrollable, beyond the official's capacity to handle. Upon someone's instruction, the announcer called for order over the loudspeaker system, proclaiming that the game was over, that it would be recorded as "no contest" with neither team the victor, and pleading with everyone to refrain from violence, leave the stadium, and go peacefully home.

This, predictably, did not satisfy everyone. But by the time the stadium lights were extinguished, everyone had left and there were no visibly wounded bodies lying on the ground.

Elements of the crowd on both sides, however—disappointed at the outcome and outraged over something they'd seen, or thought they'd seen—were determined to pursue the matter in angry conversation.

In those days, the only prominent automotive route out of town to the Ranger Highway led right through the middle of downtown Weatherford and around the courthouse square, with several cafés prominently open for business. Cars full of both local and visiting fans saw fit to stop and hopefully cool off with a cold drink or snack and postmortem discussion of the aborted football game.

Unfortunately, several of the unscheduled encounters were significantly less than cordial. Arguments ensued, some accompanied by physical blows and hands-on shoving matches.

Mayor Conrad Russell, abreast of these developments and anticipating lingering violent belligerence, had alerted the police force, instructing them to arrest and detain any and all violent individuals, both local and out-of-town people, and bring them to the city jail, with the promise that, if peaceful, they'd be released and escorted home or to their automobiles.

Weatherford had only one jail, but it fortunately contained two cells. Conrad wisely decreed that Weatherford citizens would be placed together in one cell, and all the belligerent out-of-towners in the other.

Determined to get everyone safely home without any further altercations, Conrad decreed that out-of-towners would be released first by individual family or group—one traveling carload at a time—and escorted peacefully by Weatherford police to their automobile, where they'd be met by a police car and escorted, if they wished, safely to the city limits.

Apologizing for time lost and other inconveniences, Conrad assured the cell full of locals that they would be accorded any of the same courtesies they might desire—just as soon as our out-of-town guests had been safely dispatched on their way.

Patiently, he visited privately with each out-of-town carload, ask-

With Larry Hagman, a fellow native of Weatherford, Texas, 1983. Wright was the *Dallas* star's Golden Gloves boxing coach when Hagman was in high school.
SPEAKER JIM WRIGHT COLLECTION, SPECIAL COLLECTIONS, MARY COUTS BURNETT LIBRARY, TCU.

ing for their promise that once released and in their private car, they'd drive home and not linger around Weatherford any longer that evening—for their own safety.

One by one, the small group of Ranger people left, most of them thanking Conrad for his courtesy and concern over their wellbeing.

Finally, there remained only one person in the out-of-town cell. Asked in our mayor's sweet, reasonable manner if he'd promise to get in his car and leave, the man replied:

"Mister, I'm from Michigan, and I was just passin' through your town. I just happened to see a sign that said 'Nook Café.' It seemed like a friendly place to stop for coffee. But just as soon as I got outta' my car, I was hit upside the head and knocked down in the gutter. Next thing I know, this policeman had me, and I been in jail. In answer to your question, I wasn't intendin' to drive all the way home to Michigan tonight, but, like you say, if you'll take me to my car, I'll sure leave town just fast as I can—and I'll tell you somethin' else: I won't be comin' back!"

August 11, 2010 (unpublished)

## Two Birds with One Phone

BEING MAYOR OF WEATHERFORD was a very personal thing. Personal and direct. I spent every morning at the family business and most of all of every afternoon at city hall.

But there was hardly any time, day or night, that I wasn't accessible. That was my unspoken trademark—accessibility. Local people expected that and availed themselves of its privilege. An unlisted telephone? Laughably out of the question!

Sometimes at 12:30 or 1:00 a.m., I'd receive a call from a garrulous fellow enjoying a late alcoholic libation with other fellow citizens, intent on sharing some newly occurred epiphany of great advice for the mayor.

More often, sometimes as early as 6:00 a.m., I'd hear from dear elderly ladies, alert and chipper and already involved in their daily routines.

One morning I was awakened by the telephone's imperious summons to hear an urgent complaint and plea for action from a lady on Weatherford's near south side. Three wicked boys with BB guns were shooting at the songbirds in her yard. She had installed bird houses in her trees, put out food, and erected a bird bath to attract these sweet, innocent creatures, and she thought the city had a responsibility to put an end to these dastardly depredations!

After telling her I'd "look into it" and while I was still trying to rub the sleep from my eyes, the phone intruded loudly again. This time, it was a lady on the north side, complaining bitterly of the incessant chatter of hordes of noisy sparrows and grackles that daily interrupted her unavailing efforts to get some well-earned, peaceful rest. She thought it shameful that the city was so oblivious to the veritable infestation of these loud, fractious disturbers of the peace!

As I drowsily mulled the two disparate complaints, wondering just what the city could do to be helpful, it hit me suddenly like a divine epiphany: I'd simply transfer the boys! It was the only way out.

Hopping into my car, I quickly drove to the south side neighborhood where I almost immediately spotted the armed cadre. There were four boys, not three, and I'd judge them to be eleven or twelve years of age.

I shouted to them from the car. "Hey! You guys want to hunt some birds?" I asked. "Let me show you where there's a gang of birds!"

They piled into the car, two of us in the front seat, three in the back. Happily, I knew exactly where the north side constituent lived.

I left them there to pursue their target practice, where it'd be appreciated.

I'm aware, of course, that this episode would be frowned upon by a sophisticated observer as "politically incorrect" today. Maybe even then, in a big city. But in Weatherford, circa 1950, we were blissfully free of any such compulsions.

For almost four decades in elective government, I've yearned for another opportunity to solve two serious problems in one heroic deed of direct action. None, alas, has come along.

You've no idea how triumphant I felt!

(unpublished)

# IV

# Defense and Foreign Policy

## The Bomb

FOR THE FIVE HUNDRED CIVILIAN observers witnessing for their first time the unleashed power of the atom, last Tuesday morning's blast at Yucca Flat, Nevada, lived up to its billing.

This was one show from which not even the most callous could say he had failed to get his money's worth.

You are sitting there on rocky News Nob, shivering in the chill pre-dawn, peering through your black goggles, and intently bracing yourself as the man with the microphone precisely intones "H minus five seconds . . . four seconds . . . three seconds . . . two seconds . . . one second. . . ."

You gasp involuntarily, then gape in awed silence. The world has been suddenly enveloped in a painful brilliance. Presently, your face begins to burn a little from the heat wave.

Transfixed, you watch the angry ball of flame churn in the sky for maybe seven seconds, then disappear in a boiling purple cloud that seems to foam and spill out over its own top, growing before your astonished eyes, and you can't look away.

You vaguely feel the ground moving underfoot but are wholly unprepared for the shattering blast which shouts from the mountain walls, trumpeting a destructive might equivalent to that of fifteen thousand tons of high explosive.

Thirty seconds later, you exhale. Somebody forces an outlet for his tension with a wisecrack. "At last, I've seen the light," he announces. Someone else finds his voice. "Yeah, wouldn't that just kill you?"

And you laugh a little nervously. But you can't forget it. You won't ever forget it.

Tuesday's test, with its elaborate preparations and attendant military maneuvers, was conducted primarily for the purpose of information. Much that was learned will have to await detailed inspection and evaluation by experts.

But a few practical facts, aside from those of a military character, have emerged:

1. Our cities are highly vulnerable. Conventional American architecture affords little protection. Unprepared and unsuspecting, the typical American city could be paralyzed in a fraction of a second.
2. Intelligent precautions can definitely save lives. Basement shelters and underground revetments are effective, and rescue crews, if properly trained . . . but only if properly trained . . . could be highly useful in retrieving human life from the radioactive fingers of death.
3. Present civil defense preparations are "not nearly good enough." This from FCDA Administrator Val Peterson.

It is against civilian targets that the potential toll in life and property is most appalling. House No. 1, almost three-fourths of a mile from target center, was reduced to a scrap heap. Assuming the average modern residential lot to be sixty by one hundred and fifty feet, located on a forty-foot street with a sixteen-foot alley at the back, an explosion of the Yucca Flat caliber would utterly demolish some thirty-seven hundred homes within the inner circle of total destruction.

Using the damage appraisal of Dr. Robert L. Corsbie, architectural expert for the Federal Civil Defense Administration, and the first man to inspect what remained of House No. 2, located a mile and a half away, an additional minimum of thirteen thousand homes would suffer semi-destruction.

Civil defense authorities estimate that a bomb of the type dropped on Hiroshima would take more than one hundred thousand lives if released over a large American city.

This is why, in spite of the high state of emotional excitement

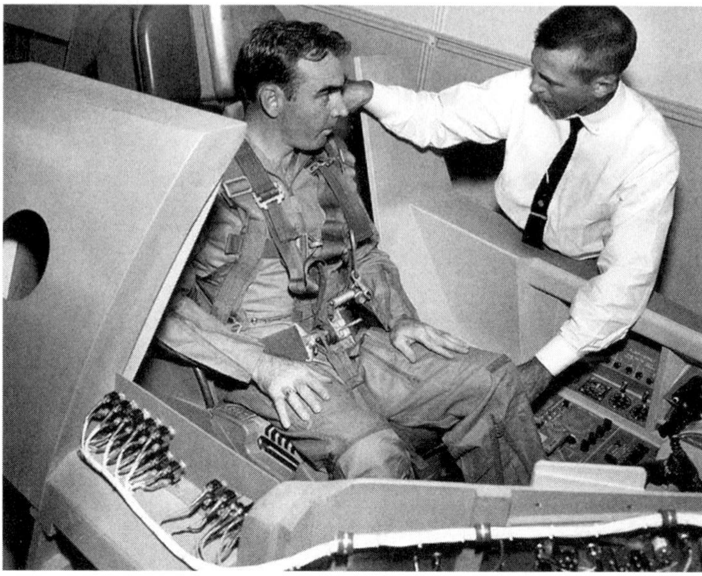

In uniform and aboard a flight simulator at Convair/ General Dynamics during the Cold War
SPEAKER JIM WRIGHT COLLECTION, SPECIAL COLLECTIONS, MARY COUTS BURNETT LIBRARY, TCU.

engendered by the weeks of feverish preparation and the prospect of viewing a historic spectacle, a note of grimness kept creeping into the briefings at Las Vegas.

Dr. Alvin C. Graves was introduced as "the leading nuclear test authority in the United States" by the panel chairman, who added significantly, "and, I sincerely hope, in the world."

What are we doing about it? At Lake Success, men like Dulles and Lodge try diligently to talk sense to the Russians. And at places like Fort Worth, men like Bob Dysart strive with about the same results to impress Joe Doaks with the information vital to his self-preservation.

Civil defense leaders from many cities gathered in Las Vegas, and the story was everywhere the same. Volunteer recruitments for all the programs—first aid, auxiliary fire and police personnel, rescue team training—are lagging far behind the quotas.

Maybe they won't drop the bomb on us after all. Maybe. But is it worth taking that chance?

Our history reminds us that the American public is a sleeping giant, slow to awaken but invincible when once aroused. That's fine . . . so long as we don't wake up with a hole in our head.

*Fort Worth Star-Telegram,* March 22, 1953

Speaker Wright and his wife, Betty, standing with former Soviet Union President Mikhail Gorbachev at the Kremlin, 1987.
SPEAKER JIM WRIGHT COLLECTION, SPECIAL COLLECTIONS, MARY COUTS BURNETT LIBRARY, TCU..

Laying a wreath at the Soviet Tomb of the Unknown Soldier.
SPEAKER JIM WRIGHT COLLECTION, SPECIAL COLLECTIONS, MARY COUTS BURNETT LIBRARY, TCU.

## Let's Make a New Beginning: 1958

"*THERE WENT OUT A DECREE from Caesar Augustus that all the world should be taxed . . .* "

As I look through the window today upon Washington . . . like Rome, a city from which decrees go out . . . I can see the severely beautiful Washington Monument. In the eye of imagination, it looks like the finger of a wise man pointing to a new star in the heavens. On the ellipse behind the White House towers the national Christmas tree, tall as a six-story building.

Aside from such landmarks, Washington is just about like any other big city at Christmastime, neither better nor worse. There is the same commercialism, the same emphasis on material things, the same congested traffic and frantic haste. And, as in every other city, the only time you can really see the light that shone over the shepherds on their hilltop in Judea is when you look closely into the eyes of a little child.

*"And she brought forth her firstborn son and wrapped him in swaddling clothes and laid him in a manger, because there was no room for them in the inn."*

Just as it was in Bethlehem, so it is in Washington in 1958. No room under the tree for another present. No room in the post office for another package. No room on our engagement pads for an additional plan. No room in the department store aisles for another shopper. And in too many hearts . . . no room for him and his message of a better way.

At the conference tables in Geneva and elsewhere men discuss more and more and settle less and less because there is no room in their minds for a new idea of peace on earth . . . still new and still largely untried after two thousand years. Our thoughts are on guided missiles with nuclear warheads, and not on the star.

*"And, lo, the angel of the Lord came upon them, and the glory of the Lord shown round about them: and they were sore afraid."*

Afraid? Well, yes, the average person in today's world is afraid.

And maybe that's one reason we stay so busy, so we won't have time to think about it.

*"And the angel said unto them, Fear not: for, behold, I bring you good tidings of great joy, which shall be to all people. . . ."*

To all people? Even to those we don't like and don't trust? Even to those who plot and plan against us? Good tidings to Democrats and Republicans alike? To the rude motorist who squeezed you out of your lane in the Christmas traffic today? Good tidings of great joy . . . even to the Russians? Well, that's what the angel said.

*". . . and on earth, peace, good will toward men."*

Peace, the word the angels sang, must have seemed as impossible a dream in those days as it does now. There was then, as now, the temporary absence of major armed conflict, the uneasy and repressed order of a Pax Romana. But real peace must be something more than just a nervous stalemate enforced by fear. It has something to do with goodwill.

Is there any real basis for goodwill? Did the angels speak the truth? Did he who lay in the sweet straw of the manger amid the barnyard noises bring into the world a flowering promise that lives and grows in the hearts of men amid even the bitter passions of this hour?

We say he did. We, who celebrate his birth, state that he did. And how strongly do we feel it?

Suppose that each of us could write a sincere and searching letter to someone . . . average as ourselves . . . in Russia, a letter to those who are the victims of a cruel history and an ugly system which has turned out the lights of Christmas. Who knows what good we might accomplish could we but establish intimate communications with these people? I'd like to write such a Christmas letter to all the plain, afraid, average men who live in Russia. And here is what I'd say:

Dear Ivan,

I'VE BEEN THINKING ABOUT YOU. I've been wondering how you were. Guess it must be mighty cold over there. It's been downright chilly here, in fact. Hope you've got a nice, warm place for the wife and kids.

We're feeling pretty warm inside right now. It's Christmastime. You see, Ivan, a lot of us have the belief that God himself came to earth in the person of a man and taught that all of us should love each other. That may sound a little silly to you, maybe a bit overly sentimental. Anyway, that's what we celebrate at Christmas.

Let me be painfully frank about this thing, Ivan, and admit that I haven't been feeling very kindly toward you lately. Guess you haven't felt exactly good about me, either. Truthfully, I suppose we've both been a little bit afraid. For one thing, we believe in entirely different economic systems. Now, I'm convinced that our system of capitalism or free enterprise is the best. But if you don't like it, Ivan, I certainly don't want to force it on you. That comes under the heading of your own business.

Why can't we just look at this thing straight and agree that we have a healthy competition going on between us to prove which system can do a better job for its people . . . and that neither one of us is going to change just to suit the other?

If we could agree on that, then maybe we could agree to a moratorium on trying to force the rest of the world to copy either one of us. Oh, I don't mean we wouldn't keep on telling people how great we think our system is, nor expect you to stop saying how well you like yours if you really do. But there just isn't any sense in trying to cram it down their throats. With armies, I mean. Starting wars and getting a lot of people killed. Why can't we just let them look at both of us, and listen to both of us, and then make up their own minds?

You know, this military business can get out of hand. That's why we're both a little nervous, isn't it? And here's the reason, the big thing we have in common. . . . I've got kids, Ivan. And so have you. My kids mean more to me than anything else in all the world. Surely you feel the same way about yours. Now there just isn't an ounce of sense in our horsing around and acting like plain fools and arranging things so that our kids will have to be killing each other someday.

My kids are thinking about Christmas, Ivan. Little starry-eyed things, they're not mad at you or at anybody.

You know what, Ivan? We folks over here are spending right at $45 billion this year on armaments. That's because we're scared of what you'd do if we didn't. I don't know quite what your folks are spending on this sort of thing, and I don't expect you do, either, but I figure it's just about the same as we're spending.

Tell you what I'd do, Ivan. I'd make a binding contract with you. We'll cut down ours if you'll cut down yours. Now, of course, it would all have to be open and aboveboard, right on the top of the table, or no-go. But I'm willing, if you are. We could start out easy.

Let's do it this way. We'll cut 10 percent from our military expenditures this year if you'll do the same thing. Right out on the top of the table, now. We'll take $4.5 billion out of our military spending this year if you'll do the same thing, match it dollar for dollar. We'll both put our money into the same fund. That'll make $9 billion for the first year.

If the deal holds, we'll double it next year. We'll both cut our current military budgets by 20 percent, and each of us will put up $9 billion next year. That'll make a total of $27 billion in the fund.

Want to help mankind, Ivan? Well, here's your chance. Here's your chance to help mankind and get rid of your fears at the same time. You like five-year plans, so I'll make you a five-year plan. Let's keep this up at the second year's rate for three additional years, and we'll have put a total of $81 billion into this fund between us at the end of five years. Neither one of us will have missed it, because it will have come out of what we'd otherwise have been putting into weapons which would just have made both of us more nervous.

We could make an $81 billion gift to humanity, Ivan.

Do you know how much $81 billion is? Well, it would build and equip a brand new $2 million hospital for every city of ten thousand or more in the world. Our medical experts say that with $4.5 billion they could absolutely eradicate malaria, typhoid, smallpox, yellow fever, and leprosy from the face of the earth. It would build one hundred and twenty thousand high schools or two hundred and fifty thousand elementary schools. It would build and stock two hundred and fifty thousand first-class libraries and it would provide twenty million four-year college scholarships. It would build twenty million modern homes to replace the world's infested slums. It would build almost a million miles of modern roads . . . enough to circle the earth several times. Take any combination of these benefits you like—it still adds up to a whole lot more sense than spending this money on the implements that kill and destroy rather than those that build and ennoble and improve.

Then, after five years we could slack off. We could reduce our contributions to the Christmas fund and give some tax relief to the folks who have been carrying the burden for so many years . . . yours as well as ours. Think of it, Ivan. Imagine what the effect would be in Russia if just 20 percent of all the money now being spent on military hardware were being plowed back into the economy and spent on the merchandise of peace! Think what it would mean in terms of automobiles and homes and household appliances!

It's a wonderful dream, isn't it, Ivan? It could be a reality if we would only play fair and square with each other and do away with needless secrecy. Of course, you'd have to know that we weren't cheating. You'd be entitled to know it, just as we'd be entitled to proof of your compliance. We could use the United Nations organization to inspect and police our operation to ensure good faith on both our parts. We'd have to open up our borders and let one another come and look . . . but what would there be to fear if we both were playing straight?

You know, Ivan, we could give the world the greatest Christmas present since the first Christmas, 1,959 years ago. We could really bring tidings of great joy and, for the first time in two millennia, the greatly troubled people of this old world of ours could obey the angels' injunction: "Fear not!"

That would be the best part, that everybody could gradually stop being afraid. If we ever got together on this we could make all the old hatreds and fears and misgivings vanish like hot breath on a looking glass.

Think it over, Ivan. We've both been trying the other way long enough. Think it over carefully. And, meanwhile, have yourself a merry Christmas.

Sincerely,
Jim

WHIMSY? PERHAPS. Perhaps there is no way effectively to get such a message through to Ivan, insulated as he is by curtains of iron. Maybe such a plan, offered by our president, could form the basis for a major breakthrough in the diplomatic stalemate. If such a sincere and honest message could be broadcasted to Ivan through the Voice of America, it might do some good. At worst, it could certainly do no harm.

*Jim Wright Newsletter,* December 1958

## Let's Make a New Beginning: 1987

Background notes relating to Speaker Wright's 1987 televised speech to the Soviets

EDITOR'S NOTE: *During the Easter break in 1987, newly elected Speaker Jim Wright, in response to a publicly announced invitation from Soviet Secretary General Mikhail Gorbachev, led an official bipartisan congressional delegation to the Soviet Union. The delegation was co-chaired by then-Chairman of the House Republican Caucus, Dick Cheney.*

*The purpose of the delegation's journey was to meet for an unprecedented series of informal talks with the Russian premier and the USSR's top legislative and military officials. Gorbachev and US President Ronald Reagan had just begun a series of exploratory talks aimed at seeking acceptable ways to relieve tensions between the two superpowers and move possibly toward the then-unspoken goal of eventually ending the thirty-nine-year-old Cold War. Officials in the US State Department had quietly encouraged Speaker Wright in his acceptance of the Soviet invitation.*

*Sensing the international pregnancy of the moment and its unrivaled opportunity to take a bold step in the direction of peace, Wright on the first morning of the talks handed Gorbachev a copy of his 1958 "Letter to Ivan." Later that day, the Speaker, now back in his hotel room, received a surprise telephone call from the Russian leader. Gorbachev explained that he'd carefully read a Russian language translation of Wright's twenty-eight-year-old letter and was moved by it.*

*To Wright's surprise, the Soviet Premier invited the American congressional leader to appear on a nationwide Soviet television broadcast and to say anything Wright would like to say to the Russian people. The Speaker called US State*

*Department officials and was enthusiastically encouraged to do so. This is believed to have been the very first time any American lawmaker had ever been granted such an invitation by the USSR's top authority.*

*Wright's carefully prepared and personally delivered speech was instantaneously being translated into Russian as he spoke it, including his closing invitation to hearers to write him a personal note to his Washington office. To his happy surprise, the letters flooded in from people, young and old, in diverse parts of the Soviet Union. A surprising number were partially or wholly in varying graduations of English, and an astounding majority were friendly in tone. These letters are preserved and available for inspection in the Wright Archives at Texas Christian University.*

My fellow citizens:

You may think it strange that I address you as "fellow citizens." I am a citizen of the USA, after all. And you are citizens of the USSR.

But there is a sense in which we are fellow citizens. We are citizens of the world. And the world is becoming a much smaller place. Science and technology have shrunk the planet Earth. It took Christopher Columbus fifty-six days to cross the Atlantic Ocean. I covered the same distance last week in six hours.

To express this fact in the most dangerous way, my hometown in Texas is only forty minutes away by Soviet intercontinental missiles from Vladivostok. And so, in that sense, you and I do live in the same neighborhood.

We can make it a less dangerous neighborhood. If combustible explosives were stored near our houses, yours and mine, or if ravening wolves were let loose in our children's playground, or if deadly poisons were left lying around within reach of our infants—you and I would want to do something about it, wouldn't we?

We'd get together and insist, for the benefit of our families, that those hazards be removed and safety precautions be taken.

Well that, in a way, is what your government and our government are trying to do in our nuclear arms reduction talks, which have been underway in Moscow this past week.

And that is what I am doing in Moscow. My name is Jim Wright. I am the Speaker of the US House of Representatives. I am here, along with twenty lawmakers of my country, at the invitation of your Secretary General Mikhail Gorbachev. We have met with Mr. Gorbachev and other members of your government.

These Soviet leaders have answered our questions with candor and honesty, as we have tried to answer theirs. We have been impressed by the sincerity of Mr. Gorbachev, by his desire to turn over a new leaf in the book of our relationship, and by his commitments to a better world for all of us and for our children—Soviet children and American children—innocent victims of the hostility and fear which we, their parents, unconsciously pass on to them.

Surely it is time for a new beginning in international relationships. Many centuries ago, an ancient Greek named Aristophanes walked among the ruins of the once-beautiful Greek temples destroyed in the Peloponnesian Wars. Out of the anguish of his soul for the senseless loss of his fellow citizens and of the treasures of his homeland, Aristophanes uttered this prayer:

*From the murmur and subtlety of suspicion*
*With which we vex one another,*
*Give us rest;*
*Make a new beginning*
*And mingle again the kindred of the nations*
*In the alchemy of love;*
*And with some finer essence of forbearance*
*Temper our minds.*

We have a great deal in common, citizens of the Soviet Union and of America. Both of our countries were born in revolution. Both continue to strive—in different ways—to achieve a better life for our people. Our two great countries have never been at war against each other. We strove together to overcome the wicked Nazi tyranny in the Great Patriotic War—in which I was then a young lieutenant flying combat missions in a Liberator bomber.

On Wednesday morning my colleagues and I visited the burial places of the heroes of your country, and I laid a wreath in the early mist of an April morning at the Tomb of the Unknown Soviet Soldier. It came to mind that twenty million of Russia's finest young people—in the bloom of their youth, with futures before them—gave up their lives that this country of yours might live. Just so, classmates and beloved friends of mine perished in that war. I looked upon the faces of the handsome young Russian guards who keep watch at that sacred place, and I thought what a tragic loss if men and women of my generation should fail the generation of these younger people, and their hopes for peace and a better life.

You see, I am the presiding officer of our US House of Representatives. We are the ones who must levy the taxes and appropriate the money for everything our government does. We have just last week concluded our annual budget process for the American nation, and I am convinced that there is something tragically wrong in both of our countries.

This year the United States will spend almost $300 billion—that's equal to about two hundred billion rubles—on machines of destruction and unproductive implements of military power. Your country will spend a similar amount on the same things. What waste that is for both of us—when human wants go unmet and legitimate needs unfulfilled in both our countries.

There are young people in our country who will not get to go to college because we have spent so much on weapons and have not left enough for student loans and grants.

In both of our countries, there are hospitals that will not be built—medical research that will not be undertaken—lives that will not be saved—because we each must spend so much on military power. And much of that bill—in our country at least—we are sending to our children and our grandchildren.

Every day this year, forty thousand people die somewhere in the world of hunger and malnutrition. And every day the nations of the world will spend $2.5 billion—much more than enough to feed and clothe them—on weapons and wasteful means of destruction.

Just think: the cost of one submarine would build a hundred and twenty-five thousand modern flats for a hundred and twenty-five thousand families—a city the size of Tula.

Our former American President Dwight D. Eisenhower, who was commander in chief of Allied Western forces in World War II, looked back upon the waste of war and said:

> *Every gun that is made, every warship launched, every rocket fired signifies, in the final sense, a theft from those who hunger and are not fed, those who are cold and not clothed. This world in arms is not spending money alone; it is spending the sweat of its laborers, the genius of its scientists, the hopes of its children.*

And so my colleagues and I have journeyed to Moscow in this season which some of us regard as holy, since it commemorates the life of one who taught that the noblest work of man is to feed the hungry and clothe the naked and care for the sick and the unfortunate.

We have come to seek, along with the leaders of your great country, a new beginning. We have different economic systems, but that should not prevent us working together.

From the beginning of time, people have found it easy to work together when they have a common purpose or a common enemy.

Today, the nations of the world hold sixty thousand nuclear warheads with a total destructive capacity one million times greater than the bomb that destroyed Hiroshima. Between us, our two nations, we hold enough destructive power to end civilization itself.

In these circumstances, it seems to me that we do have a common enemy—and the enemy is war itself. We have a common purpose, and the common purpose is peace.

As a token of our friendship, I'd like to send you a little personal gift. It has no great material value, but I would like to send you a little remembrance as a sentimental expression of our will to work together.

Here is my address—Jim Wright, The Capitol, Washington, DC, USA.

If you will write me a little note and tell me that you saw this program, I would like to send you one of these little pins that I am wearing on my lapel. It contains small replicas of flags of our two nations flying side by side.

If you will write a note to me at this address, I'll be glad to send you this little emblem with my personal best wishes.

I know that you of my generation love your children just as I love mine. You of both older and younger generations love your country just as I love mine.

And so I offer this wish for your children and for my children—and for their children: may they live in peace.

Remarks delivered on Soviet television, April 18, 1987

## Latin America: Promises to Keep

TO BE CREDIBLE, US foreign policy must be honest, principled, and consistent. Toward Nicaragua, and by extension toward much of Latin America, we have been none of these.

Once our staunchest ally in Central America, Nicaragua today is the most troublesome burr under our saddle. This adverse development shows the dangers of shortsighted policies that, lacking clear and constant purpose, forever scramble to catch up with events. We need a steadier course, based on firm principles, if we hope to improve the long-term prospects for harmony and progress in the hemisphere.

A quick glance at the history of our relations with Nicaragua is instructive.

For more than a century Nicaragua has felt the brunt of US interventionism. In 1855 a Tennessee adventurer named William Walker arrived in Nicaragua with a private army to make himself emperor. Between 1912 and 1933, a contingent of US Marines was stationed in Nicaragua almost continuously. Afterward, the first Anastasio Somoza, using the National Guard as his power base, began serving as our surrogate. He and his two sons ruled the land for forty-three years, until the Sandinista revolution in 1979.

Undeviatingly loyal to the United States, the Somozas enriched themselves in office and are widely believed in Nicaragua to have manipulated US disaster-relief funds by awarding contracts to relatives and political cronies. These abuses began to alienate the business sector, which eventually lent substantial support to the Sandinista forces.

In recent years our Nicaragua policy has veered from bemused patronage to benign neglect to outright hostility. President Richard M. Nixon's ambassador, Turner Shelton, regarded Somoza as "our best friend in Latin America." President Jimmy Carter refused to return Somoza's calls. At first our government welcomed the Sandinista victory. Last month President Reagan came close to publicly advocating violent overthrow of the Sandinista regime.

Nicaraguans know also the history of our sometimes devious involvements elsewhere in Latin America. In 1954, for instance, the Central Intelligence Agency participated in overthrowing Jacobo Arbenz in Guatemala. In 1971, in Chile, the CIA conspired to destabilize the elected government of Salvador Allende, a fact that was first officially denied by Washington and not acknowledged until after Gerald R. Ford became president.

Forbidden last year by Congress from aiding any military effort by "any group . . . for the purpose of overthrowing the government of Nicaragua," the CIA now disingenuously explains that the violent overthrow of the Sandinistas is not *our* purpose, even though it is the publicly avowed purpose of troops that we arm and train to enter Nicaragua—including some former Somoza National Guardsmen. Actions such as these make it easier for the Marxists to stir up nationalistic fervor to repulse a coming "Yanqui invasion."

Little wonder, given this history, that many Nicaraguans and other Latin Americans regard US policy pronouncements with skepticism, if not outright distrust.

The first step toward establishing hemispheric confidence in US policy is quite simply to tell the truth. Be straightforward. Renounce deception. Say what we mean clearly, and practice it. Be truthful with ourselves and with the world, including our ideological foes. Even if they dislike and disagree with us, it's better for all concerned if they know that they can trust what we say.

This is why I believe that we should firmly renounce covert involvement in schemes to overthrow governments by force. This includes Nicaragua's government, abhorrent to us though it be.

The second step is to pick a few clear policy objectives and stand by them. It isn't good enough simply to be against communism. We also must be *for* something.

Off and on we've given hope to Latin America by standing for three good things: an electoral process open to all, social and economic progress to improve the lot of the humblest *campesino* or *trabajadero*, protection of each country from military invasion or the infiltration of arms. But we have not been constant in our support of these things.

When we've stood firmly for free elections we've gained respect. President John F. Kennedy withdrew diplomatic recognition when a military junta took over Peru, then restored it when elections ratified a new government. President Lyndon B. Johnson, cooperating with the Organization of American States, threw the whole weight of our policy toward securing an electoral system in the Dominican Republic. Today we are supporting the same precept in El Salvador.

When we've sponsored programs like the Alliance for Progress, Food for Peace, and the Peace Corps, we've brought a modicum of hope and help to hungry barrios and remote villages throughout Latin America.

When we've upheld guarantees under the OAS Charter and the 1948 Rio Treaty against armed intervention across borders, we've won credibility. Surely it is in our own interest, as well as in the interest of hemispheric stability, to establish the doctrine that neither marauding expansion nor externally directed revolutions will succeed. Helping free countries to defend themselves is part of this commitment. Abiding by the doctrine ourselves is the other side of the same coin.

There are specific things that we can do, some right now, to give life and meaning to these basic principles.

Congress should pass the Caribbean Basin Initiative and thereby demonstrate that we support our president when he promises constructive measures for Central America.

Congress should approve an $80 million package now being considered to help any government in the region sanitize its frontiers from the flow of armaments.

We should encourage the efforts of Mexico, Venezuela, Panama, and Costa Rica to prevail on Nicaragua to adopt non-aggression agreements with its neighbors.

We should continue to help the embryonic democracy that is now emerging in El Salvador, leaving no doubt that we support government by ballot, not by bullet. The inspiring example of voter participation last year demonstrates that Salvadorans deeply desire and deserve their chance at free institutions. Those institutions cannot thrive while guerrilla bands terrorize the countryside and sabotage civil works.

We must accept the fact that not every society in the hemisphere can be a carbon copy of our own. We cannot insist on instant perfection. While supporting the basic forms of political liberty, let us recall that even we abolished habeas corpus during our Civil War and severely violated the liberties of Japanese-Americans during World War II.

We must not abandon dialogue with Nicaragua or write it off as irretrievably lost to Marxist tyranny. As much as any other nation, Nicaragua needs teachers, paramedics, and improved nutrition. When we failed to help with a universal health and literacy effort in 1980, Cuban "volunteers" filled the gap. Marxists have since muscled and manipulated their way to power, but most Nicaraguans are not Marxists. About 30 percent of the nation's economy depends on trade with our country. Recognizing these facts, we should be ready with creative, nonviolent initiatives to help nudge Nicaragua to recapture the goals of a progressive, pluralistic society that was originally promised, then betrayed, by the Sandinistas.

In the final analysis, wisdom requires that we be both consistent and persistent. We'll be judged in the long pull by our deeds, not our words. Even countries that do not doubt our motives question our staying power. While our generosity is well known, so is our impatience. Too often we have grown weary of, then indifferent to, programs such as the Alliance for Progress, which sought to address deep social and economic problems. By raising hopes and then aban-

Wright and Ambassador Sayre visit with villagers
at El Real, Columbia, 1971.
SPEAKER JIM WRIGHT COLLECTION, SPECIAL COLLECTIONS,
MARY COUTS BURNETT LIBRARY, TCU.

doning them, we have reaped a whirlwind of disillusionment, despair and upheaval.

There are no quick fixes, no short answers to longstanding dilemmas. There is no substitute for persevering despite setbacks. In Latin America we need to take the long view, remembering that we have promises to keep and miles to go before we sleep.

*Los Angeles Times,* June 1, 1983

## Collision Course

*Brothers, each one of you is one of us. We are the same people.*
*The campesinos you kill are your own brothers and sisters.*
—Archbishop Oscar Romero, shortly before his martyrdom in March 1980

"DAMN IT, SERGIO," I exploded in exasperation, "I'm telling you for the fifth time that the United States is *not* going to invade your country! We're *not* trying to overthrow your government!"

"Your nation's weapons are killing our people," Sergio Ramírez answered coolly on behalf of the Nicaraguan government. "Your mines are blowing up our bridges. Your bombs destroy water tanks and leave our villages without water—"

"Yes," interrupted Nicaraguan cabinet member Jaime Wheelock, "and the former Somoza guardsmen who now carry your guns are boasting that they'll be in Managua in six months to put their old crowd back in power! The United States is paying them. Your country is paying in dollars and the Nicaraguan people are paying in blood."

A huge portrait of Augusto César Sandino dominated the sparsely furnished room. So austere were the long wooden table and folding chairs in this chamber that my eyes were drawn back involuntarily to the oversized painting with its idealized version of the young revolutionary. There he stood, a study in innocence, bandolier slung over his right shoulder and on his head a tall Western hat. It was a hat of the William S. Hart or Tom Mix era, not a short-crowned Roy Rogers hat. On the youthful face was the ingenuous appeal of a young James Dean.

I sighed. These people have actually begun to believe their own rhetoric, I thought. It was April 12, 1982. Managua had undergone a striking metamorphosis in the months since my last visit. Then, in 1980, hope had reigned. Leaders in the business community were relieved to be rid of Somoza. Violeta Chamorro and Alfonso Robelo, who had just resigned from the original Sandinista junta, were sure that a new friendship with the United States could take root and flourish, based on equality rather than subservience. Enrique Dreyfus, president of COSEP (the Superior Council of Private Enterprise), a sort of national chamber of commerce, was speaking of a mixed economy and pluralistic society. Everywhere I'd looked in 1980, official slogans glorified health and learning. Billboards proclaimed: *Alfabetización es la Libertad!* (Literacy is liberty!)

Now, in 1982, those same billboards glowered with an artist's portrayal of huge US tanks trampling Nicaraguan terrain as shirtless, brown-skinned Nicaraguans fought them off with rifles. The printing trumpeted: *Triunfaramos Sobre los Yanquis, Imperialistas!* (We shall triumph over the Yankee imperialists!)

Was this a cynical manipulation of the public, a blatant appeal to patriotism as the historic excuse for surrendering liberties to police-state controls? The government, pointing to the fear of a US invasion, had just enacted the Emergency Law suspending thirteen articles of the constitution and putting the country on a wartime footing. Several Nicaraguans, including Enrique Dreyfus, had been jailed. Or could these benighted leaders be so hypnotized by their own slogans that they actually believed the United States was trying to overthrow their government by force and substitute one of our choosing?

Probably some of each, I decided. No doubt most of the country's leaders thought us capable of plotting the physical overthrow of their government. History, after all, gave precedent for paranoia. US forces *had* occupied their country for more than two decades early in the century. Sophisticated Nicaraguans thought of the forty-three-year Somoza dynasty that followed as a sort of US proxy. (Hadn't Franklin Roosevelt supposedly once referred to the first Somoza as "*our* son of a bitch"?) Within the past few weeks several US daily newspapers and two weekly magazines had published leaks connecting the CIA with armed attacks in northern Nicaragua.

Yes, I realized, Nicaraguans could actually believe we were plotting their government's overthrow. But of course we were not. We couldn't be. I had the personal assurance of Bill Casey. Like most of my colleagues on the congressional intelligence committees, I had taken CIA Director Casey's testimony at face value. He had told us solemnly of "incontrovertible evidence" linking Nicaragua's Sandinista government to "Marxist" guerrilla leaders intent on overthrowing the elected government in El Salvador. Most of the weapons used by these guerrillas, Casey informed us, were coming into that country surreptitiously from Nicaragua. Terrorist tactics by leftist forces were actually being directed by radio from a clandestine broadcasting station in downtown Managua, Casey claimed.

In the secret hearing of the House committee, several of us were at pains to get one clear stipulation: the paramilitary activities being contemplated would be designed strictly to interdict and dry up the arms flow; this was *not* an effort to start a new war. We were not organizing an invasion of Nicaragua.

"Please understand that this committee is not authorizing a war against Nicaragua's government," Chairman Edward Boland of Massachusetts admonished. Ranking Republican Bill Whitehurst of Virginia agreed.

"One thing we cannot afford," I remember telling the chief of intelligence, "is another Bay of Pigs!"

Our pink-cheeked, white-haired CIA director had a minor speech impediment that made it difficult for him to pronounce the *r* sound. Whenever Casey spoke the subject country's name it came across as *Nicawagua.* But there was no misunderstanding what he said. We were out to shut off weapons at El Salvador's border. That was all we were trying to do. I believed him.

Most of those who came with me to Central America in April 1982 still believed that story. Representative Mike Barnes of Maryland, chairman of the Western Hemisphere Subcommittee, and big George Miller of California may have been growing skeptical. But Foreign Affairs Committee Chairman Clement Zablocki of

Wisconsin and Clay Shaw, a new Republican from Florida, entertained no doubts whatsoever.

I must explain it clearly to these intense young Nicaraguans, I thought, before conditions deteriorate further. They must be made to see that all they have to do is shut off the flow of weapons into El Salvador.

"Look, gentlemen," I said, "if you're honestly worried about an invasion of your country, there is one clear way you can avoid it. Respect the territorial boundaries of El Salvador, and we'll respect yours. Just leave your neighbors alone and we'll leave you alone. You have my word for that."

What a terrible presumption! I realized this later, reflecting upon my naïve assurance. At the time I thought I was speaking the gospel. I believed that what I said had the sure backing of official US policy.

Back at the Intercontinental Hotel, Congressman Bill Alexander and I went for a swim. I was sunning when a man named Antonio asked me if I would like a drink from the bar. I remembered this man from my trip in 1980, identifying him vaguely in my mind as a hotel employee with whom I'd once engaged in conversation about the future of his country. Antonio recalled our earlier talk.

"It is unfortunate," he said, "that things have changed."

"Tell me, Antonio," I said, "do the Nicaraguan people actually believe that my country is making war against them?"

He hesitated, clearly wondering if he should speak with candor. Then he said, "My family is from the north country, up near the Coco River. A large force invaded at Christmastime. They attacked about twenty villages. They killed some people and wounded many others. They left a lot of land mines, and these have hurt many more people. My cousin lost her foot and part of her leg when one of the mines exploded as she walked along a path."

He paused. "We brought my cousin here to Managua for medical treatment. She is at my house, not far from this place. Would you like to talk with her?"

Antonio's ancient pickup truck rumbled over pockmarked

streets to the city's edge, then onto an unpaved road, coming to rest in front of a modest house of concrete blocks and a corrugated tin roof. The floor was earthen but swept clean. Cotton draperies adorned the windows. A woman whom Antonio introduced as his aunt welcomed me graciously and offered me refreshment.

Then I saw the little girl. She stood with a thin wooden crutch under her left arm. The dark, luminous eyes seemed large in her small face. Her little cotton dress was clean and neat. Her left foot was missing. She smiled at me. Suddenly my eyes filled with tears, and I couldn't speak.

I had supposed Antonio's cousin to be an adult. This girl couldn't have been more than nine, ten at the most. I didn't have the heart to interrogate her.

This, please God, was not what we had authorized—not what Bill Casey had spoken of to our Intelligence Committee. How could this little girl be involved in any flow of arms across the Salvadoran border?

It came to me with a stab of pain that US taxpayers' money, with my silent acquiescence, had paid for the planting of the land mine that had crippled this child as well as for the machine guns and bullets that had killed other Nicaraguan villagers. And most of my colleagues in Congress knew nothing about it. This was a covert operation, set in motion for the sole supposed purpose of interdicting arms.

At least in El Salvador, Congress knew what we were up to. We had publicly debated and approved military and other aid to its elected government. As majority leader, I had rallied bipartisan support for President Reagan's request. We wanted to give elective processes a chance in that small, violent country where for four hundred years no freely chosen government had been allowed to complete its term.

As Antonio and I returned over dusty roads to the hotel, my mind went back to El Salvador. Two days earlier, during dinner at the official residence of US Ambassador Deane Hinton, I had been deliberately seated beside Roberto D'Aubuisson, leader of the right-wing ARENA (National Republican Alliance) party that had just legally maneuvered its way into majority control of the Salvadoran Constituent Assembly. A retired army major with close ties to the military, D'Aubuisson was a celebrated firebrand, hated and feared by political opponents. Many suspected him of organizing and leading the secret death squads that had assassinated the late Archbishop Oscar Romero and were terrorizing the countryside. It was my mission that night, urged upon me by Ambassador Hinton, to convince D'Aubuisson that the US Congress would terminate all aid to El Salvador if under his leadership it embarked on a reign of terror. I had pressed that message as hard as I could, and I believed it to be true.

"Look, Major," I said, "you and I ought to be able to understand one another. Like you, I'm a former military officer. Like you, I'm leader of the majority in our Congress. I know what my colleagues will accept and what they won't. Basically, they serve the American people. It's only fair to tell you that a lot of people in my country are suspicious of your intentions. Our Congress will not support any government which tolerates death squads that prey on the political opposition."

D'Aubuisson, thin and ascetic, was eating little. A tense bundle of energy, he sat at my right staring into my eyes and drumming his fingers nervously on the table. He understood the message.

"We'd surely like to see democracy work in El Salvador," I assured him. "We've been working at it in my country for about two hundred years, and we've discovered that it just can't work without some tolerance for opposing views." I could not be sure that he comprehended that.

Back at the hotel, I tried to sort out my thoughts. One thing seemed clear: my government and that of Nicaragua were on a collision course that could result in a lot of bloodshed and serve the best interests of neither.

I walked out on a balcony and looked across the pockmarked

center of Managua. On a gentle rise to my right stood the monument to Franklin D. Roosevelt that had thrilled me when I first came upon it twenty-five years earlier. Above that, on a bluff overlooking downtown, rose the splendid presidential palace of the Somozas, now spurned by the Sandinista government. To the left, across a broad expanse of now-vacant land, lay the grand cathedral, the only building still functioning in the sprawling old business district, scarred by so many natural and man-made disasters.

No wonder they're paranoid, I thought. Between volcanic eruptions, earthquakes, harsh dictatorships, civil wars, and foreign military intrusions, this hard-luck country had known precious little tranquility. And none seemed likely in the offing.

Little did I suspect that for most of the next seven years I would be in the thick of efforts to resolve the twin dilemmas of Nicaragua and El Salvador. Their violence would claim the lives of a hundred thousand people, split the US Congress into warring camps, and drive the White House to the desperate illegality of the Iran-Contra scandal.

I could know none of this at the time, of course. Nor could I have supposed that I would be drawn so forcefully into the whirling vortex of the controversy, or that my efforts to find a path to peace and democracy in the region would bring me into direct conflict with the president of the United States and subject me to scalding criticism that would contribute indirectly to the end of my legislative career.

As I look back on those events today, I really don't think I could have avoided getting involved in the ways I have just described, except perhaps by being a different person. So much of what we are, what we believe, and what we do is shaped at an early age, without our realizing it. I guess I was fated to get involved.

"Worth it All: My War for Peace,"
from *Collision Course* (Brassey's, Inc., 1993)

## Give Peace a Chance: On Bipartisanship and the Central American Peace Initiative

THERE WAS A TIME when American foreign policy was made and carried out in a bipartisan manner. When I first came to Congress, Mr. Rayburn was Speaker of the House and Mr. Eisenhower was president. Our executive and legislative branches of government worked together in an atmosphere of mutual supportiveness in all questions involving foreign policy. The president confided in Speaker Rayburn—before policies were crystallized. Mr. Rayburn gave advice in private, and there was mutual support in public.

During World War II, President Roosevelt appointed a Republican his secretary of war. He sent an important message to Winston Churchill by his Republican opponent of the previous election, Wendell Wilkie. Even with the obvious wartime need for secrecy, the greatest secret of all, the Manhattan atomic bomb project, was shared with the Speaker of the House. When Speaker Rayburn asked the Appropriations Committee to provide the money for the project, he gave them his personal assurance that it was necessary. No one divulged the secret.

Trust and mutual respect continue to be essential to effective policymaking. If American policy is to be believable, it must represent a national consensus, and the world must see us practicing what we preach. Obviously, we cannot enjoy the benefits of bipartisanship if the administration conceals its purposes and plans from the Congress. As Senator Arthur Vandenberg once said to President Truman, "If you expect us with you on the landing, we must be with you on takeoff."

During the past several days, for the first time in a very long while, the administration and Congressional leaders have been engaged in a bipartisan initiative. We joined together to develop peace plans which we hoped might give some real momentum to those long-stalled negotiations in Central America.

Ultimately, it is the people of Central America who have to determine and carry out the details of reconciliation. The basic plan now being discussed was originated by President Óscar Arias of Costa Rica. But here are the key elements of the US proposal to reinforce that plan and begin some movement which, God willing, may help to end that terrible conflict and begin a process of renewal.

The centerpiece of the bipartisan plan is a cease-fire subject to outside verification. After the cease-fire, the United States will halt its military aid to the contras, and Nicaragua will stop accepting lethal aid from Cuba and elsewhere. Nicaragua will begin restoring civil and political rights. The United States will lift our economic embargo.

With respect to Nicaragua, the United States has three legitimate concerns:

> 1. That there be no Soviet, Cuban, or Communist bloc base established in Nicaragua nor any weapons of a type that could menace the United States.
> 2. That Nicaragua pose no military threat to its neighbor countries nor establish a staging ground for subversion in the hemisphere.
> 3. That Nicaragua respect the basic human rights of its own people—free speech, press, religion, and free elections—the rights embraced in its own constitution.

Beyond this, we make it clear that the United States claims no right whatever to influence or determine who the political leaders of Nicaragua shall be nor the social and economic system that country may choose. Those are matters wholly within the right of the Nicaraguan people. That's their business.

Embracing these basic principles, the United States is trying to help our neighbors—so long besieged by poverty, oppression, and war—to enjoy the fruits of peace. Peace is worth waging by single-

Speaker Wright wielding his gavel.
SPEAKER JIM WRIGHT COLLECTION, SPECIAL COLLECTIONS,
MARY COUTS BURNETT LIBRARY, TCU.

minded determination. So long as President Reagan is sincerely trying to end the needless conflict in Central America, the legislative branch and his loyal democratic domestic opposition owe that effort our unflinching help. And we join wholeheartedly in this ambitious attempt to give peace a chance. May we all ask the blessing of God on this endeavor.

Radio address, August 8, 1987

## A Lamp Unto Our Feet

YOUR HOSPITALITY is as warm as your Costa Rican sunshine, and your capacity for friendship seems as broad and expansive as your skies. Many times have I been in your beautiful country and always have carried away with me memories of the grandeur of your landscape and the graciousness of the Costa Rican people.

It is natural that the Speaker of the US House of Representatives would feel at home in your Congress, for our countries share the same values and the same fundamental ideals.

On behalf of a great many fellow countrymen in the United States, I have come to express to you—and through you to the people of this enlightened democracy—our profound gratitude for the shining example of your country, relatively small by physical measurement but large in the power of your example.

The old Chinese proverb teaches that it is better to light one candle than to curse the darkness.

Costa Rica, in the leadership of your President Óscar Arias Sánchez, lighted that candle on August 7 in the Esquipules agreement. Other nations brought their candles to Guatemala and lighted them from yours.

Each week brings some new step in one or another of the nations of Central America along the path to peace, strewn though it is with obstacles and overgrown at places by the weeds of hate and distrust.

With patience and diligence and determination and faith, we work and pray—and even dare to hope—for an end to the bloodshed which has claimed the lives of some forty-five thousand people in Nicaragua and perhaps of sixty thousand in El Salvador.

If peace comes, all the hemisphere will owe to your country a debt of gratitude, even as the world is acknowledging in its award of the prestigious Nobel Prize to President Arias.

But peace, we know, is not the mere absence of war. It is a positive thing which must be waged with the single-minded determination which nations would otherwise devote to war.

The history of civilization is the story of our continuing struggle for the nobler instincts of the human species to triumph over the baser ones.

Gibbon wrote in his *Decline and Fall of the Roman Empire:* "As long as mankind shall continue to bestow more liberal applause on their destroyers than on their benefactors, the thirst of military glory will ever be the vice of the most exalted characters."

So let us talk together of waging peace, and let us give our applause to those in whatever country who achieve victory in its pursuit.

Peace and democracy go hand in hand. And their inseparable companion is the type of economic development in which the humblest of the citizenry can share. President John F. Kennedy was thinking not only of the US but of democracies everywhere when he said: "If a free society cannot help the many who are poor, it cannot save the few who are rich."

It is our high calling as elected public officials in a democratic society to demonstrate by deeds that the legitimate social and economic objectives of a people can be achieved, and better achieved, through the constitutional processes of political democracy, without the sacrifice of individual liberties.

In neighboring Nicaragua, peace will come and economic recovery can begin when all elements of the population, true to the Arias plan, are reconciled in the equality of free speech, free press, free assembly, free worship, and free elections open to all.

In El Salvador the rule of law must supplant the violence of a bloody past and all sides accept the civilizing rule of ballots rather than bullets and reason rather than terror.

One need not travel far in our battered region to see the horrendous waste—the fields untilled and crops ungathered, the factories unbuilt and jobs unavailable, the diseases untended and children untaught—which have been sacrificed upon the altar of war.

Nor is it difficult to imagine the good that can be accomplished if the nations of Central America may turn their energies and their financial resources toward those things that unite us rather than those that divide us, those things which ennoble rather than those that destroy.

The Caribbean Basin Initiative has made a good if modest beginning, and it can be expanded to draw us nearer together and to open up opportunities throughout Central America.

But plain and ordinary people must see that they have a stake in the economic progress which it can set in motion.

No longer is it good enough for complacent governments to preserve a threadbare status quo in which plain people do not participate in progress, and succeeding generations of children are doomed to live out their lives as indebted tenants, without education, without rudimentary medical care or any real chance to own land or home or have a remunerative job.

The tree of democracy will grow and flourish if it is planted in the soil of economic growth and watered by the rainfall of a just social order.

Otherwise it will wither and die.

Costa Rica is engaging in a fascinating experiment of employee ownership in a business recently acquired from a foreign firm. Many of us will be watching it closely and hopefully. If this example of a people's capitalism can be made to work, it may light a new path toward economic development.

Working together, the nations of our hemisphere must find a means of resolving the staggering problem of debt. It does little good to open factories and expand exports if all that we sell must be consumed in interest payments.

There must be a workable plan by which people in my country and elsewhere in the hemisphere might acquire this debt through the purchase of good neighbor bonds, paid off in more humane rates of interest.

With the ending of warfare, we can concentrate together on the exciting opportunities of peace. For war is the common enemy of us all.

Next week, in my country, President Reagan and the head of the Soviet Union, Mr. Gorbachev, are scheduled to sign a treaty to reduce dramatically the number of intermediate nuclear weapons.

We earnestly hope it leads to other mutual accords on intercontinental weapons and on conventional weapons in Europe. If our two nations are successful in doing these things, it could free untold billions of dollars for productive investment in the long-deferred works of peace and human betterment.

Four decades ago, President Eisenhower, who was commander in chief of Allied Western forces in World War II, said it well:

> *Every gun that is made, every warship launched, every rocket fired signifies, in the final sense, a theft from those who hunger and are not fed, those who are cold and not clothed. This world in arms is not spending money alone; it is spending the sweat of its laborers, the genius of its scientists, the hopes of its children.*

Full development of the human potential for the humblest one among us in an atmosphere of political liberty, social justice, and human dignity, with respect and equality between nations each enjoying self-determination and practicing a policy of non-intervention, was a dream of Jefferson and Lincoln and Bolívar and San Martin and Juarez. It lives today in the minds of José Figueres and Óscar Arias Sánchez. It is shared by many in North America and embraced by enlightened men and women throughout our hemisphere.

May that dream inspire our minds and may the candle you have lighted in Costa Rica be a lamp unto our feet.

Speech to the National Legislative Assembly of Costa Rica,
December 1, 1987

## Wright's High-Risk Strategy On Central America Pays Off: Contra-Aid Victories Erase Doubts in Party

By Tom Kentworthy, *Washington Post* Staff Writer

ON MARCH 17, the day after President Reagan dispatched more than thirty-one hundred US troops to Honduras in a show of force following the incursion of Nicaraguan soldiers, administration officials swarmed over Capitol Hill to brief lawmakers on what they described as a large-scale Sandinista invasion of Honduras designed to strike a death blow against the US-backed contras.

Assistant Secretary of State Elliott Abrams told reporters that a new package of military aid for the contras was "under consideration" in the administration and that lawmakers were being given the hard intelligence information to justify a reversal of the House vote on February 3, cutting off lethal aid.

For House Speaker Jim Wright (Democrat, Texas) and his leadership, it was a critical test of their eight-month effort to repel any attempts by the White House to send more military assistance to the contras and to encourage the Central American peace plan launched in August by Costa Rican President Óscar Arias. Already, key House moderates whose votes had helped defeat the president's military aid request on February 3 were clamoring for a new package that would resume limited munitions shipments to the contras and give Reagan the opportunity to demand a congressional vote for more.

Yet if Wright was concerned that he was about to topple off the high wire he had climbed onto last summer when he joined Reagan in proposing a peace initiative that many Democrats viewed as an administration trap, he did not show it that day. Instead, at his daily news conference, Wright insisted that the new developments in Central America did not justify sending troops or resuming military aid.

As Wright left to open that day's House session, his aides handed out copies of pages 382 and 383 of the congressional report on the

Iran-Contra affair. The excerpt detailed the "intelligence misrepresentations for policy purposes" employed by the White House in the spring of 1986 during a Sandinista incursion into Honduras that the administration subsequently used to justify a $100 million aid request that Congress approved.

The Speaker's equanimity that day, and the campaign to cast doubt on the administration's version of events in Honduras, was part of a calculated Democratic strategy to ride out the storm that followed the incursion. It was based on Wright's assessment, reached through extensive and repeated contacts with both sides of the seven-year Nicaraguan war, that the Sandinistas and contras were serious about the cease-fire talks scheduled to begin the following Monday in Sapoa, Nicaragua.

"We were convinced they really wanted an agreement," Wright said.

Wright's confidence, and the Democratic strategy, paid off handsomely less than a week later, when the contras and Sandinistas reached agreement on a sixty-day truce and further negotiations toward a permanent peace. The cessation of hostilities cleared the way for last week's overwhelming votes in the House and Senate on a $47.9 million humanitarian aid package that was largely designed by Wright and was similar to his earlier plan, which the House rejected on March 3.

For Wright, the bipartisan support for the proposal he had negotiated with GOP leaders over two days last week represented a triumph that many in his own party had warned him was impossible when he embarked on his risky and extraordinary foray into Central American diplomacy last summer.

It capped what many Democrats now view as a nimble performance during which they believe Wright has consistently outmaneuvered the Reagan administration, first by quickly embracing the Arias peace plan just days after he and Reagan had launched their joint effort, then by defeating the Reagan military aid request on February 3 by promising House moderates a vote on a humanitarian

Relaxing at his Washington, DC, office.
SPEAKER JIM WRIGHT COLLECTION, SPECIAL COLLECTIONS, MARY COUTS BURNETT LIBRARY, TCU.

assistance proposal, and finally by coolly waiting out the furor that ensued after last month's Sandinista incursion and winning passage of a humanitarian aid package.

"He beat 'em," said Representative George Miller (Democrat, California). "He's the Speaker of the House, and he put the prestige of his office into the peace process and he was smart enough to let the Latinos design it, edit it, and customize it."

Last July, however, Miller was among the doubters who warned Wright that the administration was trying to snooker him by inviting him to join Reagan in the peace effort. The White House,

Democrats warned, would torpedo the effort and use its collapse to justify a new package of military aid.

"I wouldn't have given a plugged nickel for what he was thinking of doing," Miller said.

According to Representative Dick Cheney (Republican, Wyoming), the third-ranking Republican in the House, Miller and other Democratic liberals had good cause for skepticism. With the $100 million in contra aid approved by Congress in 1986 running down, and no apparent congressional consensus to provide more military aid, Cheney said, the White House strategy was to use the peace initiative to reveal the true nature of the Sandinista regime.

"A number of people involved in that effort felt that if they laid out the peace process and challenged [Nicaraguan President Daniel] Ortega to live up to it, he'd never be able to," Cheney said. "That would make it clear he is a Marxist allied with the Soviet Union . . . and we'd be able to build a consensus for military aid."

But almost immediately, that strategy was thrown off track when the Central American presidents announced their support for the peace initiative launched by Arias. Abandoning his short-lived marriage of convenience with Reagan, Wright eagerly embraced the Arias plan and encouraged the White House to do the same.

Over the past eight months, many Democrats believe the White House has consistently sought to stymie that peace process to resume military aid. "I think they have every step of the way tried to wiggle out of peace," Representative David E. Bonior (Democrat, Michigan) charged.

Wright's effort nearly faltered on March 3, when aggressive White House lobbying helped kill by just eight votes his alternative plan for humanitarian aid. That defeat, which came after all but five House Republicans supported the president, was designed to pressure Wright into proposing a tougher package—if not one with real military aid in it, at least one that guaranteed Reagan a later vote on lethal assistance if the peace process breaks down.

But the White House effort, which included warning contra leaders to stop lobbying for the Wright plan, which the contras viewed as the best they could get from Congress, may have encouraged the rebels to agree to the March 23 truce in Sapoa. "The White House felt it was better to leave our forces up in the air than vote with the Democrats," contra leader Alfredo Cesar said a few days before the cease-fire talks began. "We feel weak."

In the package adopted last week, Republicans were able to secure a promise from Wright that he would allow "fair and orderly" consideration of any future military aid request if the Sandinistas abandon the peace process.

GOP lawmakers like Cheney see that as a major concession because they do not expect Ortega will agree to a real peace and eventual democratization. "I remain absolutely convinced that he will never give up power," Cheney said. "He has used the peace process to string Congress along so the contras will wither on the vine."

Cheney also sees an institutional danger in Wright's extraordinary involvement in foreign policy, one that cuts across the grain of Reagan's success in reasserting executive branch prerogatives. "It goes beyond the proper role of the Speaker," Cheney said. "I don't think that's right."

Many Democrats, however, are delighted with Wright's performance so far, believing that he has served as an effective counterweight to Reagan administration adventurism in the region while protecting them against election-year charges that their party has abandoned the contras.

"You are looking at a role where traditionally Congress hides in the shadows," said Representative Leon E. Panetta (Democrat, California). "Trying to lead on an issue like this involves tremendous risks, yet Jim Wright was willing to take those risks."

*Washington Post*, April 14, 1988

Wright trimming a rose bush at his Washington, DC, home in 1987.
PHOTOGRAPH BY MICHAEL EVANS.

## Begin and Sadat—
## Men of War Who Risked All for Peace

THE BURIAL OF MENACHEM BEGIN on the hillside overlooking Jerusalem unleashed a flood of memories. It was thirteen years ago this month that Begin and Egyptian President Anwar Sadat, in that glad ceremony on the White House lawn, signed the historic peace treaty between Egypt and Israel.

Ironic, is it not, that these two Nobel laureates, architects of the only lasting peace between Israel and an Arab neighbor, actually began their careers as men of violence? Sadat, a professional soldier and devoted Muslim, came to manhood resenting the Jews and at one point in his youth admired Adolph Hitler.

Most of Begin's family perished in the Nazi holocaust. At age sixteen, he joined the militant youth branch of the Zionist movement. Ultimately he became a terrorist commander fighting the British in Palestine for Israeli independence. Begin ordered the 1946 bombing of the King David Hotel in which ninety-one people died. British officialdom labeled him "Terrorist No. 1" and posted a $30,000 reward for his capture.

By the time I met these two leaders in 1977, both men had changed profoundly. Mellowed in the harsh crucible of violent death, both yearned for peace.

"I have seen enough killing," Anwar Sadat said to me. "My heart is sick of it." A congressional group had traveled to Egypt to see him in the wake of his surprising statement to the Egyptian parliament that he would willingly "go to Jerusalem" in the search for peace.

Up the Nile River from Cairo, at a presidential enclave called The Barrages, the charismatic Egyptian used the presence of our group as reason for a press conference. He wanted to make clear that his statement was not merely a rhetorical flourish, like saying he'd go "to the very gates of hell." He literally wanted to go to Jerusalem, the capital of the country with which his own was at war, if he could be invited.

Two evenings later, our group met in Jerusalem with Prime Minister Begin. The Israeli leader seized this occasion to announce that he had in fact invited Sadat and that the Egyptian would address the parliament in the Knesset on the following Sunday afternoon.

Begin told me he would like for our group to stay over and be present in the Knesset for this totally unprecedented event. At first I demurred, saying we did not want to compound his problems.

We recognized the security difficulties. We knew the limited seating capacity in the legislative hall.

"There are thousands of your fellow countrymen who would give their eyeteeth to have those seats on Sunday, Mr. Prime Minister," I said. "We greatly appreciate your courtesy, but you need another set of guests like you need another war. Let us just clear out and . . ."

"You don't understand," the prime minister interrupted. "We want you to stay. We earnestly request that you stay. We believe an American presence will be extremely valuable at this particular moment."

So it was, in part, a gift of fate that we stayed as parties to that singular event that has no historic parallel. Three flags—Egyptian, Israeli, and American—flew side by side at the King David Hotel on that remarkable Sunday.

Sadat prayed at the historic mosque where a Jordanian king, grandfather to King Hussein, had been assassinated at prayer while on a similar mission of peace a generation earlier. Most of the American contingent attended services at a Catholic church on the Mount of Olives. In that ancient capital, holy to three religions, among humble people in the streets arose a spontaneous rejoicing such as I had never witnessed.

Peace did not come quite suddenly, though in retrospect it some-

With former Israeli Prime Minister Menachem Begin.
SPEAKER JIM WRIGHT COLLECTION, SPECIAL COLLECTIONS, MARY COUTS BURNETT LIBRARY, TCU.

Greeting former Egyptian President Anwar Sadat.
SPEAKER JIM WRIGHT COLLECTION, SPECIAL COLLECTIONS, MARY COUTS BURNETT LIBRARY, TCU.

times seems that way. There were months of initiatives and false starts on both sides before an actual agreement was reached at Camp David in September 1978.

President Carter recalls in his memoirs the decision "to go all out" to try to bring Sadat and Begin together for an extended personal negotiating session at a secluded place entirely removed from the ubiquitous cameras and catcalls of the media and from partisan kibitzers in both camps.

It is virtually impossible to make the concessions that lead to peace in an atmosphere dominated by skeptics and second-guessers. The need to constantly reassure zealots on the home front stiffens the intransigence of both Palestinian and Israeli negotiators today.

Wisely, the three leaders in the autumn of 1978 retreated to the bucolic sanctuary of Camp David in the Catoctin Mountains.

There, away from the spotlight's distracting glare, they worked and thought, talked and prayed for thirteen days; Carter was the catalyst, the go-between, the patient mediator. Never has an American president been so intimately engaged and hands-on in such a tireless pilgrimage of personal diplomacy.

In the end, faith paid off.

All three leaders took significant risk. Peace usually involves political hazard. Its practice often takes more courage than the practice of war.

It was the very success of the Camp David agreements that claimed the life of Anwar Sadat. Courageous, visionary, willing to strike out in a new direction and to swim upstream against the sullen tides of hatred, Sadat fell to the bullets of fanatics who did not want to be at peace with Israel.

So it was with Gandhi. And Lincoln. And Martin Luther King Jr.

Blessed are the peacemakers. Humankind with all its folly is ever in their debt.

The 1979 peace agreement between Egypt and Israel, in which I participated peripherally, may have been the high point of my thirty-four years in Congress. The signing of the Israeli-Palestinian accord is its natural sequel (no doubt its historic equal).

The ceremony was flawless, the day itself near perfect. A flotilla of fleecy clouds drifted high in the azure sky. The early autumn sun upon the noontime audience gave not the hot summer sting of a branding iron but the warmth of a caress.

Several very special moments stirred emotions like skilled fingers at the strings of an Irish harp.

The three thousand onlookers were moved to their feet as President Clinton walked forth, flanked by Israeli Prime Minister Yitzhak Rabin and PLO Chairman Yasser Arafat, sworn enemies and violent antagonists for almost a generation.

Finally, that magic moment for which everyone had waited: the handshake. The document formally signed, Arafat as if on cue turned to face Rabin and each extended his hand as Clinton, standing behind them with arms spread wide, beamed approval. That picture will endure, etched in memory, symbol of the day.

Then they spoke. First, Rabin. The old warrior's voice trembled with unmistakable emotion as he recounted the anguished tale of deaths and excruciating indignities and finally vowed: "Enough of blood and tears! Enough!"

Listening, I remembered my friend Anwar Sadat, another military careerist, and a day in Cairo in 1977 when he told me, "I have seen enough of killing! My heart is sick of it!" In the end, of course, the peace the Egyptian president won ended his life in a spray of gunfire from embittered fundamentalists who wanted war instead.

Reminiscing upon this, I listened as Arafat spoke. For years my mind harbored harsh feelings toward him. I considered him a mad terrorist at whose command innocent people died. I had never known him, of course, nor talked with him, never looked into his face.

Now I remembered the anger I felt fifteen years earlier when others refused to take seriously the peaceful intent of Israel's Prime Minister Menachem Begin, himself a former terrorist. In Begin's weary eyes I had seen the truth that even for the hardest there comes a final disillusionment with war.

There was something almost sacramental about the occasion as both sides cited the book of Isaiah. President Clinton spoke of the children of Abraham embarking together on a bold journey and even quoted from the Koran. Russian Foreign Minister Andrei Kozyrev's presence reminded us that hatreds can dissolve and former foes can be friends.

How earnestly do we want to believe all of this! Yet there are other voices, sharpened on the hard edges of ancient prejudice, that keep reminding us of the perverse, darker side of the human spirit.

Across Pennsylvania Avenue clustered two ragtag groups of hard-liners, one Jewish and the other Palestinian, whose intensity of mutual abomination drove them into an ironic alliance of opposition to the peace.

"Arafat does not represent us," read a banner in the hands of self-styled Palestinians. A fundamentalist Jewish zealot held a placard proclaiming, "Rabin is a traitor." What monstrous presumption!

Ben Franklin once wrote something to the effect that peacemakers will have to get their reward in heaven because they find precious little here on earth.

A long road over tortuous terrain lies ahead for the pilgrims of peace who, in Clinton's words, "have embarked together on a bold journey." Still to be resolved are difficult questions of long-denied diplomatic recognition, the exact nature of Palestinian autonomy, the future of Jerusalem and the Golan Heights. Solutions will require patience and understanding.

They also demand something even more important: forgiveness. Without this, there can be only nervous and suspicious accommodations ready to erupt in renewed violence, but never peace. Peace means forgiveness. A new beginning means closing the book on past wrongs, of which both sides are guilty. In Rabin's word, enough!

Some people, unfortunately, do not want to forgive. Maybe they cannot. But all their pent-up hostility and anger can never erase the wrongs of the past, only give continued excuse for vengeance begetting vengeance begetting vengeance.

Surely evidence exists that the peacemaker's life is more at risk than the war maker's. Consider Sadat, who wanted Egyptians to live at peace with Israelis. Or Mohandas Gandhi, who pleaded with Hindus and Muslims to coexist in freedom. Or Abraham Lincoln, who preserved the Union for North and South. Or Martin Luther King Jr., who had a dream of black children and white children walking hand in hand. All died at the hands of assassins who feared peace.

Walter Lippmann, in one of his final columns, said he had ceased to believe in the perfectibility of human nature but still believed in its improvability.

I am not certain that I believe even in that. But I do rejoice that in the ancient cradle of civilization, things are moving again in the right direction. And I am convinced that there is a spark within each of us that responds to the groping, finer spirit in humankind that knows that we are intended by an almighty wisdom to find the ways to live in peace.

In 1987, I pleaded with Cardinal Miguel Obando y Bravo to assume the role of negotiator between the warring factions in Nicaragua. Just as he was agreeing to take on that thankless task I said, "Blessed are the peacemakers."

"*Los niños del Dios,*" he responded. The children of God.

*Fort Worth Star-Telegram*, March 15, 1992

## Build Bridges, Not Walls

TODAY I INVITE YOU to focus your minds on two familiar models of construction, two things we see every day. I want us to think about walls and bridges.

Let us consider these familiar forms not merely as structures of wood or masonry or metal, but in their broader symbolic sense. Almost everything we do in society builds either a wall or a bridge.

Either we open our minds to new thoughts by bridges of learning, or we close them by walls of prejudice which reinforce our ignorance.

Either we inhibit economic and social opportunity and restrict human growth by impenetrable walls of class distinction, or we build bridges of brotherhood. Walls divide people; bridges unite them.

Today in the senseless violence that engulfs Bosnia we see a modern reenactment of an ancient tragedy. It is the tragedy of those who perpetuate emotional walls of hatred and fear that separate race against race and religion against religion and resist all efforts to build bridges of reconciliation.

Some governments build walls with the intention of protecting their people, only to discover that the walls have imprisoned and diminished them. In the third century, BC, the Chin Dynasty in China built the world's longest contiguous wall to surround and insulate their country from what its leaders considered the evils of foreign influence. Nobody could get in or out. Behind this wall, China languished for eighteen hundred years and fell hopelessly behind the rest of the world because it had erected a barrier which mankind's new discoveries and increasing knowledge could not penetrate.

The invisible Iron Curtain that Soviet leaders drew across Europe forty-five years ago had essentially the same purpose—to seal off the people of the Communist bloc countries from outside information, outside ideas, and outside influence. As a consequence, Eastern Europe withered intellectually and crumbled economically.

The Berlin Wall, topped by shards of broken glass, was a hideous example of that state of mind.

Those who erect artificial impediments to the free flow of international trade are creators of economic walls. Those who like to censor books and restrict the free expression of ideas are builders of intellectual walls.

In my country for many generations those who enjoyed the privileges of political power built legalistic walls to protect their exclusive levers of authority. They propounded legal and economic barriers to keep negroes and other ethnic minorities from voting, and from sharing fully in the opportunities of a free society.

In Mexico it was not greatly different. Here too, for several centuries, were those whose man-made walls divided race against race and class against class, condemning many of their countrymen to perpetual peonage.

But as the poet Robert Frost has written: "Something there is that doesn't love a wall, that wants it down!"

On the other side, we have people and institutions that build bridges. This very university was conceived as a bridge, a two-way educational and cultural bridge across the chasms of ignorance, misinformation, and alienation that too long separated our two nations and our two peoples.

After all, there is much more that unites us than there is that divides us. The legacy of Father Miguel Hidalgo and Thomas Jefferson is essentially one. That of Benito Juarez and Abraham Lincoln is the same. These emancipators strove to build bridges over which the very humblest of their countrymen could escape the prison walls of lifelong denial.

Even today, the internal problems of our two republics contain remarkable similarities. They differ only in degree. Both of us undergo explosive population growth. We both are struggling to expand our economies more rapidly so that there will be productive work for all. We both are becoming more urban and less rural, with all the environmental and social problems that this change brings.

And today our national leaders, President Carlos Salinas de Gortari and President Bill Clinton, are striving to remove old walls of alienation and build in their places new bridges of commerce, new bridges of culture, new bridges of friendship.

Let me suggest to each of you that the most useful and most psychically rewarding work of life is to be a builder of bridges.

St. Francis of Assisi said it most eloquently of all:

*Where there is hatred, let me sow love;*
*Where there is injury, pardon;*
*Where there is doubt, faith;*
*Where there is despair, hope;*
*Where there is darkness, light;*
*And where there is sadness, joy.*

We might add: Where there is a wall, let me build a bridge.

My political mentor was a wise old man named Sam Rayburn who said, "The way to have a friend is to be a friend, and the way to be understood by others is to make the effort to understand them."

My countrymen have not always done that in our dealings with Mexico and our sister republics of the hemisphere.

Sometimes we have assumed, somewhat arrogantly, that we knew best, and have tried to impose our economic methods and our cultural preferences upon our neighbors.

Official US policy too often has responded to Latin American alarms like a fire engine kicking up great clouds of dust as it rushes south to drown the flames in a spray of cold water, then retreating just as quickly—leaving the hapless inhabitants to deal with the wreckage and the ashes and water-soaked landscape.

"Living beside the United States," a Mexican friend once told me, "is like sleeping beside an elephant. It can roll over in the middle of the night, meaning you absolutely no harm, and crush the life out of you."

An old aphorism claims that when the United States sneezes, Mexico comes down with pneumonia. The reverse is true, as well. When Mexico suffers economic calamity, and its people can no longer purchase goods, then factories close and people go jobless in the United States. When Mexico's economy revives, then my countrymen, second only to Mexicans themselves, are the first to enjoy its benefits. Our futures are inseparably linked.

Closer ties are in our economic self-interest. The nations of Latin America, with Mexico at the forefront, have always been my country's best trading partners. For most of the twentieth century they have bought more of its goods than any other region, and they sell more of theirs to the United States than to any other country. Seventy cents of every import dollar spent by Mexicans comes to the United States. Therefore, the surest way to enhance our exports is for the Mexican people to enjoy greater buying power, becoming better customers for their own goods as well as for those of the United States.

On the threshold of a new century, we must build bridges of mutual understanding. The United States must understand the pride that pulsates in Mexico's veins, respect its institutions, be sensitive to its sovereignty, and identify with its principle of non-intervention. Mexico in turn must realize that our desires for a mutual commitment to improved wages and labor conditions are born of sincere concern.

Neither country would benefit by a return to the practices which prevailed prior to the Revolution of 1910, when foreign investments in Mexico flourished and reaped huge profits for the investors while the Mexican people lived in abject poverty.

If our new agreements embrace the twin ideals of free trade and fair labor standards, history will applaud us. For human labor is not just another commodity—like beans or timber or steel or cotton fabric—to be traded as cheaply as possible in the world marketplace. Labor is life itself. Let us remember that laws are the means, but people are the ends.

Under the leadership of President Salinas, Mexico is removing walls of protectionism and inviting investments in areas long forbidden. If the new relationship is to endure to the mutual benefit of our two countries, investors must not commit again the errors of the past. Let us greet the new century with a new ideal of socially conscious capitalism, or as Costa Rican President José Figueres once said, "ethics applied to economics."

If we are honest we will acknowledge that there are differences as well as similarities in our cultural histories. We need not apologize for these differences. Instead, let us respect them, and even celebrate them. Those of us who have come to love Mexico love it the more because of those differences. If it were not for our cultural diversity, the hemisphere would be as bland and colorless as the desert.

As for me, I am ceaselessly impressed with the marvelous panorama of cultures that make Mexico like a tapestry in which each thread contributes its own distinctive coloration. I am impressed with Mexico's marvelous blending of the old and the new—with the timeless tranquility of its countryside, and with the modern structures which arise in its cities to sparkle against the backdrop of an ancient and honorable civilization like newly cut diamonds in a setting of old gold.

Having come to Mexico frequently for more than forty years, I am impressed anew on each arrival at the genuine warmth of Mexico's welcome. I observe that amidst the world's busy changes, in the Mexican soul there still is time for hospitality, for calm reflection, for enjoyment of friendship, and for compassion to the humblest creature. For me these have come to symbolize the spirit of Mexico, and I would never want to see that change.

And so, as I call you forth, members of this graduating class, to be builders of bridges—bridges of learning, bridges of human understanding, bridges of conciliation of differences, of improved relations, and hemispheric progress—I wish for each of you and for your family, that there may be . . .

*Sunshine on your garden every morning,*
*A song in your heart every night,*
*Good work for your hands,*
*A straight path for your feet,*
*And a dream for your mind;*
*The hands of a good friend knocking at your door,*
*Happiness at your hearthside,*
*And God's blessings to you always.*

Commencement speech, University of the Americas,
Puebla, Mexico, June 4, 1993

## The Spanish-American War: America's Coming of Age

ONE HUNDRED YEARS AGO TODAY, Theodore Roosevelt's Rough Riders, along with volunteer military contingents, embarked enthusiastically from Tampa Bay and were enroute to Cuba and a series of successful skirmishes known as the Spanish-American War. Their impressive efforts and Spain's quick surrender catapulted the United States into its twentieth-century role as a world power.

That war, officially declared by Congress on April 25, lasted only a few weeks and was described by then-Secretary of State John Hay as a "splendid little war."

Like the Persian Gulf conflict of 1991, it produced quick, easy victory, dramatically showcasing America's military superiority.

For our country, there was only brief fighting, and very little dying, but a newfound glory that brought a sort of unifying closure to the bloody divisiveness of the Civil War just as, almost a century later, our one-sided routing of Iraq from Kuwait seemed to cure America's national hangover from Vietnam.

But the "splendid little war" in the Caribbean and South China seas did much, much more. It thrust America, almost against its national will, into the big, complex world of global responsibilities that we have increasingly shouldered throughout the twentieth century.

Not everyone reacted joyously. So fixed were House Speaker Thomas Brackett Reed's convictions against expanding American hegemony or assimilating Filipinos and Puerto Ricans into an American amalgam that he resigned the Speakership rather than participate in the new roles that the Spanish-American War thrust upon his country.

By 1898, America was already a political inspiration, and

arguably the world's foremost industrial power. Ours was the model for popular people's movements on every continent. And reports of our emerging egalitarian prosperity and open opportunity were drawing waves of immigrants, magnet-like, from stale and hopeless cells of stratified poverty throughout the world.

But aside from the Monroe Doctrine and our pre-Civil War flirtation with the "Manifest Destiny" credo, America's interests had been largely domestic. We'd been content to mind our own business and plow our own acres. Didn't George Washington admonish us to beware of entangling alliances?

Now, suddenly, with Spain's faded empire so decisively vanquished, we emerged like a young giant upon the world stage. It was a sort of national coming of age, with elements both awkward and heroic.

Changes in style and quality of American life swept across the scene with that war. One of those, championed by William Randolph Hearst, was an entirely new style of journalism, infinitely more colorful and entertaining and certainly more influential, if lamentably less reliable.

It was Hearst's crusading newspapers whose screaming headlines and extravagant claims stampeded public opinion, ultimately driving Congress into declaring war.

Ben Procter, in his authoritative and revealing new book on Hearst (*William Randolph Hearst, The Early Years, 1863-1910*), shows how the flamboyant publisher used his *New York Journal* to seize quick advantage of a tragic explosion to kindle nationwide outrage and fan it into a war cry.

The arrogant Spanish overlords of Cuba had sunk the battleship *Maine* in Havana Harbor, killing two hundred and twenty-six US servicemen, asserted Hearst immediately. By 6:00 a.m. the next morning, a *Journal* extra was on the destruction, "BY AN ENEMY'S SECRET INFERNAL MACHINE."

On February 20, after four days of sensationalized finger-pointing, the *Journal's* bold headline claimed "PROOF OF A SUBMARINE MINE." Following issues featured purported quotes from underwater divers supplying "positive proof" that the Spanish, in spite of their denials, had masterminded the gory disaster. (Years later, official examinations of the hull would speculate that the *Maine* had blown up internally, probably from combustion or accidental fire in the coal supply, setting off explosions of the adjacent ammunition stores.)

Hearst had been crusading to free Cuba from Spanish rule, the goal of repeated Cuban uprisings since at least 1878. The *Journal* had championed Cuban rebels, once fictionalizing a daring "rescue" of a saintly young nun from a corrupt Spanish prison. Public support was rising for the Cuba Libre cause. The sinking of the *Maine* was an irresistible instrument with which to whip sentiment to a level of frenzy.

With a sense of high idealism, Congress adopted by joint resolution a firm commitment to Cuban independence as its justification for war. "The people of the island of Cuba are and of right ought to be free and independent," proclaimed Congress, demanding that Spain relinquish power and directing President McKinley to use armed force if necessary to achieve that end.

Congress declared further that the United States "hereby disclaims any disposition of intention to exercise sovereignty, jurisdiction, or control over said island except for pacification thereof, and asserts its determination, when that is accomplished, to leave the government and control of the island to its people."

It didn't work out that way. Cuban General Calixto Garcia and other revolutionaries who'd fought beside our troops to liberate the island were cut out of the negotiations and out of governance, to the bitter disillusionment of Cuban patriots.

McKinley appointed an overseer, Governor General Leonard Wood, who said that any Cuban without at least $250 represented a "social element unworthy" of the ballot. "Let him not vote." We didn't yet know how a democracy could exercise world power.

A century later, Hawaii is a state; Puerto Rico soon may be; the Philippines are free and mostly friendly; ours is the undisputed mantle of world preeminence. We still haven't made peace with Cuba. Perhaps it's time.

*Fort Worth Star-Telegram,* June 14, 1998

## If It Must Come to War: Haunted by History

IT SEEMS THE DIE IS CAST. Within days, regardless of any decision or indecision in the United Nations or elsewhere, American troops will invade Iraq. President Bush, having doggedly pursued this goal for many months, apparently feels he cannot now alter it.

If war comes, in keeping with our tradition, we'll close ranks in support of America's uniformed services, praying for a swift victory, which our overwhelming military superiority makes all but certain. At least this first deadly all-out offensive should be soon over, and Saddam Hussein either dead or deposed from power.

In a few days, I'll expect to go out to Fort Worth's Naval Air Station with other patriotic local citizens to salute and embrace young men and women called to join our fighting forces in the Middle East. Even we who've questioned the necessity of this immediate conflict know it wasn't the making of these brave youths who're willing to offer their lives in service to our common country.

My family, I guess, is fairly typical. My father led an infantry company to France to avenge the *Lusitania* and fight the "war to end wars." I dropped bombs on Japanese targets to avenge Pearl Harbor and universalize the "Four Freedoms."

My son saw service in Vietnam, avenging the Tonkin Gulf attack among other atrocities, and supporting South Vietnamese independence. An earlier distant relative, I'm told, was with Sam Houston's ragtag forces at San Jacinto, avenging the Alamo and Goliad and securing Texas independence. So it goes. We're good Americans. That's how we were raised.

President George W. Bush, some observers insist, has been planning this "preemptive" move against Iraq since before the September 11, 2001 outrage. They believe that Bush, dedicated Christian, has long felt a sense of personal mission to "remake" the Middle East and see removal of Saddam as a start in fulfilling that project.

Bush would like to create a "free and democratic" Iraq, friendly to our country. On its surface, a worthy aspiration.

Still, I can't help being haunted by history. We're beginning the twenty-first century very much as we began the twentieth.

In 1898, we declared war on the Spanish governors of Cuba. Aside from commercial considerations, our noble aim was to "liberate" the people of that benighted land from foreign oppressors so they could enjoy the blessings of a "free and democratic" society, friendly to us.

As a mobilizing justification, Americans were urged to "remember the *Maine*," after the US battleship *Maine* was blown up and sunk off Cuba's shore—presumably by Spanish forces.

In hindsight, we now have evidence that the *Maine* was not torpedoed at all but apparently sank from internal engine combustions that split the hull. Still, that slogan fired up the troops to throw out the wicked overlords so the Cuban people could be "self-governing."

For the next sixty years, we were at pains to ensure, through a series of paternal interventions, that Cuba's chosen leaders were the "right" people, and friendly to us.

At the end of that six decades, the Cuban people, rankling and resentful under our tutelage, followed the fiery rhetoric of Fidel Castro to throw off the yoke of US paternalism. Their message to us, the political equivalent of that old TV commercial: "Please, Mother, we'd rather do it ourselves."

The *Maine*'s sinking was not the cause of the Spanish-American War, any more than the September 11 disaster was the cause of our invading Iraq. It provided, however, a jingoistic rallying cry useful to those (among them, crusading publisher William Randolph Hurst) who'd already decided to invade and "liberate" Cuba.

Let us pray that, having triumphed militarily, we'll be wise enough this time to avoid setting off sixty years of shadowy intrigues and bloody revolutions launched in the name of "self-determination," while we persist in trying to remake ancient Iraq in our own image.

Democracy is not taught in torture dungeons or at the ends of bayonets. It is a product of understanding and a sense of equal rights.

What's needed most are patient, peaceful, and sincere efforts at understanding and mutual respect on the part of leaders, opinion makers, and plain people of both worlds. Creating a climate conducive to this—aye, there's a vision worthy of one's finest efforts, a mission for a lifetime. Whoever undertakes that mission—Jew, Christian, Muslim, or none of these—will engage in God's true work.

March 16, 2003 (unpublished)

## The Folly, the Futility, of Threats

IT WAS AUTUMN, 1933—almost seventy-four years ago. I was ten years old, a sixth grader at William James Junior High School. We were coming back from lunch break, all intent on getting into afternoon classrooms on time.

Suddenly, I felt the hard jolt of two hands upon my back, and the force of a body pushing me. Turning, I saw the source. With clenched fist, instinctively and without thinking, I hit him on the jaw. The other boy recoiled, appearing surprised.

He probably hadn't meant his forceful shove, nor I my uncalculated response, as expressions of personal dislike.

Both intuitive actions, however, were irretrievable: I could not withdraw mine, nor he retreat from his. He had shoved me violently; I'd struck him in the jaw.

"Take that back!" he ordered.

"Not until *you* take yours back!" I responded.

Then I recognized him, a boy called "Dub." I'd encountered him once with two of his buddies along Sycamore Creek. They were from Daggett, I recalled, a school in an adjacent neighborhood.

"You'll be sorry," Dub insisted.

"Who said so?"

A crowd was gathering, encircling us—among them friends of mine, and at least a couple of his. Neither of us could back down now, not in front of our buddies.

Almost instantly, the crowd parted. There was a large hand on my shoulder, another on his. It was Mr. Knute Buster, the principal.

"Go to your classes," he said to the others. The crowed vanished. He took Dub and me into his office.

There Mr. Buster convinced each that the other was an okay guy, that it was all a mistake. We didn't really want to fight each other. We were letting "foolish pride," in the principal's words, push us into a public brawl. We could, in fact, be friends, he told us. Under his watchful eye and insistent urging, we shook hands. Then each of us departed for our separate classrooms.

We didn't exactly become close friends, but we always greeted one another by name and neither of us, from that moment, had any trouble from the other.

Men raised in the macho culture of a Texas boyhood in the 1930s will recognize the situation. Dub and I, each with friends watching, were required by unwritten rules, unyielding as an umpire's call, to stick by our guns when challenged. But for Mr. Buster's calming intercession, we'd have had to fight it out.

My question: Where, in the culture of grown up men and women, is Mr. Buster today when we need him?

A week ago, Vice President Cheney made a televised appearance in front of a rack of US warplanes on an aircraft carrier off the Iranian Coast in the Persian Gulf. He was lecturing not the Navy and Marine personnel assembled, but the leaders and people of Iran.

Cheney's message, paraphrased: We're right here in your face, and we've got bombs. We'll not let you enrich uranium, or interfere with shipping of oil in the gulf, or send weapons into Iraq, and we won't let Iran "dominate" politics in this region.

In fairness to Mr. Cheney, let's call it a warning. The problem is that Iranians are sure to have seen and heard it as a threat. A verbal salvo across Tehran's bow. And why just now, when we're scheduled to meet in days for long-delayed civil discussions about Iraq's future?

Sometimes tough-guy talk simply hardens the opposition. Consider: President Bush's verbal attack on North Korea just when South Korea was trying to pursue détente; blunt rejections of the UN's plea to let the search team finish its work before attacking Iraq ("The time for talking has past," Bush quipped). Then, the "bring 'em on" taunt.

In contrast, I remember a day in 1957. Muslims had built a magnificent temple of worship on Washington's Massachusetts Avenue, convenient to many foreign embassies. President Eisenhower was invited to inspect the sanctuary as part of the building's dedication.

As cameras clicked and film rolled, the president of the United States very deliberately removed his shoes, in obeisance to Islamic custom, before entering the holy space. Some Americans criticized the gesture. But Dwight Eisenhower didn't have to prove how tough he was. He preferred to show we could also be tolerant, welcoming, and gracious.

The moral: If we're really strong, in more ways than just money or muscle, we don't have to keep reminding folks of it.

May 20, 2007 (unpublished)

# V

# Defining Moments

Wright in his mid-thirties.
SPEAKER JIM WRIGHT COLLECTION, SPECIAL COLLECTIONS, MARY COUTS BURNETT LIBRARY, TCU.

## True Believer

A TRADITIONALIST would say that I did practically everything wrong in my first bid for public office. Certainly I broke most of the conventional rules for anyone wanting to serve in the Texas Legislature. I took sides in other races, publicly supported the losing candidate for governor, managed to alienate the Speaker-to-be of the House in which I sought membership, spoke out needlessly on the most controversial issues, accosted the state's dominant economic interests, and opposed the governor-elect at the state Democratic convention. To the well-established power structure in Texas, I was as abrasive as sandpaper. I insisted that I was conducting an "educational" campaign. Seasoned political observers were sure that I was acting like a damn fool. "If there was a mistake you didn't make," my friend I. B. Hand later chided me, "it was only because you didn't think of it." And maybe he was right.

I wanted more money for the public schools, better pay for teachers, paved farm-to-market roads, an improved public welfare program, and a statewide water plan to develop a base for modern agriculture and industry—and I wanted to pay for all these things by levying severance taxes on oil and gas and sulfur. I also wanted a new and modern state constitution, a stiff lobby registration law, and year-round salaries for legislators. And it wasn't the platform so much as the way I went about expostulating it which must have made me a curiosity on the dirt road hustings of Parker County.

Disdaining the logic of directing appeals to natural self-interest, I'd speak to the educators about the need for farm roads, to farmers about the need for more adequate teachers' pay, to the old folks about water for Texas's future, and to the business community about why we ought to tax oil and gas. This, I insisted, was the *statesmanlike* way to go about campaigning. I had little patience for Lloyd George's sage dictum that the first duty of statesmanship was to get elected. Just *be* a statesman, expose the public to the truth, and elections will take care of themselves: that was my naïve article of faith at the mature age of twenty-three. I believed in the perfectability of man and was determined to be its instrument.

"Texas ranks first among the states in oil production, first in natural gas and sulfur. We rank first in carbon black; first in cattle, cotton, wool, and mohair," I would expound to my listeners in sweaty rural high school gymnasiums and under open-air church arbors throughout the county. Most of my auditors probably had come to size up the candidates for sheriff or county commissioner. Austin, after all, was a pretty far piece away.

"But, my friends, our state ranks a miserable thirty-eighth in education! We rank thirty-eighth in per capita income, thirty-fourth in aid to the elderly, well below the median in our literacy rate, below the norm in wages paid to our industrial workers and in the income of our average farmer. And Texas ranks forty-eighth—last among the states, mind you—in aid to dependent children! We ought to hang our heads in shame. Or better still, redress the balance!"

It always got some applause. It was strong doctrine and had the further merit of being statistical truth. But I'm not precisely certain just how smoothly it went down gullets long accustomed to the soothing syrup of being told how Texas was best in everything!

(unpublished)

## Resignation Speech

MR. SPEAKER, FOR thirty-four years I have had the great privilege to be a member of this institution, the people's House, and I shall forever be grateful for that wondrous privilege. I never cease to be thankful to the people of the Twelfth District of Texas for their friendship and their understanding and their partiality toward me. Eighteen times they have voted to permit me the grand privilege of representing them here in this repository of the democratic principles. Only a few days ago, even in the face of harsh news accounts and bitter criticisms, they indicated in a poll taken by the leading newspaper in the district that 78 percent of them approved of my services, and that includes 73 percent of the Republicans in my district, and I'm very proud of that.

And you, my colleagues, Democrats and Republicans, I owe a great deal to you. You have given me the greatest gift within your power to give. To be the Speaker of the United States House of Representatives is the grandest opportunity that can come to any lawmaker anywhere in the Western world. And I would be deeply remiss if I didn't express my sincere appreciation to you for that opportunity. I hope that I have reflected credit upon the people of my district who know me best, perhaps, and upon the people of this House who, next to them, know me best.

I am proud of a number of the things that we've done together while you have let me be your Speaker. I am proud of the record of the 100th Congress. Many people feel that it is the most responsive and most productive Congress in perhaps twenty-five years. And all of you who were here in that Congress had a part in that. Many of the things we did were truly bipartisan in character.

Together, we made it possible for great leaps forward to be made in such things as our competitiveness in the world. Together, we fashioned the beginnings of a truly effective war on drugs to stamp out that menace to the streets and schools and homes of our nation. We began the effort to help the homeless. We still have work to do to make housing affordable to low-income Americans so that there won't be any homeless in this country. We did things to help abate catastrophic illness, and to provide welfare reform legislation, clean water legislation, and a great many other things that I shall not detail. For your help, your great work, and for permitting me to be a part of this institution while that was happening, I thank you. And I shall forever be grateful for your cooperation.

And I love this institution. I want to assure each of you that under no circumstances—having spent more than half of my life here, this House being my home—would I ever knowingly or intentionally do or say anything to violate its rules or detract from its standards.

Now all of us are prone to human error. The Speaker of the House is, in fact, the chief enforcer of the rules of the House and it's really a wonderful thing that any member of the House may at his will bring question against any other member—and under our rules that has to be looked into—and I have no quarrel with that, nor any criticism of people who serve on the Committee on Standards. It's a thankless job, and we have to have such a committee.

For just about a year, I have ached to tell my side of the story. That to which I have to respond keeps changing. But today, silence is no longer tolerable; nor for the good of the House is it even desirable. And so without any rancor and without any bitterness or any hard feelings toward anybody, I thank you for indulging me as I answer to you and to the American people for my honor, my reputation, and all the things I've tried to stand for all these years.

For the past year, while the Committee on Standards has had these matters under advisement, I have ached for the opportunity to speak. Almost daily I besought them to let me come and answer whatever questions they had on their minds. Finally, on the fourteenth of September, they gave me one day in which to do that. I gratefully went and spent the whole morning and the whole afternoon answering as candidly and as freely as I possibly could any question that anyone would ask, and I believe when I left everyone was reasonably well satisfied.

Suffice to say that the five original charges that had been lodged were dismissed. In their place, however, came three additional charges. Well, some said sixty-nine. The sixty-nine are merely a matter of multiple counting of the three. And in April, the committee said that they thought there was some reason to believe that rules may have been violated in these three basic areas. I owe it to you and to the American people to give a straightforward answer on those three areas. I'm convinced that I'm right; maybe I'm wrong.

I know that each of us, as Benjamin Franklin suggested, should be careful to "doubt a little of his own infallibility," but before those charges were issued as fast leaks, filtered out almost daily, tarnishing my reputation and by inference spilling over on the reputation of this institution, I pleaded for the privilege to come and answer those questions before charges were made. Under the rules that was not permitted to me, and they were formally made.

And so let's look at them, one by one, dispassionately. The committee has raised these three basic questions. It doesn't say that there is "clear and convincing proof" that I violated the rules. It doesn't say that they know I violated them. It just says they have some reason to believe I may have. And for these last few weeks I've been trying to find that and get an opportunity to address it. Now is the day—I'm going to do it now.

The three questions are these:

Did my wife Betty's employment, at $18,000 a year for some four years, by a small investment corporation which she and I formed with friends of ours, George and Marlene Mallick, and the attendant benefits of that employment—the use of an apartment when she was in Fort Worth on company business and the use of the company-owned car—constitute merely a sham and a subterfuge and a gift from our friend, Mr. Mallick? Was Betty's employment and those things related to it a gift?

You've read in papers the suggestion made by committee counsel that I may have received up to $145,000 in gifts from my friend, Mr. Mallick. Half of it, $72,000, was Betty's income, Betty's salary. The other half involved the use of a car and the use of an apartment on a per diem basis. Now, whether it's right or wrong, let's look at it. Betty's employment. Was that a gift?

First question I suppose you might be asking: Why was Betty working for the corporation? Why did we put her to work at $18,000 a year? The answer is really very simple. She was the only one of the four of us who had the time and the inclination to look into the investment opportunities that our investment corporation was created to explore. George Mallick, my partner, was too busy looking after his own interests; he had business interests of his own. Marlene Mallick was raising a family. I was busy being a member of Congress and majority leader. I didn't have any time to spend on it. Betty alone, among all others, had the time and the opportunity and the experience and the desire to give effort and energy to exploring and promoting investment opportunities.

She did indeed perform work, and it paid off for the little corporation. She did it well. She studied and followed the stock market on regional stocks—buying and selling—some of them I brought into the corporation that I'd owned personally—my personal estate. She advised us of when was a good time to sell and when was a good time to buy. And the corporation made some money on those regional stocks, not a lot of money by some people's standards, but we made some money.

Betty paid for her salary several times over. She maintained very frequent contact with a drilling company that was drilling a series of gas wells, exploratory gas wells in West Texas in which each of the four partners had an interest, having borrowed money from the corporation in order to do that. She visited the site of drilling and maintained contact with the company for us in that instance. She went to New York and studied the gemstone business, and the corporation made an investment in gemstones—made some money on that. She looked into the possibility of the corporation building apartment complexes for young people, but concluded that the interest rates were unfavorable. Betty spent a considerable amount of time studying the wine industry, which was then just getting started in Texas, and she made an economic study that concluded it was too speculative for a little corporation of our type. She looked into other prospective investments such as a small, limited partnership in the movie *Annie* and a prospective venture in sulfur extraction, but advised against both of those investments, and it's lucky for us that she did because people invested in it and lost money.

Now I want to include for printing in the record affidavits from several business people who know from their personal experience and attest to the work that Betty did in this regard, and there will appear in the record at this point an affidavit by Pamela L. Smith, one by K. F. Schnider, one by John Freeman, one by Luis A. Ferris Jr., and one by J. D. Williams—all attesting to their personal knowledge of these things that Betty did in working for the corporation for $18,000 a year.

The outside counsel employed by the committee that suggested that Mrs. Wright's employment somehow amounted to a gift—I don't know why but he assumed that the services she rendered couldn't have been worth $18,000 a year. How he concludes that she didn't perform duties is to me a mystery. On page twenty of the statement of alleged violations, you'll find a very strange suggestion based on a statement that (quote) "There was no evidence either supporting or establishing that the money paid to Mrs. Wright was in return for identifiable services or work products." Now, frankly, I don't know exactly what Mr. Phelan means by "work product."

You want so many pages of cancelled shorthand notes? So many pages of typed manuscript? She wasn't a carpenter. Is a woman's mental study and her time and her advice not to be counted as a work product? How the committee could conclude that there was no evidence that Betty performed duties is very puzzling to me. They

Wright delivering a speech to the House of Representatives when he resigned the Speakership.
SPEAKER JIM WRIGHT COLLECTION, SPECIAL COLLECTIONS, MARY COUTS BURNETT LIBRARY, TCU.

don't offer any evidence that she did not. When I was before the committee that wasn't one of the things that was being considered. They didn't ask me to go into any elaborate detail, as I have just done, to tell of the things that she did. They assumed that there was no evidence.

Ah, but there was evidence! The two people of whom questions were asked aside from myself, Mr. Mallick himself, and Pamela Smith, both testified that she did work. Mr. Phelan's report says that they couldn't identify but maybe twelve days in the whole four-year period in which she worked. That's an inaccurate representation of what they said. Pamela Smith, both in this affidavit and in her testimony before the committee, clearly said she saw Betty there from five to seven days every month, and on weekends. And she spoke of her knowledge of her doing work in Washington and New York and elsewhere. So, there's evidence.

Well, is one to conclude that my wife's services to our little corporation were worth less than $18,000 a year? It's not worth it? For most of her adult life, Mrs. Wright has been a businessperson. She's been an officer in a large hotel, an officer in a successful real estate and construction firm, a professional staff person on a congressional committee. She was making more than $18,000 when she worked at the congressional committee.

And here's the irony, the supreme irony. In 1976, when I was elected majority leader, Betty voluntarily left her job as a professional staff person on the committee, so as to avoid any criticism of this institution or of her husband on the ground that we both were on the public payroll. How many colleagues in the House and the Senate do you know whose wives are on the public payroll doing good work? And you know, Betty didn't want to be the cause for even unfounded criticism. She was legally entitled to continue. She had that job before our marriage, but she chose to leave to save the institution and her husband from unwarranted criticism. That's the kind of person she is.

Now, it just seems to me that there isn't any justification at all for anybody's even raising a question about whether she earned $18,000 a year. Should a member of Congress have to prove that his wife earned that much money? Bear in mind, this money was not paid by Mr. Mallick; the money was paid by the corporation of which Betty and I were half owners.

Now, in addition to her salary as a gift, outside counsel contends, in his summing up the $145,000 in "gifts," that Betty had the use of a company car. That's true—she did. For the first three years, it was used largely by Mr. and Mrs. Mallick. It wasn't Mr. Mallick's car. It was the company car. The company bought and paid for it. We owned half of it. The next four years Betty had most of the use of it.

Now, I've done what I can to resolve any doubt. I want to do the right thing, the honorable thing. I bought and paid for that car out of my personal funds. The trustee of my blind trust, at my instruction, paid the corporation full book value for the car on the day Betty first started driving it on company business, through the whole time she had it in her possession, plus interest! The interest amounted to about $9,000. What more can I do?

Now concerning the apartment, Betty and I have been more than anxious to do what's right and honorable about that. We didn't think there was anything wrong with paying a per diem rate. The apartment was not held out for rent to anybody else. It wasn't owned for rental purposes. The Mallick family didn't want anybody else in the apartment. They owned about five apartments in this apartment complex. They held them out for their employees, for their family. There wouldn't have been anybody in the apartment paying any amount of money at all if they hadn't permitted us when we were in town—and Betty was doing company business—to occupy the apartment. We paid on a daily basis for our use of that apartment.

Meanwhile, in an effort to resolve any doubt, last year I told Mr. Mallick that I didn't like the situation being criticized. He said, well, Ralph Lotkin, the committee counsel, said that it was all right. It was in the paper—printed in the Fort Worth paper four years ago—a statement quoting the chief counsel of the Committee on Standards, Mr. Lotkin, saying he didn't see anything improper with it. I relied on that.

Nevertheless, last year I said to George Mallick, "I want to buy the apartment, George. I'll pay you for it." I did. I paid the amount suggested and appraised by two real estate persons in Fort Worth, $58,000. Now if anybody thinks that's too low a price, I'll sell it to you today for $58,000.

Well, I just wanted to clear the air, and remove doubts, and say, if we made a mistake, we've done what we can to set things right. I don't think we violated any rules. I think you're entitled to know that. My respect for you leads me to want to tell you that.

The second alleged violation continues on the assumption that Betty's employment and these little benefits that she had were gifts. And then it further assumes that George Mallick, our friend and business partner, had a direct interest in influencing legislation, which would make it illegal for us to accept gifts from him.

Now how do they arrive at that suggestion? I've known this man for more than twenty-five years. He's been my friend—a good, decent, hardworking man of Lebanese extraction. His father had a wholesale grocery store there. His grandfather came with a wagon, a cart to Georgia. He's been successful, moderately so. Never once in all the years I've known this man has he ever asked me to vote for or against any piece of legislation. Not once. That's not the basis of our friendship—it is not how our relationship goes. You have friends like that. They don't ask for anything. All they want is to be a friend. Not one time has he ever asked me to intercede with any administrative agency of government in behalf of him or of any institution in which he has interest. Not once, not once.

So how do they say that he had a direct interest in influencing legislation? Well, on page fifty-eight of the committee report, it is suggested that simply because he was in the real estate business and that he had some oil and gas investments, the committee might *infer*—that's the word—the committee might *infer* that he could be deemed a person with an interest of a direct nature in legislation. The committee suggests he might have an interest in the tax code. Well, who doesn't? I mean every taxpayer's got an interest in the tax code.

Everybody who ever expects to receive social security has an interest in the social security code. All people have an interest of some kind in the *results* of legislation, don't they? That's not what we are talking about. We're talking about whether or not they have a direct interest in trying to influence the course of legislation.

Now where would you go to find out what that means—if somebody wanted to associate with you some way and be in business with you some way back home in a perfectly legal way—whether he had an interest in legislation or not? Who would you consult if you were in doubt about it? I wasn't in doubt, but suppose you were. Wouldn't you think you'd consult the publication of the committee? Or consult the people that wrote the rules?

Well, the people who wrote the rules don't think George Mallick had an interest in legislation. David Obey was the chairman of the committee that drafted those rules. He asserts clearly, unequivocally, emphatically, unambiguously, both in an affidavit that he wrote and a report he wrote for the *Washington Post* that the rule doesn't fit George Mallick's case. He doesn't have an interest in legislation as defined under the rules that David and his committee wrote.

Harold Sawyer, former Republican member from Michigan, who served on that committee along with David Obey, says the same thing. I have here an affidavit from Mr. Sawyer in which he states exactly that same conclusion. And there's an affidavit of Donald F. Terry, who is currently employed by the Commitee on Small Business, but was a staff member on the Commission on Administrative Review, which was charged in 1976 with the responsibility for drafting new rules for the official conduct for the House. Most of what he refers to has to do with the question of book royalties. Now I shall come to that next, but in these matters these three people, who had a great deal to do with writing the rule, say that's not what they intended when they wrote the rule. I offer these for printing in the record.

Where else might you turn if you were in doubt? Might you not possibly go to the commitee itself and see what advisory opinions it has given? Here is the publication the committee sends to all of us to tell us what is and is not legal. Each year we receive this as instructions for filling out our financial disclosure statement. Appendix E is advisory opinion number ten, which defines who has a direct interest in legislation under the law. It says that "If the member does not believe that the donor of the gift has a distinct or special interest in the congressional legislative process which sets him clearly apart from the general public," well, "then the member should feel free to accept such gifts." That's the official advice from the committee given to every member. And then it defines in the summary who has an interest in legislation as prohibited under the rule.

Four classes, that's all: registered lobbyists—George Mallick's not a registered lobbyist; somebody who employs a registered lobbyist—George Mallick never did that; somebody who directs or operates a political action committee—George Mallick has never done that; or, finally, any other individual which the member *knows*—not should know or ought to suspect or ought to infer—but which the member *knows* has a distinct and special interest in influencing or affecting the legislative process. Not just somebody who's got an interest financially in the outcome of legislation—not at all! Somebody that you know has a direct or special interest in influencing the outcome of the legislative process, which sets that individual apart from the general public. Well, that was just simply not the case with George Mallick. And so he had no direct interest in any legislation that anybody could define.

Now we have motions before the committee—to set that aside, set aside that presumption of a man's having a direct interest in legislation if you haven't got a reason to believe he has. The only thing that they have suggested is that in 1986 his son borrowed money from a savings and loan to build a little shopping center of his own, wholly apart and foreign to any investments that Betty and I had—nothing to do with them, at all—his son, and that in 1987 the lending institution had to foreclose.

But the period when Betty was employed, presumably as a gift, was 1981 to 1984. Now, he couldn't have known in '81 and '84 that his son was going to borrow money in '86, and the thing would go bad in '87, and that the economic decline would make it impossible to pay off his note on time. He couldn't have known that. And anyway, would you stretch the thing to the point of saying that just anybody who has a member of his family that owes money to a bank or a savings and loan is forbidden? Of course you wouldn't. That covers more than half the citizens in the country.

The people who wrote the rules don't believe that he's covered. The people who have been interpreting the rules don't believe he's covered. And, so I think under all reasonable circumstances that motion ought to be agreed to—if rules mean anything, if we're not just going to turn the whole thing on its head and change the rules by whim every time we turn around.

Now the only other basic question—just one that remains in the statement of alleged violations—concerns the sale of a book, a little book called *Reflections of a Public Man,* which I wrote and which was sold sometimes in bulk quantities. The people who bought it gave it away to other people—students, newspapers, public officials, and members of their organizations. And I wanted them to. You know, I wanted to get the widest possible distribution of the book. A book that you write is kind of part of you. You think of it as a child almost. It's probably not great literature, but I like it. Marty Tolchin of the *New York Times,* John Silber, President of Boston University, Jim Lehrer of the *MacNeil/Lehrer Report,* and Dr. William Tucker, Chancellor of TCU, all said nice things about it, and I appreciate that.

Now, the contention of the committee, as I understand it, is that this book project—on which I got three dollars and a quarter for every book that sold—was kind of a sham and a subterfuge itself and an overall scheme for me to exceed and violate the outside earning limitations of a member of Congress.

Do you think that I'd do something like that? The purpose of the book—three dollars and a quarter is what I got out of it, and I didn't get any advance—was to publish something that could be sold at a small price and get wide distribution. If monetary gain had been my primary interest, don't you think I would have gone to one of the big Madison Avenue publishers, the houses there that give you a big advance? Hey, I know people who received advances before a single book sells from those big companies—twice and three times as much as I got in total sales of those books.

If there had been a scheme to get around outside earning limits, that's what I might have done. I hear that a woman author of a book called *Mayflower Madam* got $750,000 in advance royalties. I don't know that to be true. Our former speaker, Mr. [Thomas P.] O'Neill [Jr., (Democrat-Massachusetts)], is said to have received a million dollars for his excellent and readable book in advance, before any of them were sold. I have read that a woman named Kitty Kelly has received as much as $2 million in advance royalties for a book she's written on Nancy Reagan, which, as I understand it, is not even an authorized biography. Well, so much for that.

It is true, I think, that people on my staff were eager to sell these books. They knew I wanted them sold. I've got to accept some responsibility for that if it was wrong, but the rule doesn't say it was wrong. It couldn't have been an overall scheme to avoid outside earning limits because the rules are clear. They're not equivocal. The rules expressly exempt royalty income. And that too is attested to by David Obey. And it's attested to by Donald Terry. There wasn't any exception; book royalties were exempted. Now maybe they shouldn't have been. You know, maybe somebody got the impression that buying a book was the price of getting me to make a speech. I never intended that impression. I never suggested that. I hope that friends of mine did not.

Of all the books that were sold, the outside counsel suggests that seven cases involved instances where individuals associated with organizations to which I made speeches bought multiple copies of the books and distributed them among members of the organization or others. Now I have not been permitted to see the copy of their testimony, so I don't know what exactly they said. I've asked people on my staff, did you tell these folks that they had to buy these books or I wouldn't make a speech? They said no, they didn't.

The total amount, as I figure, from all of those sales that it involved is about $7,700—that's what I received. You know, I will do whatever is necessary, whatever is right. If those people were under the impression that I wasn't going to make a speech to them unless they bought a bunch of books, if they want their money, I'll give them that money. I don't want the money. That's not important. What's important is a person's honor and his integrity.

During that three-year period when the counsel says there are seven instances where I made speeches to groups and they bought copies of these books, seven groups, seven instances, I made at least seven hundred speeches for which I didn't get any honorarium. I didn't offer to sell anybody a book. Nobody had the chance to buy a book. Do you suppose if I'd done an overall scheme, it would have been a wider kind of an experience than that? I'm just saying to you that I didn't intend to try to violate the outside earning limitations and I don't believe legally that I did. Some of the rest of you make a lot of speeches. How many speeches do you suppose you make that you don't get anything for? Most of us do.

Well, what can I do? One other thing about the books that I suppose needs elaboration. It involves the allegation in the statement of alleged violations that a man named S. Gene Payte—a reputable businessman in Fort Worth—paid for more books than he got from the publisher. It is claimed that they didn't deliver enough books to him. Now that's what was said in the report of the outside counsel. S. Gene Payte, upon reading that report, issued an affidavit that is not ambiguous at all. Here's what Mr. Payte says. I'll read, in part, this affidavit and put the whole thing in the record.

He says,

*I have read the report of special outside counsel Richard J.*

> *Phelan on the preliminary inquiry conducted pursuant to the committee's U9 resolution as it relates to my testimony. I also have reviewed the transcript of my deposition testimony. The report and also the conclusions reached by the special counsel ignores much of the most pertinent testimony in the transcript, takes certain statements out of context, distorts clear statements of fact, and in general fails fairly and accurately to summarize the matters as to which I testified.*

The conclusion reached by the special counsel that—I quote from the outside counsel's report—I violated what the rule calls for was based upon a categorical assertion that "Gene Payte did not receive the books." The special counsel asserts Payte testified—and I'm quoting—that he only "received between three hundred and five hundred copies of the whole book for $6,000" and makes the flat statement, "Gene Payte did not receive the books"—citing as authority Payte's transcript.

Now, here's what Payte says:

> *On the contrary, I did not so testify. I stated not once, but three times that I believe one thousand books were delivered to me (transcript 27, 40, 41). The special counsel ignores this testimony. Instead, he cites transcript 77 and that citation does not support the special counsel's assertion. Transcript 77 shows that Congressman Myers, not I, made the comment. "I believe you said you received three to five hundred." I did not confirm that recollection—my reply being I would like to have all the books; in fact I never so testified.*

So this is a copy of that affidavit, which I should like to submit for the record—together with a copy of a letter that was sent by the committee to Mr. Payte after he issued this affidavit, telling him he ought not to comment.

What do you think of that? A private citizen, a reputable citizen of my community, misquoted in a document published at public expense, sent widely to newspapers throughout the country, widely cited as authority, uncritically assumed to be accurate. The citizen being misquoted issues an affidavit to straighten it out, so that he is not misquoted in the public record. And then he's warned by the committee that he might be held in violation and in contempt of Congress if he doesn't shut up. First Amendment rights supersede any rules of any committee. And any citizen of the United States ought to have the right to have his own testimony correctly characterized and not be threatened or silenced by a House committee. Any House committee owes to the citizen of the United States that right and that privilege.

Well, those are basically the matters that are pending before the committee and our motion to dismiss. Those motions could clear the air. Rules are important, just like the constancy of what a law means is important to a citizen to resolve these particular legal issues as to what constitutes "direct interest in legislation" and whether or not book royalties are exempt, as the rules say they are. I think it's important for the motions to be ruled upon, and I earnestly hope that the committee will look at it from that standpoint and grant our motions.

Members are entitled to know what the rules mean and if they still mean what they meant when they were written and promulgated. Now maybe the rules need to be changed. If so, let's change them in a legal, orderly way. Let's vote on it. Let's vote to change them. Maybe the whole process needs some change and clarification. You know, the House may want to consider establishing a House counsel to whom members can look for official advice and then rely on that advice. The rules of the committee itself might need some reconsideration. Having gone through this agonizing experience for about a year now—I mean, almost every day there's a news story in a newspaper leaked, without any chance for me to know what's coming next and no chance for me to go to the committee and answer it and say, "Hey, wait a minute, that's not correct; that's not right."

Maybe the committee—as it's currently required to sit as kind of a grand jury and petit jury both—ought to have a different composition, rather than those who issue the statement of alleged violations being the same people who have to judge them. I think it clearly is difficult to expect members who've publicly announced a reason to believe there's a violation to reverse their position at a hearing stage and dismiss charges against a member. Maybe once a report of alleged violations is issued, the committee rules ought to allow the member to respond expeditiously. You know, to deny a member the opportunity to reply quickly can cause serious political injury. It's unfair. Once alleged violations are announced, the committee ought to just immediately release to the member all the evidence that it could have to indicate that that's happened. In my case, for example, the committee has yet to release any witness testimony or documents that it obtained during the investigation.

Why hide the evidence? What's there to hide? This ought not to be the kind of proceeding in which strategic maneuvering is allowed to override fundamental relations of fair play. Now, I urge the abolition of the gag order too, which the committee said forbids any witness who comes and makes a deposition from discussing publicly or telling his side. And the charges which the committee concludes are unfounded should not be published and widely disseminated, as though they were true and bore the imprimatur of the committee's approval.

Well, there are other things you want to consider. I'm not trying to give you an exhaustive list. I know there are others who have views that are equally relevant. Perhaps we want to consider an outright abolition of all honoraria and speaking fees altogether. Maybe we want to do that—I don't know; it's up to the House—in exchange for a straightforward, honest increase in the salary for members of all three branches of the government. It is intolerably hurtful to our government that qualified members of the executive and legislative branches are resigning because of the ambiguities and the confusion surrounding the ethics laws and because of their own consequent vulnerability to personal attack. That's a shame. And it's happening.

And it is grievously hurtful to our society when vilification becomes an accepted form of political debate, and negative campaigning becomes a full-time occupation; when members of each party become self-appointed vigilantes carrying out personal vendettas against members of the other party. In God's name, that's not what this institution is supposed to be all about. When vengeance becomes more desirable than vindication, and harsh personal attacks upon one another's motives and one another's character drown out the quiet logic of serious debate on important issues—things that we ought to be involving ourselves in. Surely that's unworthy of our institution and unworthy of our American political process. All of us in both political parties must resolve to bring this period of mindless cannibalism to an end! We've done enough of it!

I pray to God that we will do that and restore the spirit that always existed in this House.

When I first came here, all those years ago, 1955, this was a place where a man's word was his bond, and his honor and the truth of what he said to you were assumed. He didn't have to prove it. I remember one time Cleve Bailey of West Virginia, in a moment of impassioned concern over a tariff bill, jumped up and made an objection to the fact that Chet Hollifield had voted—in those days we shouted our answers to the votes, and Hollifield was back there in the back, and Bailey said, "I object to the gentleman from California's vote being counted. He came down and voted late. He was not in the chamber when his name was called and therefore he's not entitled to vote."

It was a close vote. Speaker Rayburn grew red as a tomato and I thought he was going to break the gavel when he hammered. He said, "The chair always takes the word of a member." And then because I was sitting over here behind Cleve Bailey, I heard other members come and say, "Cleve, you're wrong. Chet was back there behind the rail and I was standing by him when he answered; his answer just wasn't heard." And others said, "You shouldn't have said that." And Cleve Bailey, a crusty old West Virginian, came down here and abjectly, literally with tears in his eyes, apologized, for having questioned the word of a member. Now we need that.

Have I made mistakes? Oh, boy, how many? I made a lot of mistakes. Mistakes in judgment, oh yeah, a lot of 'em. I'll make some more. Recently, let me just comment on this briefly, because it's such a sensational thing and injury's been done to me in this particular moment because of it. John Mack—many of you remember him, know him—I think a lot of you like him, respect him. I helped John one time in his life when he was about nineteen or twenty years old. I didn't know him, never had met him.

I didn't know the nature of the crime that he had been convicted of. I knew only that John Mack was a young man who my daughter had known in high school, and my daughter was married to his brother. That's how she knew about John. And she mentioned it to me. All I knew was that he'd been convicted of assault and that he'd served twenty-seven months in a Fairfax County jail. Contrary to what's been published, I did not interfere with the court. I didn't suggest anything to the court. I didn't have anything to do with his sentencing. I really didn't know and didn't inquire. Maybe that's bad judgment. I didn't inquire as to the exact nature of the crime.

The sheriff's office in Fairfax County called and asked me if I would know of any job that I could help this young man get. They wanted to parole him. They said he said he'd been a model rehabilitative prisoner. And I gave him a job as a file clerk. You know, $9,000 a year. After that, he really blossomed and grew and developed and those of you who know him can't conceive—as I never could conceive when finally just two years ago I read in the newspaper—the precise nature of that crime. It just didn't fit his character. Married and had two beautiful children, wonderfully responsible, and I think he had become a very fine person.

Now, was that bad judgment? Yeah, maybe so. It doesn't have anything to do with the rules, but it's gotten all mixed up with it. I don't think, though, that it's bad judgment to try to give a young man a second chance. Maybe I should have known more about it, but in this case I think he has turned out well and I don't believe that America really stands for the idea that a person should forever be condemned. But I think maybe he ought to have a second chance. And that's what I thought in the case of John Mack, and good judgment or bad, that's it. I believe in giving somebody a second chance.

Have I contributed unwittingly to this manic idea, this frenzy of feeding on other people's reputations? Have I caused a lot of this? Maybe I have. God, I hope I haven't. But maybe I have. Have I been too partisan? Too insistent? Too abrasive? Too determined to have my way? Perhaps. If I've offended anybody in the other party, I'm sorry. I never meant to. I would not have done so intentionally. I always tried to treat all of our colleagues—Democrats and Republicans—with respect. Are there things I'd do differently if I had 'em to do over again? Oh boy. How many may I name for you?

Well, I tell you what. I'm going to make you a proposition. Let me give you back this job you gave to me as a propitiation for all of this season of bad will that has grown among us. I will give it back to you. I will resign as Speaker of the House effective upon the election of my successor. And I'll ask that we call a caucus on the Democratic side for next Tuesday to choose a successor. I don't want to be a party to tearing up the institution—I love it.

To tell you the truth, this year it has been very difficult for me to offer the kind of moral leadership that our organization needs, because every time I've tried to talk about the needs of the country, about the needs for affordable homes—both Jack Kemp's idea and the idea we're developing here—every time I've tried to talk about the need for minimum wage, tried to talk about the need for daycare centers, embracing ideas on both sides of the aisle, the media have not been interested in that. They wanted to ask me about petty personal finances.

You need somebody else. So I want to give you that back. And we'll have a caucus on Tuesday. And then I will offer to resign from the House some time before the end of June. Let that be a total payment for the anger and hostility we feel toward each other. Let's not try to get even with each other. Republicans, please don't get it in your heads that you need to get somebody else because of John Tower. Democrats, please don't feel that you need to get somebody on the other side because of me. We ought to be more mature than that.

Let's restore to this institution the rightful priorities of what's good for this country. And let's all work together and try to achieve them. The nation has important business and it can't afford these distractions. And that's why I offer to resign.

I've enjoyed these years in the Congress. I am grateful for all of you who have taught me things and been patient with me. Horace Greeley had a quote that Harry Truman used to like: "Fame is a vapor, popularity an accident. Riches take wings; those who cheer today may curse tomorrow; only one thing endures—character." I'm not a bitter man. I'm not going to be. I'm a lucky man. God has given me the privilege of serving in this greatest institution on earth for a great many years, and I'm grateful to the people of my district in Texas. I'm grateful to you, my colleagues—all of you. God bless this institution. And God bless the United States.

Resignation speech delivered before the
US House of Representatives, May 31, 1989

## A Morn When History Was Made: The Twentieth Century Owes Much to the Longest Day

TOMORROW MARKS THE FIFTIETH anniversary of D-Day. News and entertainment media have anticipated its celebration so fully that its actual coming seems almost anticlimactic.

For the past two weeks, we have luxuriated in a sea of nostalgia, while waves of memory have reminded us again of that heroic time when we were the good guys and America was united.

Surely the Normandy invasion on June 6, 1944, was one of history's seminal events. The six thousand ships crossing the English Channel on that fateful dawn represented the greatest armada ever assembled.

Seldom if ever has the result of a battle been so crucial. Midway through the last century, Sir Edward Creasy wrote a scholarly book titled *Fifteen Decisive Battles of the World.* He judged and ranked them by the degree to which their outcome influenced the future.

Creasy chose the Battle of Marathon in 490 BC as history's most consequential. From that Greek victory over Persia, he wrote, the entire direction and progress of Western civilization was determined. Because of it, the Athenian glorification of learning and ennoblement of the individual were to take hold and expand.

If battles are ranked by their effect upon future generations, fifty years may be too short a span to give us history's perspective. But surely the entire last half of the twentieth century has been profoundly shaped by the victory that stemmed from the D-day invasion.

It could be said that on that day America's greatness as a world power emerged. True, British and Canadian troops participated valiantly in that landing. It was the largest exercise ever conducted under a joint international command.

This very fact serves to mark the final end of American isolationism. From that point forward, we have been involved in the world, sharing its fortunes and its woes. The enemy we vanquished was formidable, a juggernaut of oppression and terror that had run roughshod over Europe and posed a credible threat to the future of freedom.

The twisted genius of Germany's Third Reich, for all its malignant hate and demonic evil, was inventive, resourceful, and determined. The lightning speed of the blitzkrieg that bypassed the Maginot Line, the scientific prowess that fueled the Wehrmacht and Luftwaffe with synthetic fluid made of soft brown coal long after Germany ran out of oil, and the world's first guided missile were only a few of the wicked products of a strong and proud people driven insane by appeals to their latent nationalism.

My generation of American youth who did the actual fighting could not have triumphed except for superb leadership and an almost total national commitment that America has not enjoyed before or since. I got my wings and second lieutenant's commission in December 1942, ten days before my twentieth birthday. My experience was not unique.

It was a time when heroes were permitted, and there was an unashamedly religious faith in our common destiny. Three dynamic personalities—President Franklin D. Roosevelt, Prime Minister Winston Churchill, and General Dwight D. Eisenhower—dominated the era, infusing the millions of young Americans, Brits, and Canadians just like me with zeal for our cause and confidence in our mission.

Churchill, by the indomitable force of the spoken word, kept hope and confidence alive in Britain during the long months of its nightmarish ordeal while that embattled island race, outgunned on the ground and in the air, bore alone the brunt of the Nazi onslaught.

"Never in the history of human conflict," he said of the outnumbered Royal Air Force, "has so much been owed by so many to so few." Reeling from the tenuous escape from Dunkirk, Churchill challenged the British to "so bear ourselves that, if the British Empire and its Commonwealth last for a thousand years, men will still say: 'This was their finest hour.'"

Roosevelt provided the unifying personality around which our own nation rallied, converting its peaceful industry to war production. Within three short years, we were not only supplying ourselves but providing more than one-fourth of the armaments needed by our Russian and British allies.

We all remember those electrifying first words of Roosevelt's war message to Congress: "Yesterday, December 7, 1941—a date which will live in infamy . . ." Only last year did I see at the National Archives FDR's actual platform copy. He had scratched through the typed word *history* and inserted his substitute, *infamy*, in his own handwriting.

By D-day, I had served a tour of combat duty in the South Pacific and been returned to train new aircrews. I remember Eisenhower's radio broadcast, the businesslike crackle of his deep voice: "A landing was made this morning on the coast of France." And Roosevelt's fireside chat when our president led the nation in prayer.

Not only a general, Ike was a diplomat. Only by an end run to King George VI did he dissuade the sixty-nine-year-old Churchill from personally accompanying the English assault troops on their deadly mission. The king, after hearing Ike, vowed that if Churchill went, he also would feel compelled to go. That ended it.

In America, it was total mobilization. Entertainment figures, movie producers, and songwriters all participated eagerly. Americans who had never seen Europe got teary-eyed over *White Cliffs of Dover* and *The Last Time I Saw Paris.* War correspondents like Ernie Pyle and Edward R. Murrow glorified the GI Joes and humanized our leaders. For once they overlooked the petty flaws. They let us have our heroes.

*Fort Worth Star-Telegram,* June 5, 1994

## Never Young Again

MAYBE THE GREATEST DAY of Kennedy's presidency came on June 26, 1963, when he stood on the balcony of Berlin's city hall, one hundred and ten miles deep in Communist territory, and set off a thunderous demonstration with his ringing declaration, "*Ich bin ein Berliner.*" No symbol of the Cold War was as enduring, or as defining, as the Berlin Wall. Nor, from the Soviet standpoint, as self-defeating. President Kennedy's appearance in Berlin dramatized the differences between the two sides more strongly than anything else he had done or would do.

A few days earlier, on June 11, Attorney General Nicholas Katzenbach escorted two black students into the University of Alabama, walking past Governor George Wallace, who'd vowed to "stand in the schoolhouse doors" to protest court-ordered integration. In August, James Meredith, grandson of a slave, became the first black to graduate from the University of Mississippi.

Later that summer, on August 28, more than two hundred thousand demonstrators assembled jubilantly but peacefully along Washington's grand grassy National Mall, facing and surrounding the Lincoln Memorial, as Dr. Martin Luther King Jr. held them, and a national television audience, spellbound. A long-subdued impulse to gender equality also began to find its voice that year as a forty-two-year-old housewife, Betty Friedan, published *The Feminine Mystique,* which dissected the boredom and long-subdued personal identity of many American women. Her book called for a liberating life plan that would glorify the expression of their human individualities. Unconsciously, for the most part, I was a male chauvinist. I had been all my life. Quite naturally—unquestioned—that state of mind pervaded my background, and the culture in which I had been reared. As though taking a distasteful draught of medicine, I resolutely read Ms. Friedan's book, mentally resisting her conclusions, but reluctantly reexamining my matrix of biases.

All this was part of the intellectual ferment that bubbled up during those brief three years. America was, for the moment, young, unfettered by the cynicism that would creep up on us. The vitality of the historic moment held me in its grip the day Vice President Johnson asked me to help him organize a tour of personal appearances in Texas in November for President Kennedy.

From the moment the presidential trip was suggested to me, it commanded my enthusiastic attention. As envisioned by Johnson, the two-day tour would touch down in our state's four biggest cities—Houston, Dallas, San Antonio, and Fort Worth—and end with a statewide dinner in Austin. I talked with Governor John Connally. Always a little more pragmatic than I, he focused on the fundraising potential of an Austin dinner. My instinctive emphasis was on crowd building—exposing people to Kennedy and his message—but I promised Connally I'd try to help him sell $100,000 worth of tickets in Fort Worth and environs, including parts of West Texas. But it wasn't enough to expose John Kennedy to our community's elite—its civic, political, and business leadership. I wanted plain citizens to have a chance to see and hear their president. Against resistance from some of the itinerary's planners, I held out for a very early, pre-breakfast public appearance on a huge parking lot, which filled the city block adjacent to that occupied by the Fort Worth hotel where the breakfast would be held. I knew there were thousands of working people who loved the president and couldn't attend the breakfast even if invited, since most of them had to punch in for work at 8:00 a.m. But they would show up eagerly for a 7:00 a.m. chance to see Mr. Kennedy in person. There was one hitch. The whole city block, including the parking lot, was owned by William A. Moncrief, a colorful independent oilman and philanthropist, an early pioneer of the Texas petroleum industry—and hardly a Kennedy supporter. His first reaction was to decline the request, but John Connally and I both worked on him, appealing to his sense of civic duty. "Monty," as he was affectionately known, finally relented.

This much nailed down, I turned to the fund-raising chore I had taken on at John Connally's request. Tickets to the Austin dinner were $100 each, and I was out to raise $100,000. This translated to one thousand paid tickets. First, I assembled a fair cross-section of Fort Worth's business and professional community. About a hundred or so showed up.

Then I got together the labor leadership of our area, and with the help of David and Marjorie Belew (she was our state Democratic executive committeewoman) and committeeman Garrett Morris, I assembled all our Democratic precinct chairmen for individual ticket sales. Next, I got on the telephone and called friends in nearby Central and West Texas counties—as far away as Brownwood, a hundred and thirty miles distant. In all, I got pledges exceeding my ticket-sale commitment and saw checks totaling about $78,000. Fund-raising was never my forte, but it was and is, as Boston mayor James Michael Curley succinctly described it, the mother's milk of politics.

The first day of the president's Texas trip was a tour de force. The entire series of speeches was an elaboration upon the New Frontier theme. In San Antonio, Kennedy dedicated his remarks to the twin frontiers of space and medical science. At Houston that afternoon, he spoke to a state convention of the League of United Latin American Citizens (LULAC). His message addressed the Alliance for Progress. Jacqueline Kennedy followed with a few words spoken to the group in Spanish. The two of them wowed the Hispanic crowd. That evening, in Houston's spacious coliseum, the chief executive addressed a dinner honoring veteran Congressman Albert Thomas, first elected in 1936 when, as Kennedy pointed out, Houston had fewer than two hundred thousand people. But there, as elsewhere, the president's focus was on the future. By 1990, Kennedy anticipated, America would need three times as much electric power and four times as much water. This look ahead justified the list of specifically enumerated Texas water and power development projects being authorized that year by Congress, including

Alongside John F. Kennedy in downtown Fort Worth, Texas, hours before the president was assassinated in Dallas, November 22, 1963.
SPEAKER JIM WRIGHT COLLECTION, SPECIAL COLLECTIONS, MARY COUTS BURNETT LIBRARY, TCU.

desalination plants. We also would need by 1990, he prophesied, the capacity to serve three times as many college students, and airports to accommodate five times as many passenger miles. He predicted a $2 trillion economy "in this century."

The speech was a sign of the times. We believed everything would be bigger and better, and we could help make it that way. Exhilaration kept us from exhaustion as the traveling party flew to Fort Worth. It was after ten o'clock when the big presidential plane touched down at Carswell Air Force Base in my hometown. But a large official welcoming party awaited. Mrs. David Belew presented Jacqueline Kennedy a huge bouquet of yellow roses. Then the president spotted a large number of airmen and their families, roped off from the runway apron by a chain-link fence. They were applauding lustily.

"Take me over to the fence, Jim, and introduce me to some of these good people," he said. But their exuberant cheers as we walked toward them and passed along the fence shaking hands drowned out any attempt I might have made at an introduction. They wanted to touch him. I marveled again at his energy. But by now we all were tired. It was almost midnight. Tomorrow would be November 22.

On that Friday morning, which today seems an eternity ago, it would have been hard not to feel that the nation and this man who so perfectly symbolized it were in their finest hour.

The events of November 22, 1963, burned themselves indelibly into my memory. No sitting president had visited Fort Worth since 1936, when Franklin Roosevelt rode in an open touring car down Main Street. The lilting joy of hosting my president and presenting him that morning to my people in my hometown would give way only hours later to the stark trauma of the assassination in Dallas and the unutterable pathos that followed. But I didn't know this as I stood, so early, looking out the window, waiting expectantly for dawn.

The day began to the patter of raindrops on the streets outside Fort Worth's Hotel Texas, where the president and his party were billeted. The rain had begun during the night, and I had been unable to sleep, worrying about its effect upon our first scheduled event, the 7:00 a.m. outdoor appearance on which I had personally and so doggedly insisted. A damp crowd was already assembling, some in rain gear. Then, at six-forty, the rain stopped and the sky began to clear. "The luck of the Irish," I thought, with an enormous sigh of relief.

I walked to the elevator, rode up five floors, and spoke to my boyhood friend and then city detective, Harvey McMahan, who stood in the corridor. I knocked at the door of the president's suite. He was ready.

The crowd outside was tumultuous with joy. In that inimitable way in which he gave himself, John Kennedy walked past the flatbed trailer rigged for a speaker's platform and directly into the assembled crowd of people. He obviously enjoyed going among them, shaking their hands, feeling the press of their hopes and aspirations. The little group accompanying the president onto the trailer consisted of Vice President Lyndon Johnson, Texas Governor John Connally, state senator Don Kennard, committeewoman Marjorie Belew, and chamber president Raymond Buck.

"Where's Jackie?" somebody shouted.

"It takes Jackie a little longer to get herself together," the president answered. "But, then, she's prettier than we are. After all, nobody ever asks what Lyndon and I were wearing."

As he talked, another crowd was gathering at the breakfast. But he would not bring himself to leave, so hungry were the people assembled on the rain-soaked asphalt lot to hear him and to clasp to themselves forever the imprint of his personality. Almost whimsically, I thought of the words of that last stanza of his favorite poem:

*But I have promises to keep,*
*And miles to go before I sleep,*
*And miles to go before I sleep.*

The breakfast was a great success. Kennedy spoke of national defense, of Fort Worth's historic contribution since its inception as a cavalry outpost in 1849 (I had given speechwriter Ted Sorenson that background and was pleased the president used it), and of our role in the world. Kennedy went out of his way to pay me personal praise: "I am glad to be here in Jim Wright's city. . . . He speaks for Fort Worth, and he speaks for his country, and I don't know any city that is better represented in the Congress of the United States than Fort Worth." At this, my friends set off a loud stampede of applause that lasted too long. I didn't even have the grace to be embarrassed.

Everybody was in an ebullient mood.

Enroute from Carswell Air Force Base to Dallas Love Field aboard Air Force One, I talked with President Kennedy. Someone had shown him a copy of the *Dallas Morning News,* which contained a scurrilous display advertisement accusing the president of treason. What a boorishly rude and inhospitable thing! Any self-respecting newspaper, I thought, would have rejected such a vulgar advertisement on the day the president of the United States was visiting the city. Kennedy was puzzled by the extreme right-wing fanaticism that seemed to pervade the upper echelons of Dallas. "What makes the twin cities, Fort Worth and Dallas, so different?" he asked.

I suggested that the right-wing viewpoint so rampant in Dallas was instilled and cultivated by daily exposure to the very newspaper that published this singularly offensive ad. John Connally attributed the city's extremism to economic causes. Large banks and insurance companies, not factories, provided the bulk of Dallas employment. The work force was white collar, non-unionized, he explained. President Kennedy was intrigued with the question, said he'd like to discuss it further, maybe enroute to Austin later in the day.

We arrived in Dallas. The sun shone brightly. The president deliberately chose to ride in an open convertible with the top down, rejecting the official limousine with a protective bulletproof bubble top, which the Secret Service was recommending. Jack Kennedy wanted to show his identity with the people and his faith in them. He wanted to see their faces and for them to see his. Jack Brooks, Dallas Congressman Earl Cabell, and I rode in the fifth or sixth car, separated from the presidential and vice-presidential vehicles by several cars of media representatives.

What a contrast to that day three years earlier when Kennedy, then a candidate, had last ridden through the downtown Dallas streets! On that day in 1960, the noontime crowds in the Dallas business district stood in stony silence, neither smiling nor applauding with any vigor. This November day in 1963, they waved lustily and cheered heartily as the presidential car rode slowly past them.

The motorcade now inched its way through downtown Dallas. The president's car was approaching a grassy knoll filled with people. The vehicle in which I rode had rounded the corner past the old courthouse and was heading north toward the Texas School Book Depository warehouse when the first shot rang out. We were startled, suddenly alert. Then a second crack from the same rifle, its echo reverberating. I thought, "How foolish! Someone's trying to fire a twenty-one-gun salute with a rifle." Then the third shot, the cadence slightly off. I knew quite suddenly that this was no salute. Something was wrong!

There were three clearly audible shots. Of that I am absolutely certain. They all were from the same rifle. If any other shots were fired, they would have had to come from a weapon with a silencer. Within minutes, a witness named Howard Brennan told police that he had seen a young white male firing a rifle from a corner window on the sixth floor of the book depository.

Congressman Cabell's wife, Dearie, also reported seeing the gunman at the window.

We were turning west at the intersection below that depository window as we saw a scene of pandemonium in the president's open vehicle. Jacqueline Kennedy, inexplicably, was facing backward, looking to the rear, her fashionably clad torso leaning over the back seat of the convertible. Then the car suddenly lurched forward and speeded up the ramp of the Stemmons Freeway. Vice President Johnson's car followed in swift pursuit.

Now we passed the grassy knoll. The crowd was stunned. In people's faces was a look of sheer horror. Some were crying. What they had witnessed held them traumatized. I saw a uniformed policeman running uphill, as if trying to find the gunman.

Short minutes later, we arrived at Parkland Hospital as the president was being carried inside. The back seat of the car in which he rode was stained with great quantities of fresh blood. We feared the

Waving to the crowd with President Kennedy and Vice President Johnson in a Fort Worth motorcade, November 22, 1963.
SPEAKER JIM WRIGHT COLLECTION, SPECIAL COLLECTIONS, MARY COUTS BURNETT LIBRARY, TCU.

worst as we entered the hospital behind the group accompanying President Kennedy. It soon was confirmed. John F. Kennedy was pronounced dead at 1:00 p.m.

Connally, riding in the seat directly in front of the president, had been grievously wounded but would recover. Nobody knew at this moment if the killing had been the work of a lone madman or part of a well-organized conspiracy. Someone suggested there might be a ream of assassins. Jack Brooks broke the silence. "Lyndon, we need to get you out of here as soon as possible. Nobody knows where a gunman may be hiding." Secret Service men quickly agreed.

"But first," insisted Jack, "you need to be sworn in."

Lyndon, stunned at the thought, seemed about to demur.

"This is no time to hesitate, Mr. President," said one of the Secret Service men.

Someone asked who could administer the oath. Brooks never lost his presence of mind. He was cooler in that crisis moment than I. He suggested federal judge Sarah T. Hughes. Called by telephone, she agreed to meet the presidential party at Air Force One, standing by at Love Field. There Lyndon B. Johnson took the oath of office, Lady Bird Johnson and Jacqueline Kennedy at his side.

To describe the depth of sadness that engulfed us that day defies the vocabulary. In Washington, one of the New Frontiersmen said to Larry O'Brien, "We'll never laugh again." Kennedy's chief apostle replied, "Yes, we'll laugh again. But we'll never be young again."

For several days most of us moved about in a cloud. The trip back to Washington . . . long queues of people, which streamed through the Capitol all Saturday night and into Sunday to pay respect at the casket as it lay in state in the rotunda . . . the little boy, John, unaware of the finality of what had happened to his father, saluting the flag . . . the long, slow march to Arlington Cemetery . . . all this burned itself into our memories.

Was there a conspiracy? Conceivably. Lyndon Johnson, in fact, felt that there was one. He believed, at least for a time, that the assassination was somehow the work of Castro, upon whose life an unsuccessful attempt had been made by people reportedly traceable to US intelligence. It is at least possible that, at this stage of the Cold War, zealous agents from the Communist bloc, either in Europe, Asia, or Latin America, could have been involved somehow. But I emphatically do not believe that the Warren Commission or any of its members engaged in a deliberate cover-up. Whatever shortcomings may be seen in their product are, in my firm judgment, honest errors. I knew four of the members personally, and they were honest men.

Now we look back after all these years and seek meaning. How unreal it seems. How beyond our capacity to fathom. How incongruous and paradoxical that, in the cosmic fitness of things, so premature an end to so fine a life would come at such a time and in such a seemingly senseless way. Yet, as deathless as immortality are some of the things he said and did. After a hundred years, perhaps, the children of this land may still recite and apply to their lives the timeless challenge of that inaugural address: *Ask not what your country can do for you—ask what you can do for your country.* Men and women of compassion may find enduring confirmation in Kennedy's 1962 message to Congress: *We are not developing the nation's wealth for its own sake. Wealth is the means—and people are the ends. All our material riches will avail us little if we do not use them to expand the opportunities of our people.* And just perhaps it may not be forgot: *If a free society cannot help the many who are poor, it cannot save the few who are rich.* These, I think, are among the things John F. Kennedy would have us remember.

from *Balance of Power* (Turner Publishing Co., 1997)

Following a year of aerial combat service in the South Pacific, then First Lieutenant Jim Wright sought out his old college classmate Joe Sutton (left), who was serving at Carswell Air Force Base in Fort Worth. (1944)

SPEAKER JIM WRIGHT COLLECTION, SPECIAL COLLECTIONS, MARY COUTS BURNETT LIBRARY, TCU.

## Long Night's Flight From Home

IN THE LATE EVENING of April 24, 1943, the first of twenty-nine B-24 bombers, manned by skeleton crews, lifted off from the airstrip at Hamilton Field, just north of San Francisco. We were en-route to Hickam Field, Hawaii, where we hoped to put down at about seven-thirty the next morning. We flew singly, not as a formation. Takeoffs were scheduled five minutes apart.

This was the first of five legs in the overseas movement of the 380th Heavy Bomb Group, known to a small circle within the Army Air Corps as "The Flying Circus." We were four squadrons, each consisting of nine planes and crews.

Seven elite crews, including that of Group Commander Miller, had preceded us by two or three days. Our crew, part of the 530th Squadron, would land eight days later at Amberley Field near Brisbane, Australia, the final destination of our almost ten thousand-mile journey.

Eager as we'd been to get into the action, that first night was, for me and for most of us, a tense and anxious one. The long over-water flight in the dark was a new experience, throbbing with adventure and fraught with uncertainties. There I was, at age twenty, a second lieutenant trained as a bombardier with some cross training in navigation and metrology and maybe forty hours of "stick time," certified as "combat ready," embarking on this first night leg of our journey into the Pacific combat zone.

Like most of the others in our group, I'd never flown anywhere nearly this far over water, nor so far in the dark with no view of earth below. Of the four classic forms of navigation we'd studied, two were completely off the table for this journey.

It was impossible to radio ahead for instructions or to get a directional fix on a radio beam. All of our bases in the mid-Pacific were maintaining absolute radio silence, which forbade any effort to contact Hickam or any point enroute. "Pilotage"—the plotting of a course by visual observation and orientation with landmarks—was out of the question, too. It was dark as pitch, and there simply weren't any landmarks. Nothing but shoreless miles of ocean.

Even dead reckoning—our oft-practiced discipline of setting a compass heading and crabbing into the wind just enough (as figured by vectors drawn on a piece of graph paper) to compensate for the wind's force and direction—was compromised. There was no way to know the direction and velocity of winds at our altitude after we'd left the coastal zone for which weather forecasters had briefed us back at Hamilton Field. This was before the day of radar equipment, and even our drift meters were useless, as the very waves below were in constant movement.

The only reliable check upon our compass, or proof of our precise location enroute, was in the heavens. Our twenty-four-year-old navigator, Pat Mullins of Boston, kept his handheld sextant busy taking "fixes" on the recognizable stars to reassure us that we weren't being blown off course. Pat was good at what he did. At thirty-minute intervals, he would "triangulate" our precise position on planet Earth by drawing straight lines from each of three heavenly bodies, plotting our own moving location. When the three lines intersected at the same point in our path, we all breathed easier. At least we knew exactly where we were. Gus Connery, our pilot, would make corrections whenever the stars showed us that vagabond winds had blown us four or five degrees off course.

There were six of us in the "skeleton" crew—pilot, copilot, navigator, bombardier, flight engineer, and radio operator. During the long moments between navigational fixes that night, each of us was alone with his private thoughts in those deep mental silences that somehow surmounted the hypnotic drone of four propeller engines.

As the dark night swallowed us and we inched farther and farther west above the broad ocean, our minds drifted back, clutching past images—the last embrace with loved ones, the fond and funny things of home—then lurching into the unknowable future, I trying to embed in my memory the silhouette shapes of all the Japanese military aircraft—the Zekes, the Zeros, the Rufes, the Jakes—then always springing back to the pregnant present, straining our eyes to perceive the illusory outline of any island chain, anywhere amid the miles of ocean still in front of us.

Maybe what made the night a nervous one for us all was really the subliminal awareness of broader uncertainties ahead. We all covered such doubts as we had with bravado. The tension evaporated as the first fingers of sunrise, tinting the sky faintly behind us, began to light up the path ahead. Suddenly, there on the horizon before us at one o'clock, loomed the dim outline of an island. It was the easternmost of the Hawaiian chain. Broad smiles lighted all our faces. Later, each admitted to the others that, for all our feigned confidence, we'd been "just a little uneasy." Scared as hell might have been more like it.

from *The Flying Circus* (Lyons Press, 2005)

# ABOUT THE EDITORS

James W. Riddlesperger Jr. is professor of political science at Texas Christian University. He has published dozens of articles and encyclopedia entries and is the coeditor of *Presidential Leadership and Civil Rights Policy*, and coauthor of *The Austin-Boston Connection: Five Decades of House Democratic Leadership, 1937-1989*; *Texas Politics*; and *Lone Star Leaders: Power and Personality in the Lone Star Delegation* (a joint project of The Center for Texas Studies and TCU Press, 2011).

Anthony Champagne is professor of political science at the University of Texas at Dallas. He has written about legal representation of the poor, the election of judges, Texas politics, and congressional history. In addition to his coauthorship of *The Austin-Boston Connection* and *Lone Star Leaders*, Champagne's books include *Congressman Sam Rayburn*; *Sam Rayburn: A Bio-Bibliography*; and *Judicial Politics in Texas: Partisanship, Money, and Politics in State Courts.*

Dan Williams, professor of English at TCU and former chair of the English department, is the director of TCU Press. A specialist in early American print culture, Williams has published three books, including *Pillars of Salt: An Anthology of Early American Criminal Narratives.* He is coeditor of *Liberty's Captives: Narratives of Confinement in the Print Culture of the Early Republic* and *descant: Fifty Years*, and has published numerous articles in the areas of crime and captivity narratives.

# INDEX